IMAGES
of America

THE BATESVILLE AREA

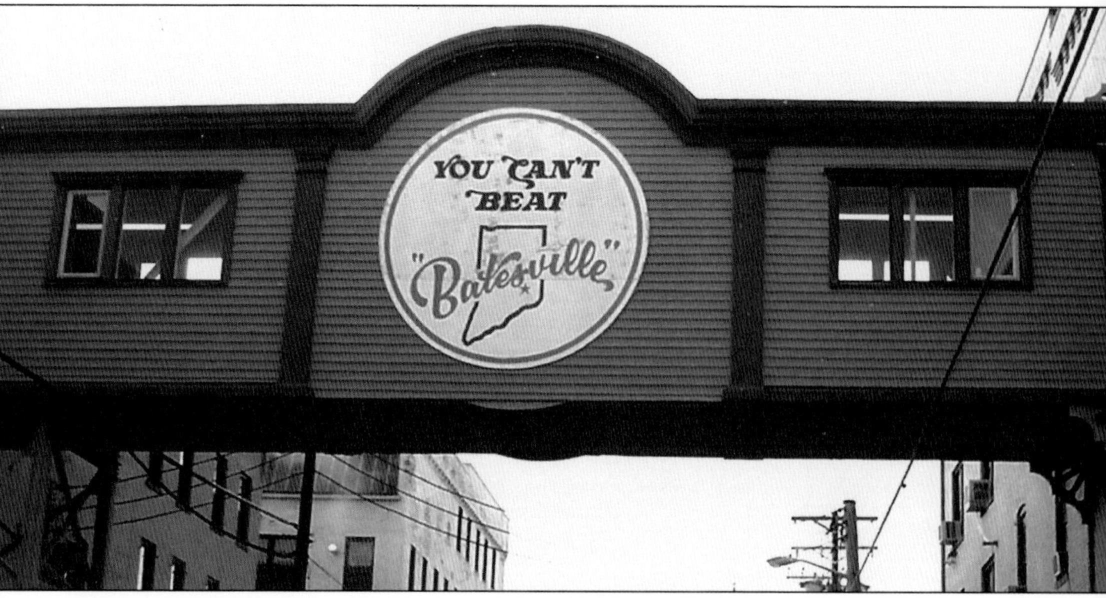

This sign on the catwalk over Walnut Street boasts, "You Can't Beat Batesville," which developed into the slogan for the City of Batesville. It was conceived in 1983 by a group of students from Batesville High School, who were planning for the next 20 years of progress for the city of Batesville. A contest was held to come up with a slogan to be used in their planning process, and this was the winner. (Jean Struewing.)

On the cover: George M. Bessler rode in his new automobile over the streets of Batesville Tuesday evening, October 20, 1903. The automobile was constructed at the Bessler factory in Batesville. The construction differs from all other automobiles, being projected according to Bessler's own ideas and suited for rough usage and country roads. Pictured in the automobile are George Bessler and driver is Herman "Meuse" Bessler. (Alma Miller and Georgann Flory.)

IMAGES
of America

THE BATESVILLE AREA

S. Jean Struewing
for the Batesville Area Historical Society

ARCADIA
PUBLISHING

ISBN 978-0-7385-6132-5

Published by Arcadia Publishing
Charleston, South Carolina

Printed in the United States of America

Library of Congress Catalog Card Number: 2008930083

For all general information contact Arcadia Publishing at:
Telephone 843-853-2070
Fax 843-853-0044
E-mail sales@arcadiapublishing.com
For customer service and orders:
Toll-Free 1-888-313-2665

Visit us on the Internet at www.arcadiapublishing.com

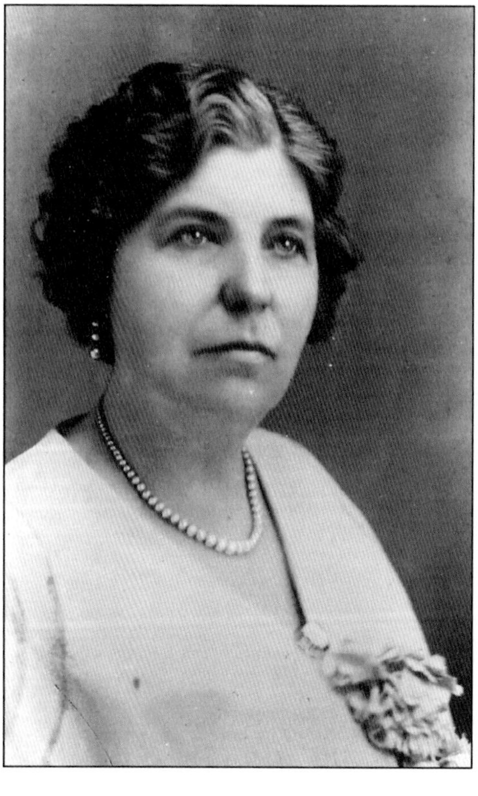

This is Minnie E. Wycoff, the author of *Builders of a City*, from which most of the text was taken for the captions in this book. She never had her book published before her death, but her family had it bound into three volumes, unpublished and exactly as she had typed it on a manual typewriter. (Pat Hare.)

Contents

Acknowledgements 6

Introduction 7

1. Batesville's Beginnings 9

2. Transportation 15

3. Public Buildings 23

4. Churches and Schools 31

5. Factories 41

6. Entertainment 49

7. Retail Businesses 61

8. Homes 81

9. People 93

10. Centennial Celebrations 121

ACKNOWLEDGMENTS

Without the book *Builders of a City* by Minnie E. Wycoff, I could not have written this book. It is my bible for any facts about Batesville, Indiana. Thanks must be given to Pat (Wycoff) Hare, the granddaughter of Minnie E. Wycoff. Minnie had never managed to get her book published before her death. Her manuscripts were discovered in a suitcase in the attic after she died. It covered the history of this area from when the Native Americans roamed this territory up until the year 1933. When the Batesville Area Historical Society became a reality in 1999, we approached Pat to see if she would give us the rights to publish a condensed version of Minnie's books to sell as a fund raising project for the society. Pat graciously gave us permission, and the shortened version of Minnie's history of Batesville is available from the society. She has also given her permission to use any of the facts in Minnie's history to include in this book. We sincerely thank Pat for this privilege. She has also given many pictures from her dad, Paul Wycoff, and from Minnie's estate to use in this book. Numerous other photographs herein are compliments of the Batesville Area Historical Society, (noted as BAHS). The Batesville Area Historical Society has made every effort to ensure the historical accuracy of the captions and regret any inadvertent inaccuracies that might have escaped their attention. Courtesy names are shown in parentheses at the end of the captions. My thanks and appreciation goes to Ken Baran for proofreading the text and to all the donors of these valuable items. Please visit the Batesville Area Historical Society Web site at www.batesvilleareahistoricalsociety.org.

INTRODUCTION

Just outside two exciting cities, there is a piece of country waiting for you. Batesville is a charming, easy paced community where backyard gardening and front porch conversations are still a part of the everyday lifestyle.

Batesville lies conveniently between two of the Midwest's most dynamic cities: Cincinnati, about an hour to the east, and Indianapolis, about an hour to the west.

Batesville itself combines the prosperity of strong economic growth through industry with the slow pace of a country town. Founded in 1852 and situated in the scenic hills of southeastern Indiana, it is a community of approximately 6,500 friendly, family-oriented, forward-thinking people.

Places to live in Batesville are as diverse as its people. Small, picturesque farms are interrupted with roomy subdivisions and warm, solid, century-old homes on tree-lined streets.

Batesville's early beginnings are tied to a Dutch boy's dream of owning and working a piece of farmland in southeastern Indiana. Teunis Amack, 18 years old and newly married, purchased 120 acres of government land in Ripley County's Laughery Township in 1837. He cleared the land, used the logs to build a home, barn, and outbuildings, and dug a well.

After working the land for 15 years, Amack was approached by representatives of the John Callahan Trust Company. The group bought land for what they thought would make a perfect spot for a railroad right-of-way and to establish a town. In 1852, Amack sold his land to the trust company, and a town was laid out in 45 lots.

Running from Lawrenceburg to Indianapolis, the railroad ran through the center of the acreage utilizing water from Amack's well and timber from his land to power the steam locomotives. Joshua Bates, one of the members of the Callahan Trust Company, built the first house on lot number one. Undoubtedly the town received its name from Joshua Bates.

In the period from 1867 to 1892, at least nine furniture, coffin, and novelty factories were in operation, using the extensive stands of hardwood timber in this area. The hardwood forests became the area's wealth. As the trees were used and the land cleared, farming became an important occupation for this area and remains so today.

Agriculture is both a way of life and a major industry in the fertile area that surrounds Batesville. More than half of Indiana's acreage is farmland, and the state is among our nation's leading producers of grain.

Industry in Batesville runs the gamut from small, highly skilled entrepreneurs to progressive corporations international in scope.

It is to industry that Batesville owes its strong economic base. Besides offering varied employment opportunities, industry contributes generously to the recreational and social needs of the community.

The Sherman House is one of the oldest buildings in Batesville. It was opened on November 9, 1852, and was named for Gen. William Tecumseh Sherman. In 1923, Hillenbrand Industries purchased the Sherman House and over the next 10 years added four additional buildings to the property.

Batesville residents make quality education for their children a priority. Equally vital is excellent medical care. Batesville is fortunate to have its own hospital, Margaret Mary Community Hospital, a modern medical facility that exceeds the capacity standards for the community it serves. First-rate care for cancer patients at the Hansen Center is further evidence of Batesville's superior resources.

One

Batesville's Beginnings

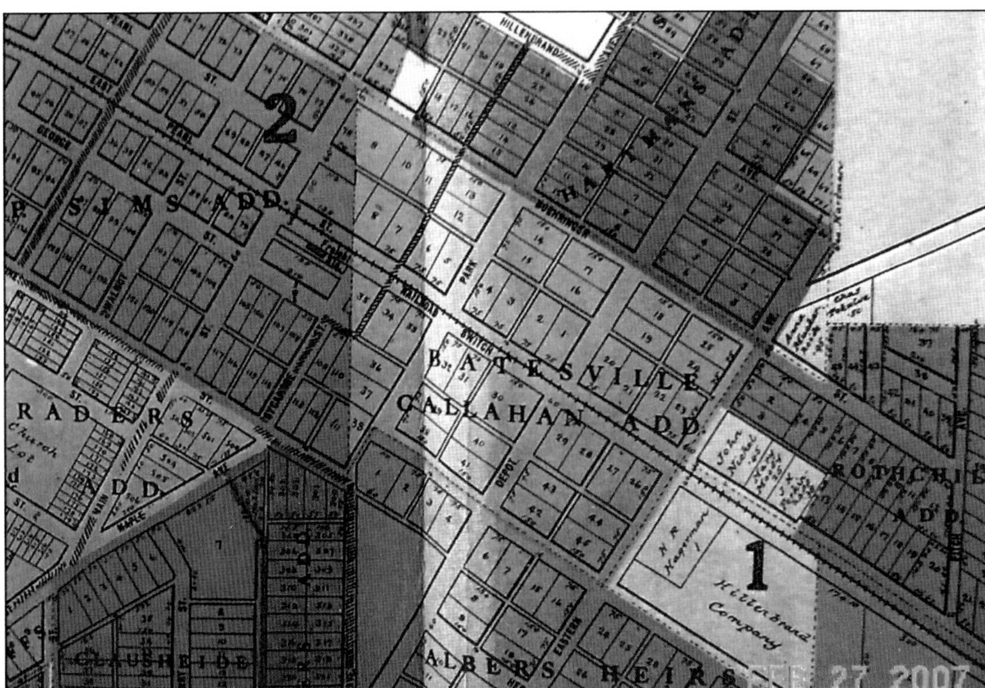

This map of Batesville, from the Standard Atlas of Ripley County, was published in 1921. The center addition, labeled "Callahan Add," consisted of the original town of 45 lots. The southern border was South Street, the eastern border was Eastern Avenue, the northern border was Boehringer Street, and the western boundary line went on a diagonal line from Boehringer Street back to South Street. The original layout occurred this way because the railway was surveyed to connect Lawrenceburg and Indianapolis in a direct line. (BAHS.)

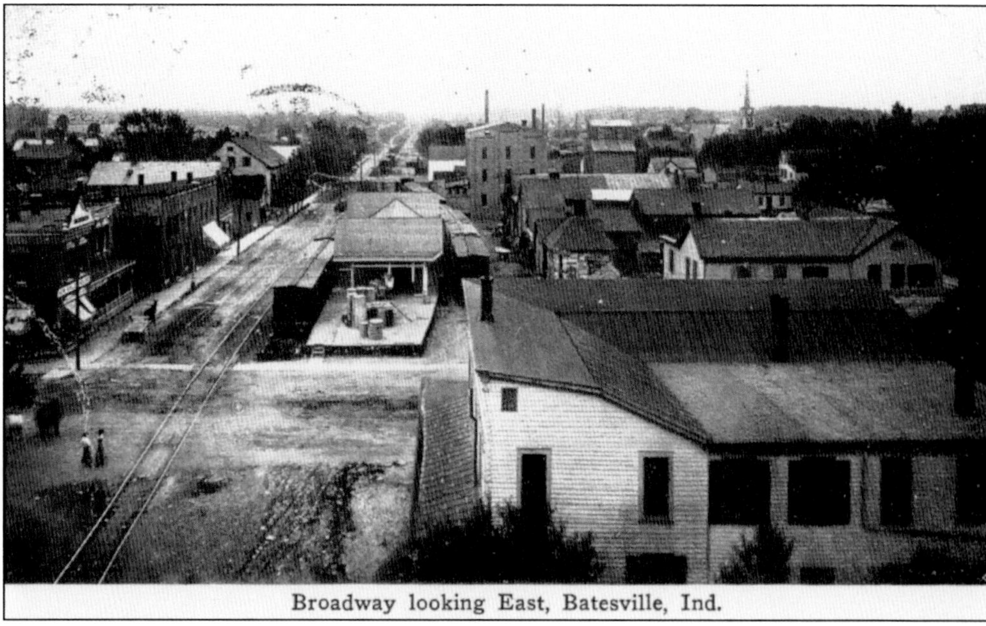

This was the second location of the train depot. It was moved from Depot Square to this site, just two blocks west, in 1915. It was situated directly across from the Sherman House at the southeast corner of Main and East Pearl Streets. The last passenger train to pass over this old railroad bed of 1852 was on July 2, 1906. (Don Karbowski.)

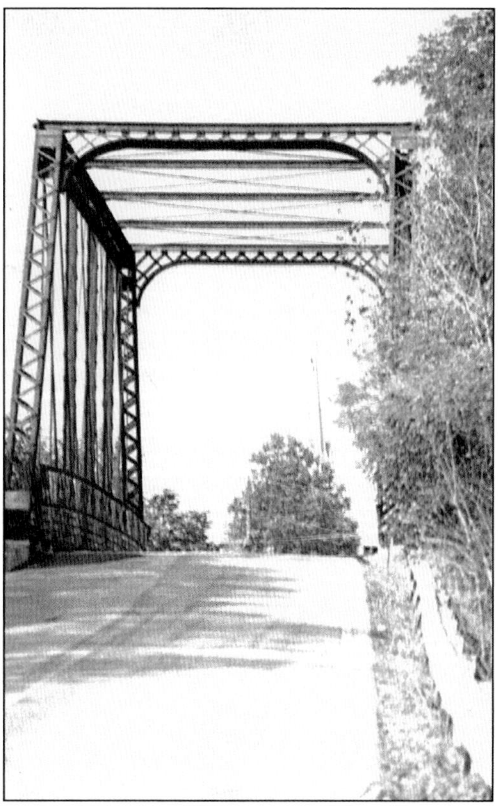

This historic bridge was known as the Overhead Bridge to most people in Batesville. It was built in the spring of 1922. As motorists entered Batesville through the Overhead Bridge from the south, on Highway 229, they could see the St. Louis Church steeple framed inside the structure of the bridge. (Jean Struewing.)

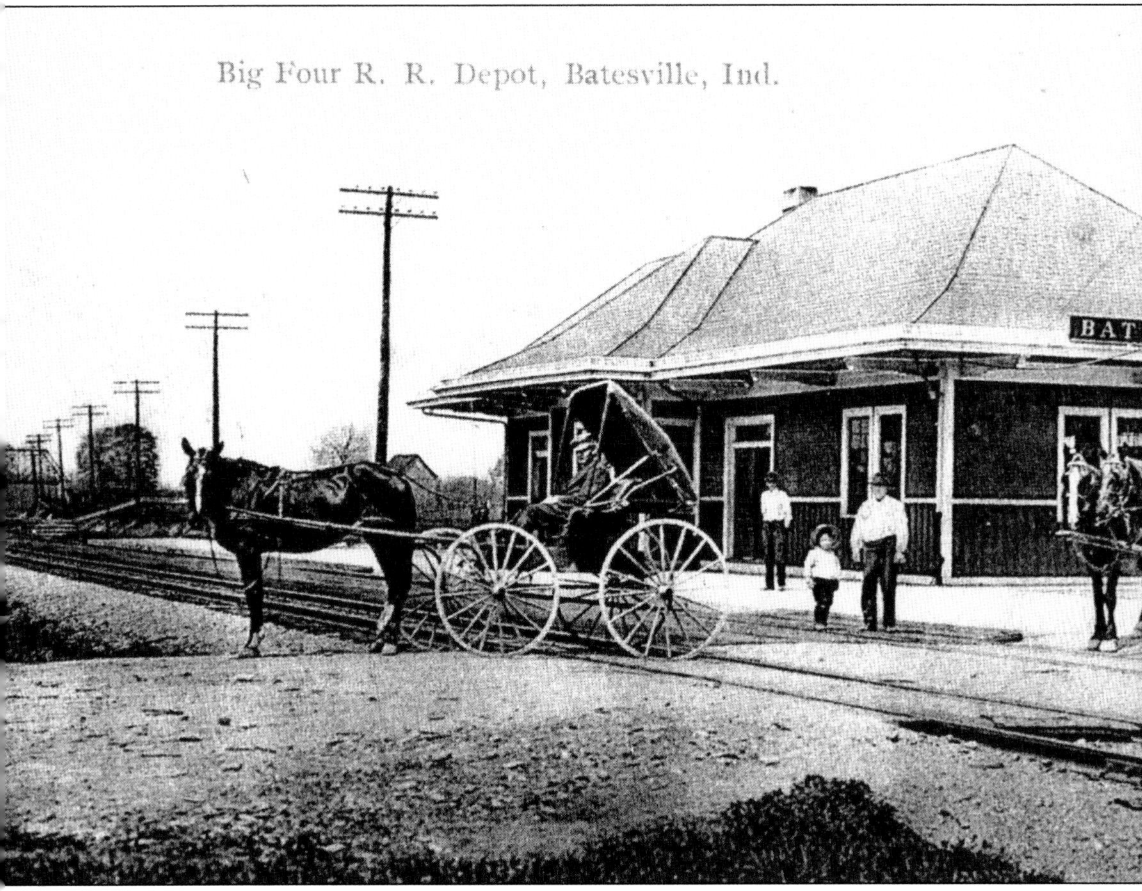

As the town grew and traffic increased, a new passenger depot was built south of town near Liberty Park. A new line of rail to take the railroad out of the downtown area was proposed to run one-quarter mile south of the original line. The selection of the right-of-way presented some difficulty, as the Fair Association owned part of the land of the proposed route. A compromise was struck by agreement to locate the new passenger depot near the entrance of the fair grounds (Liberty Park). The new depot was built in late 1905, and the railroad itself finished in 1906. People in the picture are an unidentified timber buyer for Hillenbrands (in the buggy), Roy Behr as a child, and Jacob Behr standing next to Roy. The tall man in the background is "Spot" Doll's dad. (Margaret Tangman.)

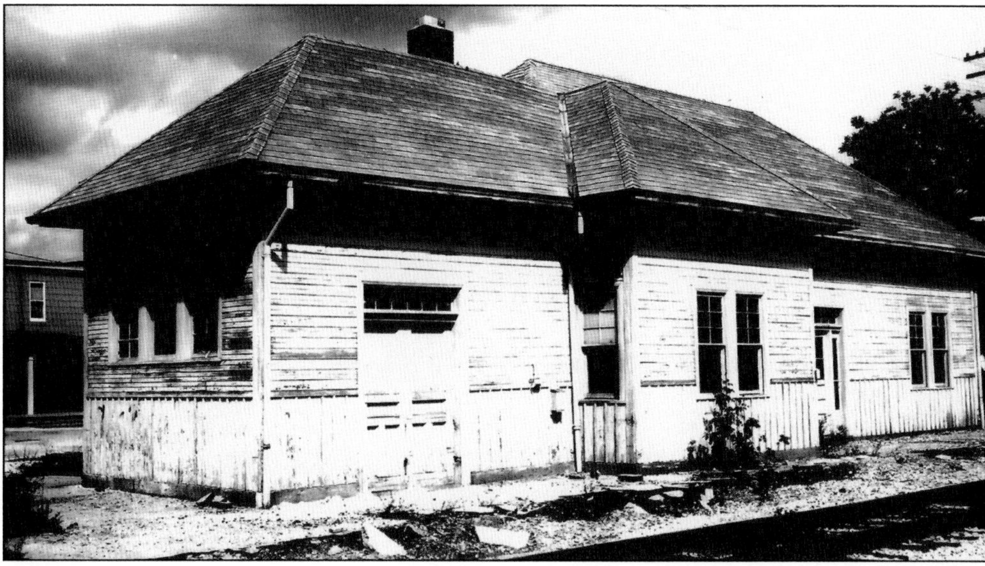

With the introduction of the automobile, the trains slowly vanished, and by the early 1970s, the train depot began to deteriorate. This picture was taken in 1976, and soon afterward the old depot was torn down. Today this is the site of Doug Bessler's used car dealership. (Jean Struewing.)

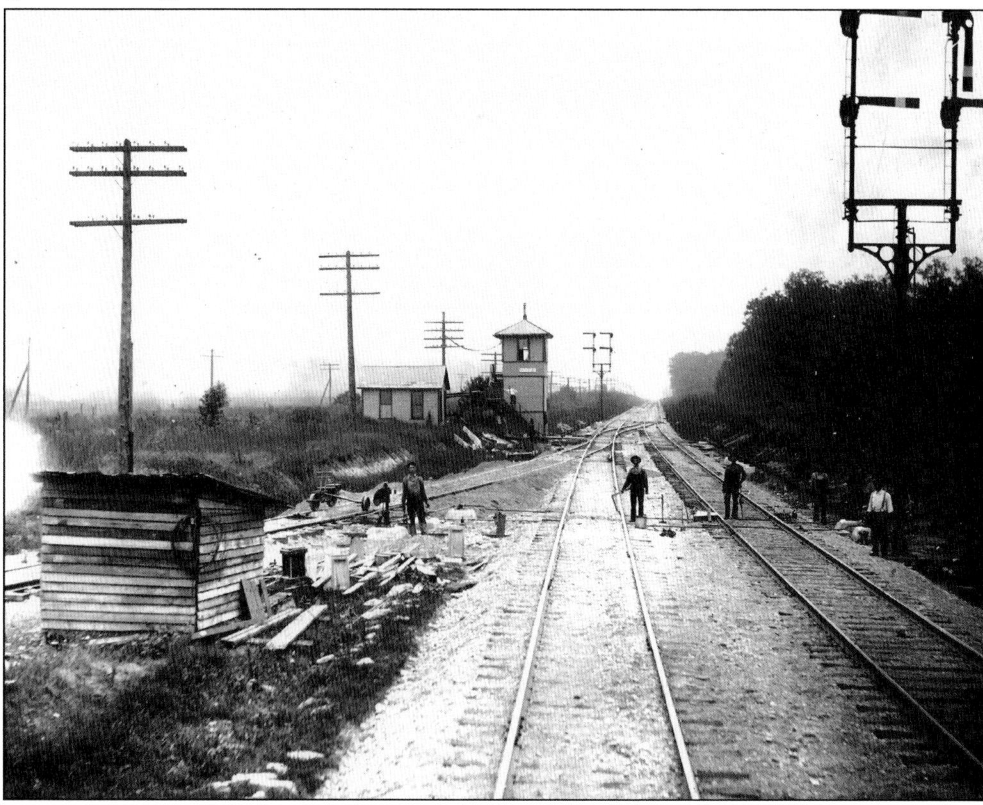

This picture shows the railroad signal tower on the main railroad line east of Batesville toward Morris. The signal tower was built new in 1898. (Paul Wycoff.)

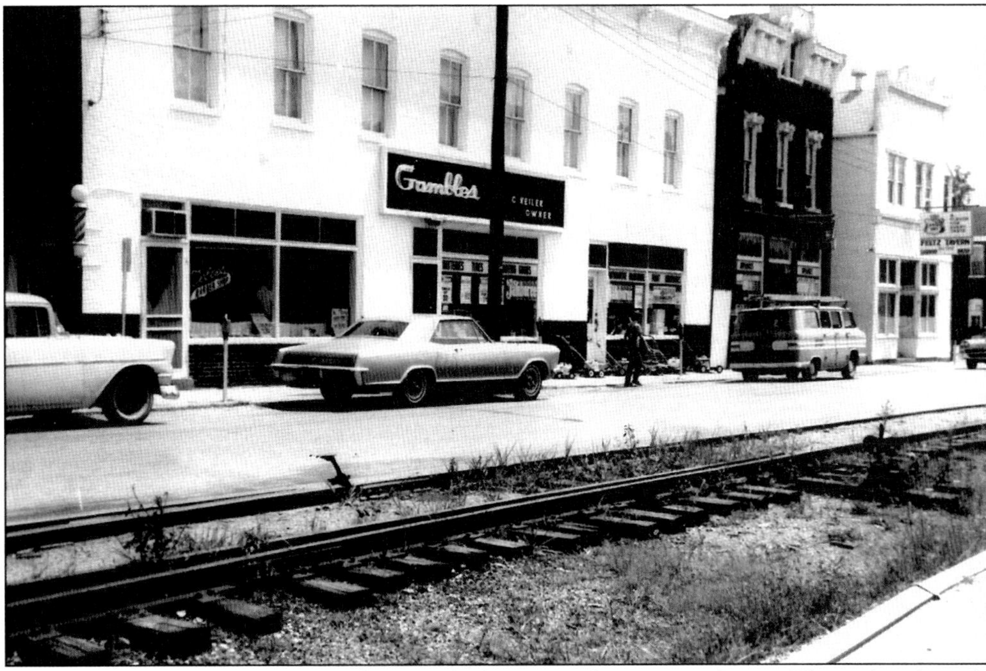

This photograph shows East Pearl Street looking east from Main Street. The railroad tracks ran straight through downtown Batesville in the 1950s, but by this time, the tracks were used infrequently because the main passenger depot was now south of town. The stores along the tracks are, from left to right, Telles Barber Shop, Gambles Department Store, Robert Schene Radio Repair, and Feltz's Tavern. (Batesville Women's Study Club.)

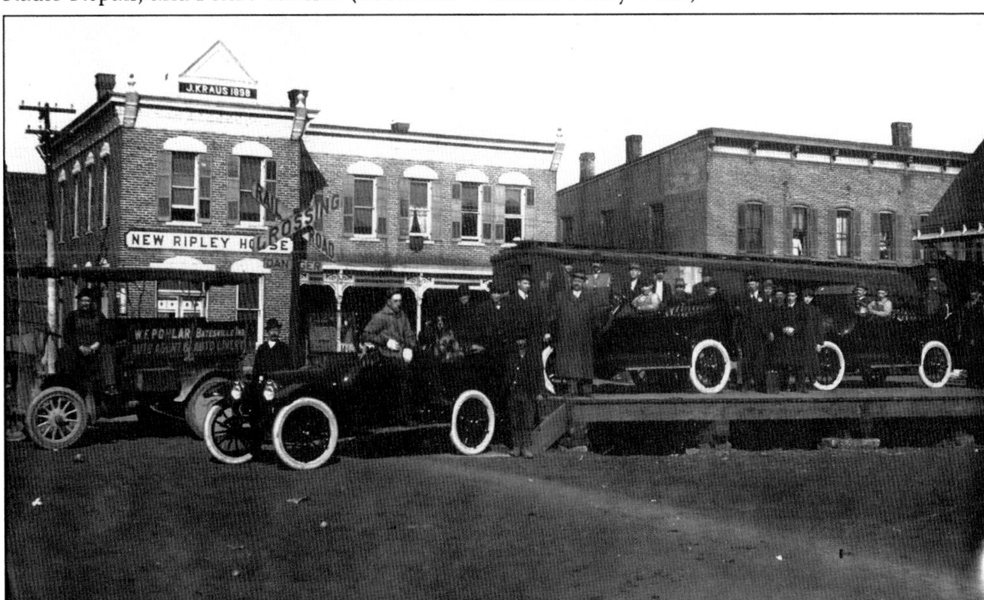

About 1910, the first carload of Buicks arrived in Batesville by rail. This photograph shows the Buicks being unloaded at the freight depot on East Pearl Street. Bill Pohlar is in the first car, as he owned the dealership. In the background is the New Ripley House, which stood at the northeast corner of Main and East Pearl Streets. (Paul Wycoff.)

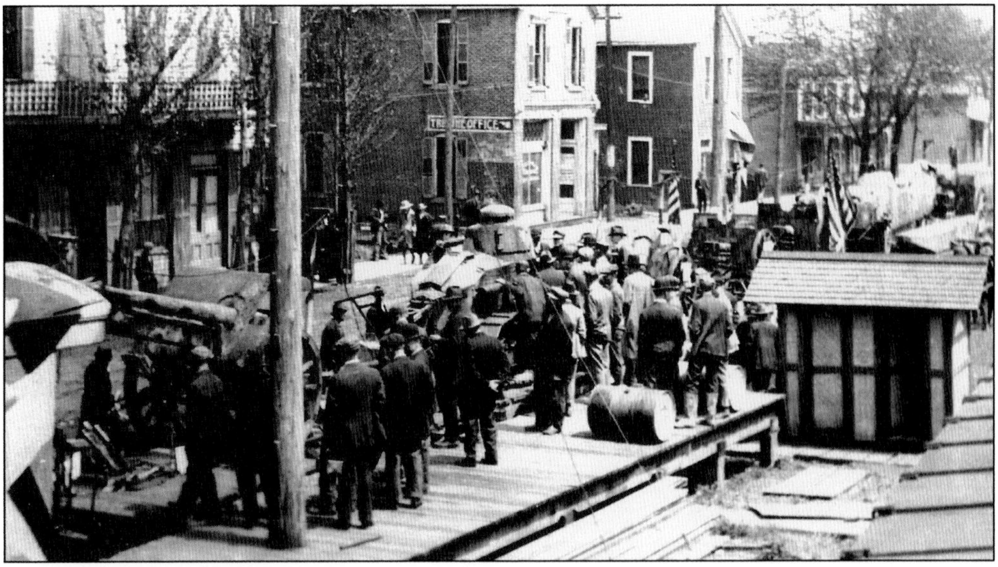

This photograph, taken in the early 1920s, shows what appears to be a load of farm equipment arriving on the train. The partially obscured sign on the building across from the train track reads "Tribune Office," to identify the offices of the *Tribune* newspaper. The *Tribune* was on East Pearl Street, and the other newspaper, the *Herald*, was on Boehringer Street. Later they merged as one newspaper. (BAHS.)

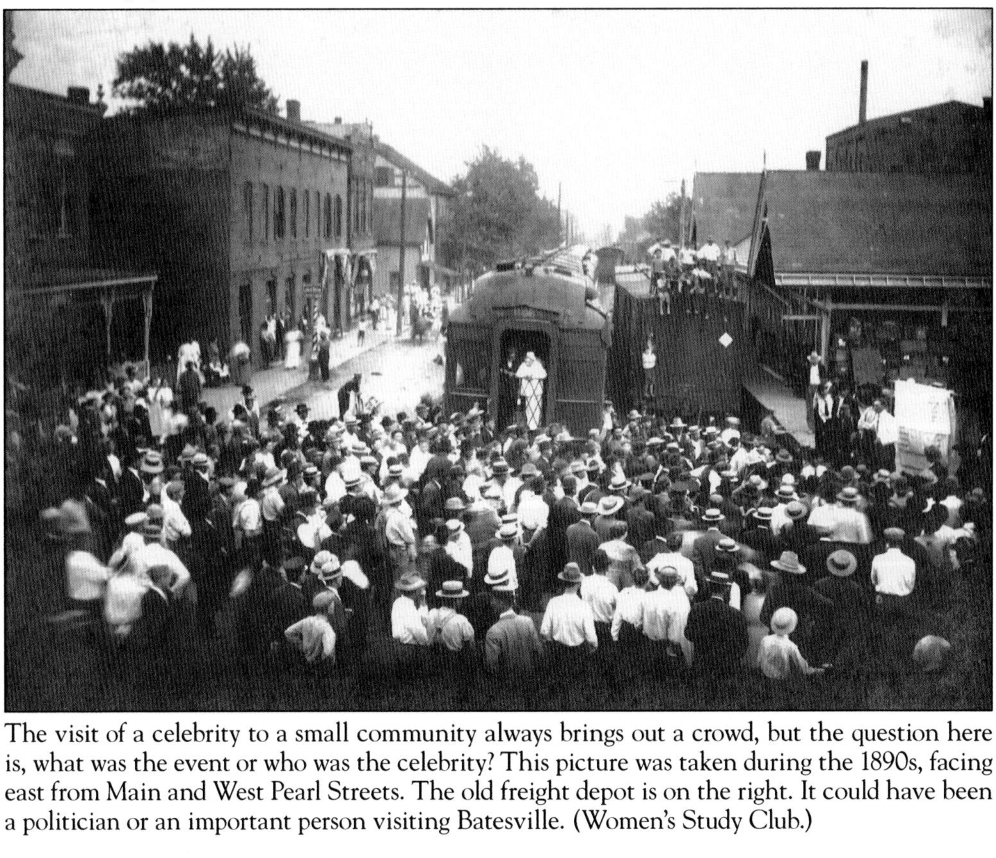

The visit of a celebrity to a small community always brings out a crowd, but the question here is, what was the event or who was the celebrity? This picture was taken during the 1890s, facing east from Main and West Pearl Streets. The old freight depot is on the right. It could have been a politician or an important person visiting Batesville. (Women's Study Club.)

Two

TRANSPORTATION

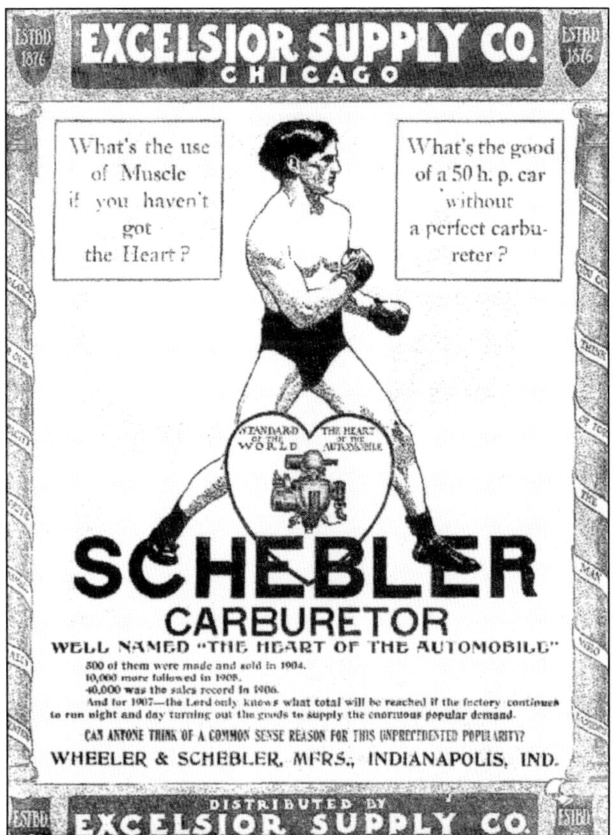

"The Heart of the Automobile" was the slogan that Franklin County resident George Schebler used to advertise the carburetor he invented. This advertisement appeared in *Motor Age* magazine in 1907. The preliminary work on this carburetor was done in 1901 and 1902. In 1904, Schebler began its manufacture in connection with the Central Motor Car Company. Schebler eventually sold out, having acquired a handsome profit. (Schebler family.)

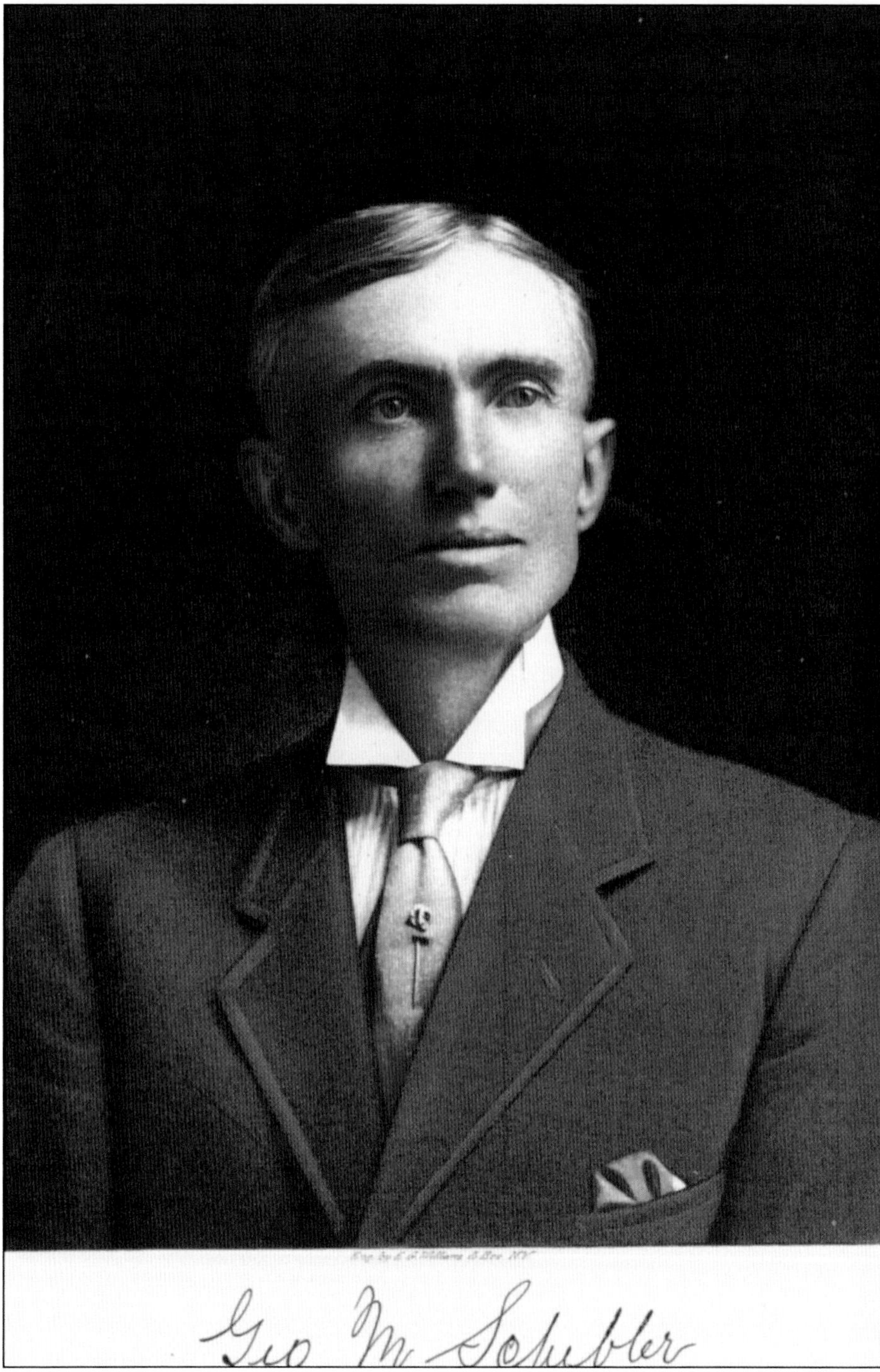

George M. Schebler, the inventor of the well-known carburetor that bears his name, was born at Saint Peter, Franklin County, September 29, 1865. He was the son of John and Katherine (Thalheimer) Schebler. George was educated at the parish school in Hamburg, Indiana. Until he reached adult age, George was engaged in farming on the old home place. His invention of the carburetor brought him fame and fortune. (Franklin County Atlas.)

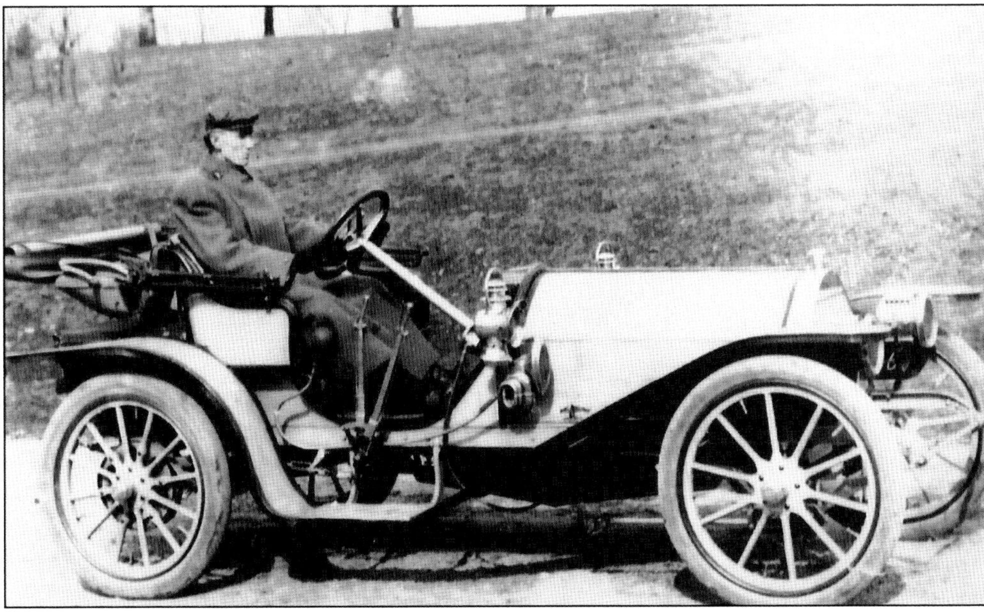

George is shown in his automobile on his farm north of Batesville. He was a very energetic and enterprising gentleman who devoted a considerable portion of his life toward his invention of the carburetor. His mechanical and financial reputation extended throughout the length and breath of the country. He is one of those men whom Franklin County delights to honor because of his splendid achievements. (Ruth Lecher.)

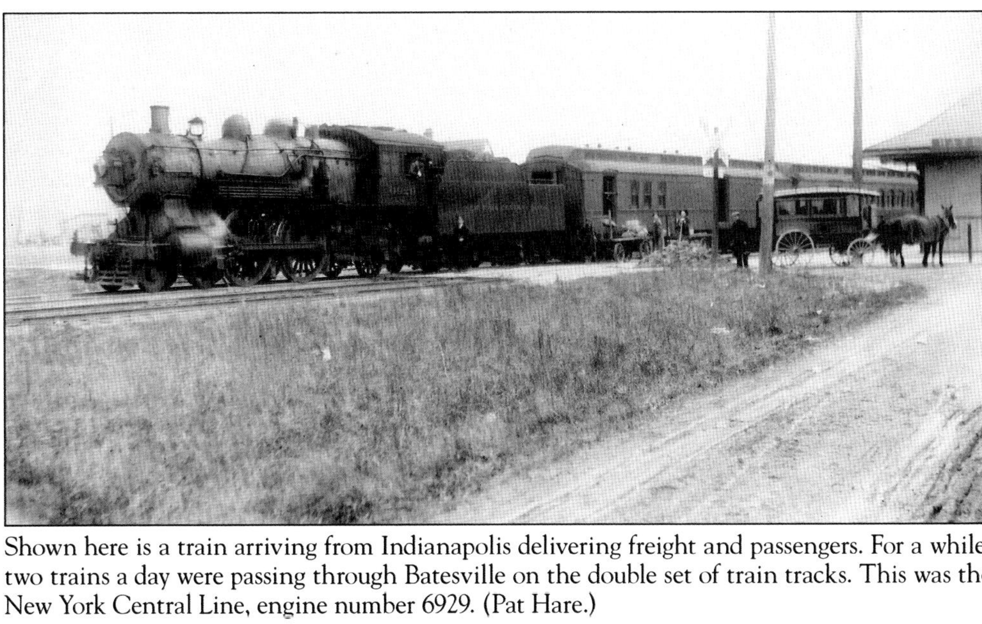

Shown here is a train arriving from Indianapolis delivering freight and passengers. For a while, two trains a day were passing through Batesville on the double set of train tracks. This was the New York Central Line, engine number 6929. (Pat Hare.)

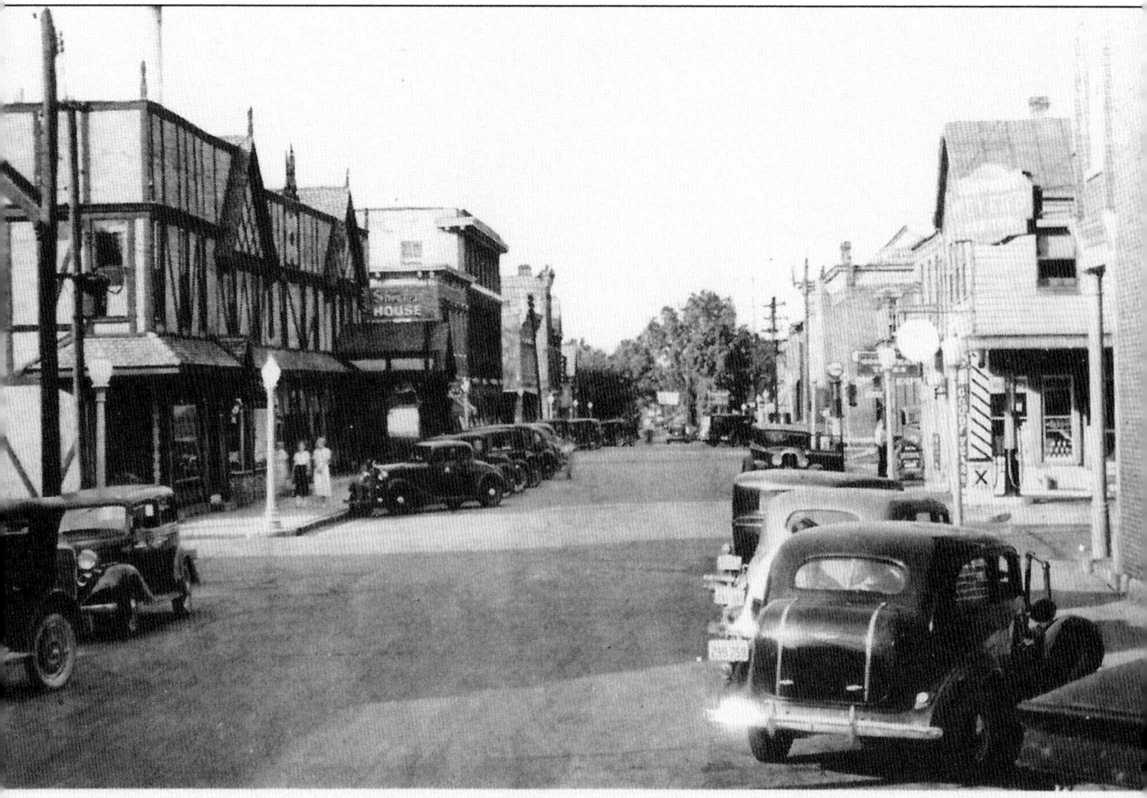

NORTH MAIN ST. - BATESVILLE, IND.

In the 1940s, this is how the business district on Main Street appeared looking north from George Street. On the right is Meyer's Hardware and Furniture Store. John Meyer built the large brick building at the corner of George and Main Streets and moved the hardware business into this building. Next is the Zim-Bat Tire Company, owned by Jack Zimmerman. Continuing on the right side is the New Ripley House; John Kraus, builder and proprietor of the hotel and bar, built this building in 1898. Several years after Kraus's death, the New Ripley House was modernized by the addition of bathrooms and modern plumbing. On the left is the expanded Sherman House, with Stewart's Dress Shop on the corner, operated by Leota Stewart. Next was the Gannon Jewelry Store, which was operated by Irene and Jesse Gannon and then the entrance to the Sherman House. Next to the Sherman House is the American Furniture Company building. (BAHS.)

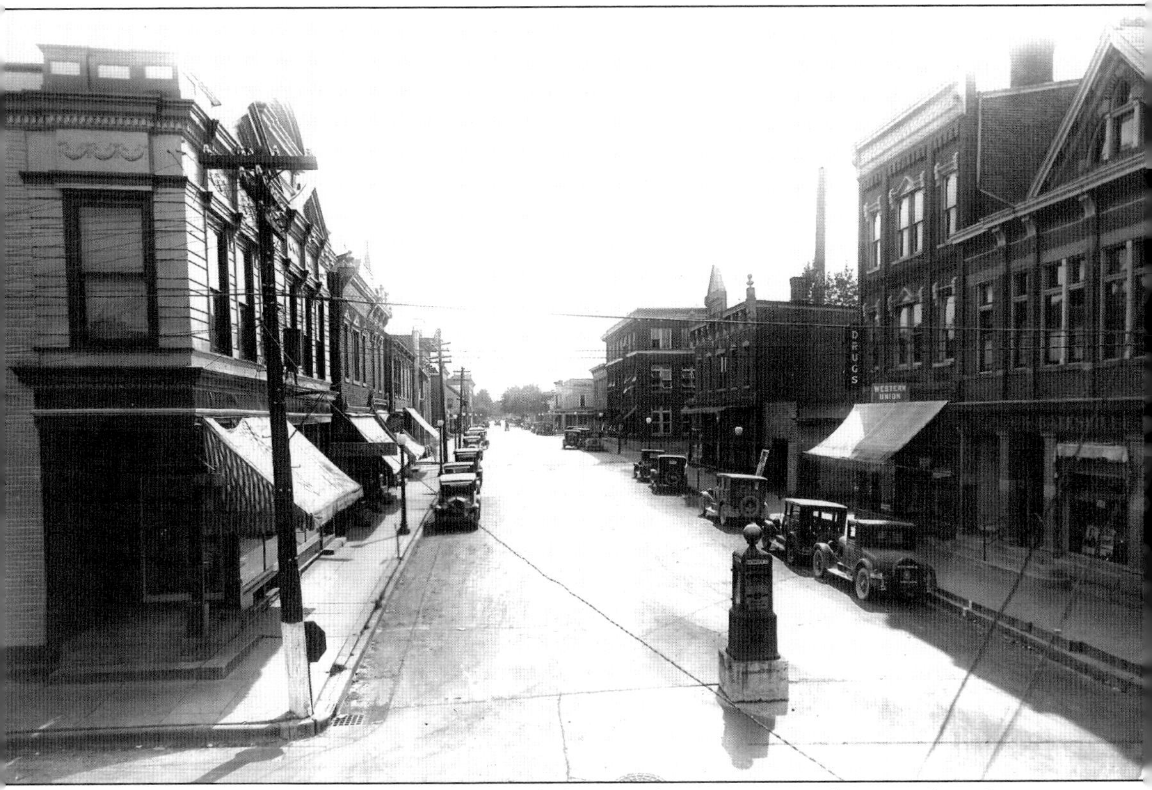

This picture shows Main Street looking south from Boehringer Street. This was when the post office occupied part of the Home Outfitters store. The post office sign is visible just beyond the awning on the left. Next on the left is the Kramer Bakery (circular sign) whose second floor was occupied by attorney Paul Wycoff. Next on the left is the Brockman Shoe Store and then the Benz meat market. Across a small alley is the First National Bank building. On the right side of the street is the Batesville State Bank and Blank's Drug Store. The next building is the Wilker Company building, which sold dry goods and was later known as Giesins. Further south, across West Pearl Street, is the American Furniture Company. Hitching posts lined the street on both sides. (Paul Wycoff.)

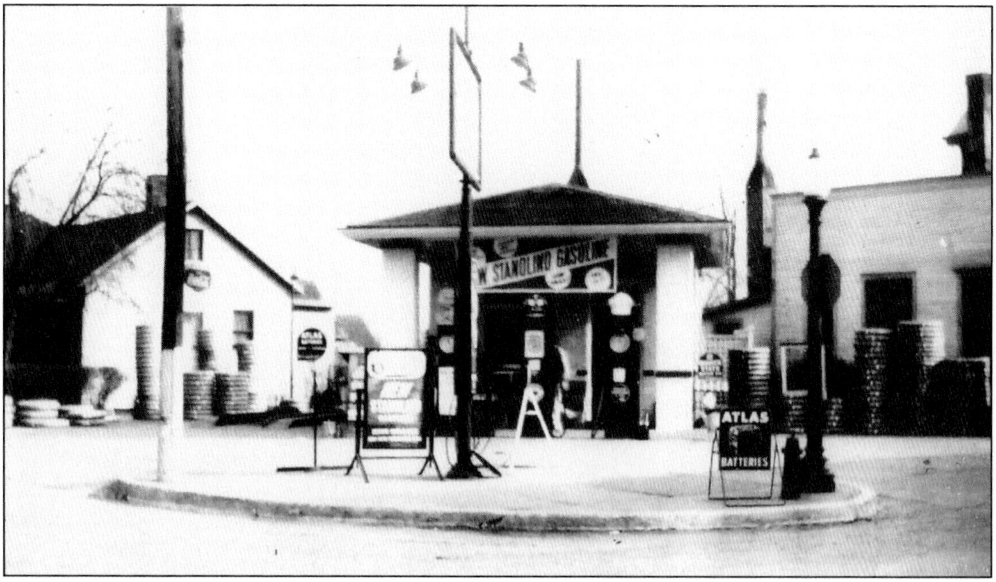

The Standard Oil Service Station was very small when Maurice Hellmich purchased it in 1929. Today this corner is where Fran Telles has his barbershop. Besides gas, Hellmich sold tires, batteries, motor oil, and serviced automobiles. Because of the countless tires that Hellmich sold, he was called "Tire King of Batesville." Highway 229 eventually went right past this location. (Sue [Hellmich] Hill.)

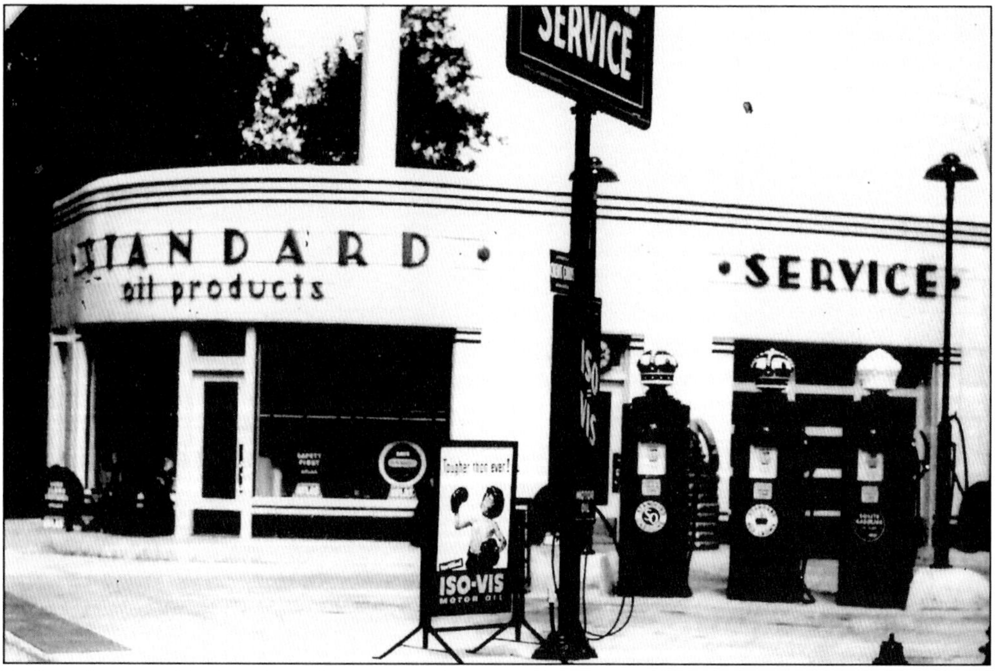

Hellmich remodeled, enlarged, and modernized the original gas station in 1940. At the completion of his update project, he held his grand opening. The executives from the Standard Oil Company were there to participate in the celebration. After many years at this location, he moved his station north of Batesville, where the BP Station is now, near Interstate 74, Highway 229, and Highway 46. (Sue [Hellmich] Hill.)

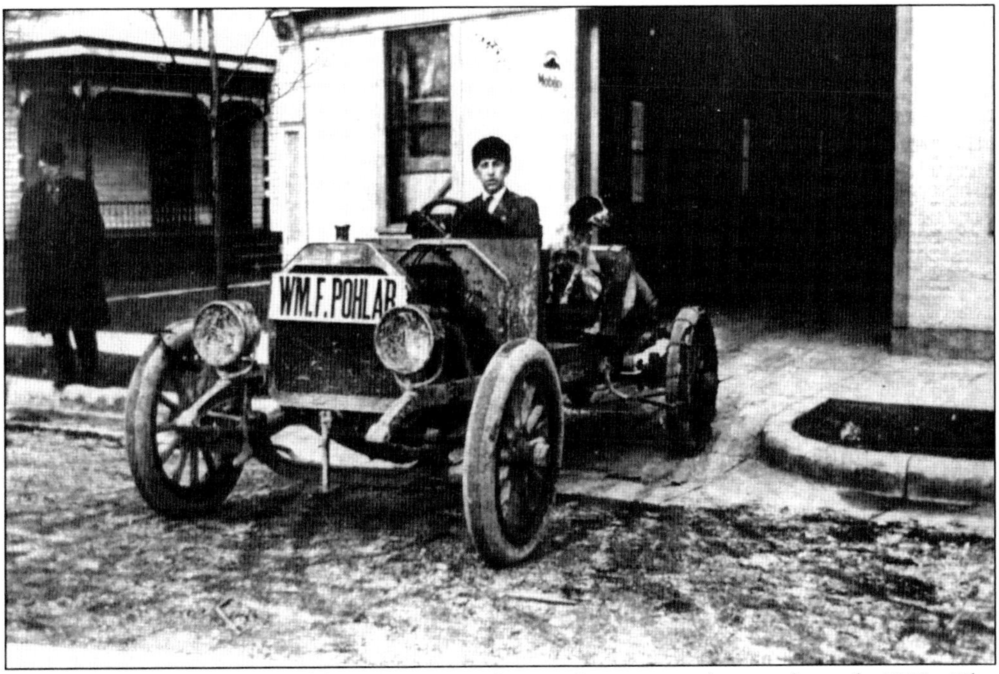

This picture of William F. Pohlar's Garage on George Street was taken in the early 1900s. The garage was located across from the post office where Hill-Rom has one of their factories. It looks like Pohlar is ready for some tortuous driving. Look at the chains on his back wheels. (Anne Koester.)

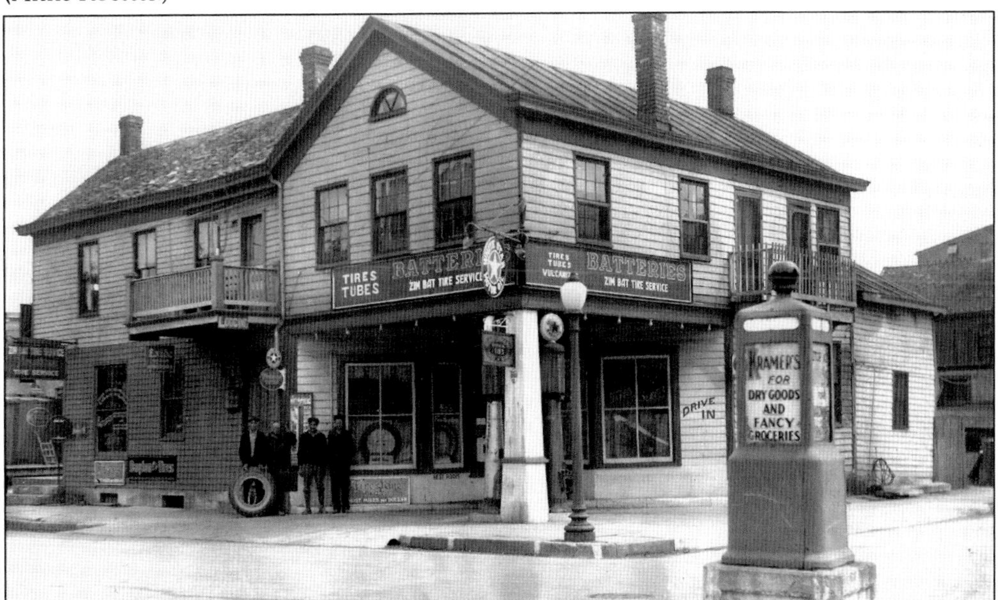

The Schene building was at the northeast corner of Main and George streets, in the early days. In late 1926, the lower floor of the Schene building was vacated and remodeled into a drive-in gas, repair, and supply business for automobiles called Zim-Bat Tire Service and was operated by Jack Zimmerman. Later he moved his station east on George Street to where Ken's Auto Repair is today. (Rosie Fisher.)

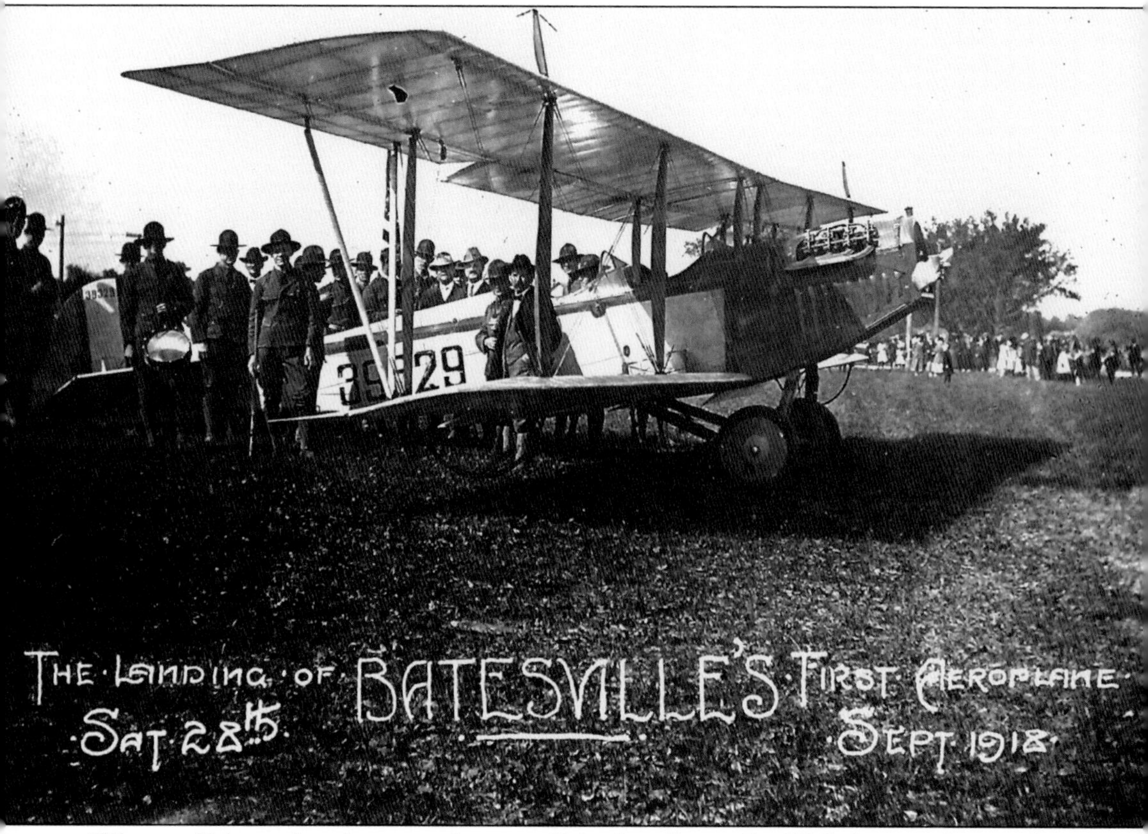

Who would have thought an airplane would land in Batesville. Well the very first airplane, which was army plane "39929," landed north of the city in George Schebler's cornfield around 9:00 a.m. on September 28, 1918. It later flew on to Versailles and other parts of Ripley County. The Liberty Guards were stationed at the field to perform police and guard duty while the plane was on the ground. Among the dignitaries at the landing was then mayor of Batesville, George M. Hillenbrand. The aviator of the airplane was Lt. H. L. Hill. (Susie Canfield.)

Three

Public Buildings

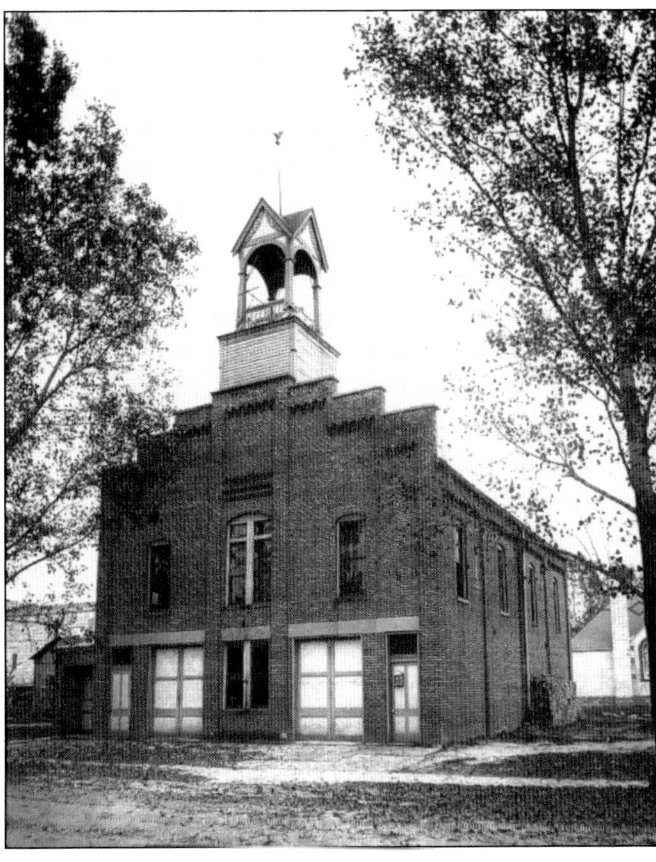

Batesville Town Hall, two stories high, was erected in 1887. This was 35 years after the platting of the town and five years after its incorporation. In February 1888, a cupola and bell tower was added. It became city hall in 1909. (Women's Study Club.)

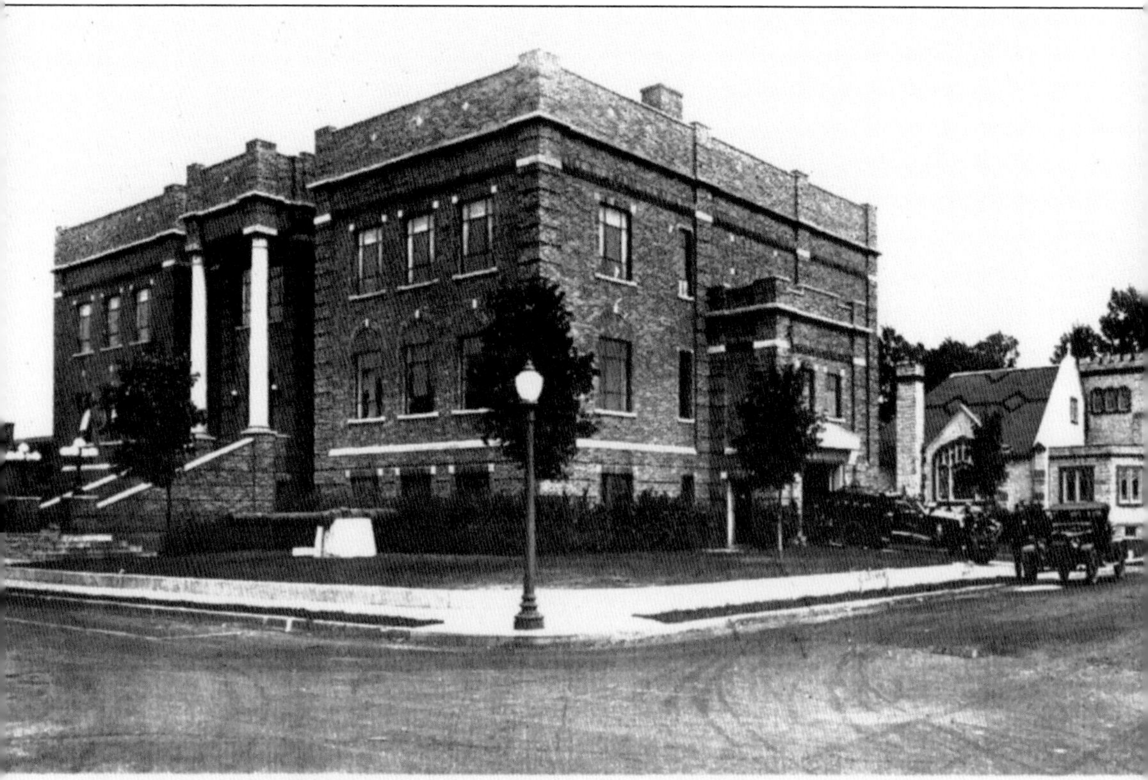

MEMORIAL BUILDING - BATESVILLE, IND.

The Memorial Building, which was built as a monument to the men and women who answered the call to duty during World War I, was completed in late 1922 and early 1923. Architect Karl P. Hinkel from Connersville was selected to design the Memorial Building. The plan included a gymnasium and kitchen (both on the basement level), council chambers, a community room, an auditorium, and stage, all on the second floor with dressing rooms, restrooms, and lobby. A balcony was included in the auditorium plan large enough to seat 300 people, and the main auditorium seated 500. The material to be used was brick, hollow tile, cement, and tile throughout. The basement plans included a fire engine room and jail cells. The top floor was to have three large rooms for the use of the American Legion. To the right of the building is Fred Brummer, fire chief, with his new car that the city bought for him. In the back of the building is the Bethany church. (Margaret Tangman.)

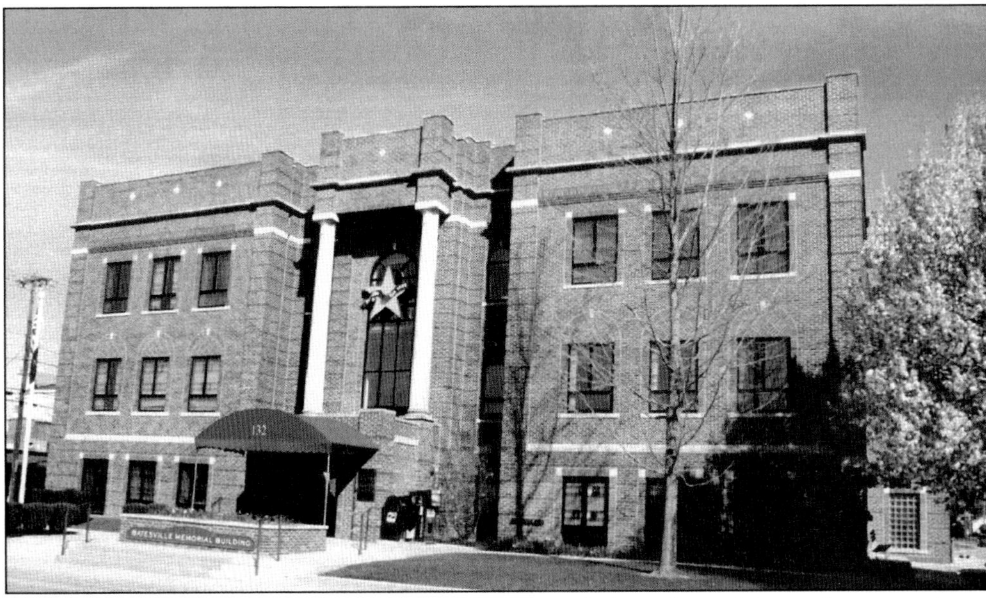

On September 11, 1993, the Memorial Building was rededicated to celebrate the renovation of this historic landmark. The long staircase seen in the previous photograph was removed and the entrance was moved to ground level. W. A. Gutzwiller Company was the contractor for the project, and Designhouse, Inc. was the architect. The lighted yellow star was placed above the entrance at the beginning of the sesquicentennial celebration in January 2002. (Jean Struewing.)

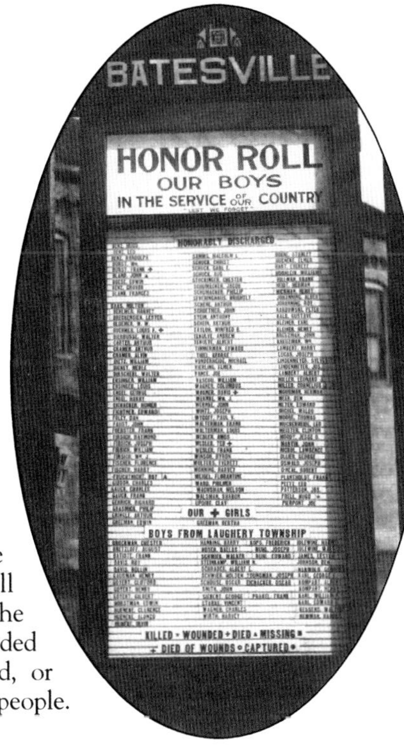

"Lest we forget," is the barely visible last line of the caption at the top of this honor roll that stood on the front lawn of the Memorial Building. The honor roll lists the names of men and women in the service of the country during World War I. The honor roll included those who were killed, wounded, missing, captured, or died of wounds. It stood as a tribute to all military people. (Women's Study Club.)

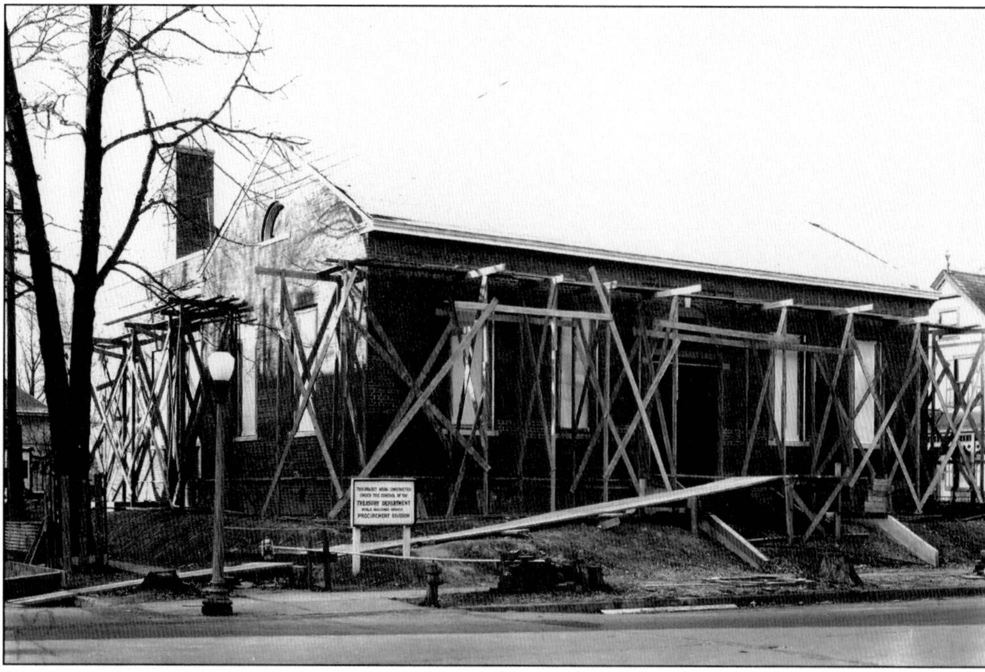

Besides a phone system, the town needed a reliable mail system. Batesville's mail delivery began in 1917. The post office was located in stores during its early existence. One of the first post offices was in the back of the Home Outfitters store on Main Street. Construction on the current post office began in 1936. (Women's Study Club.)

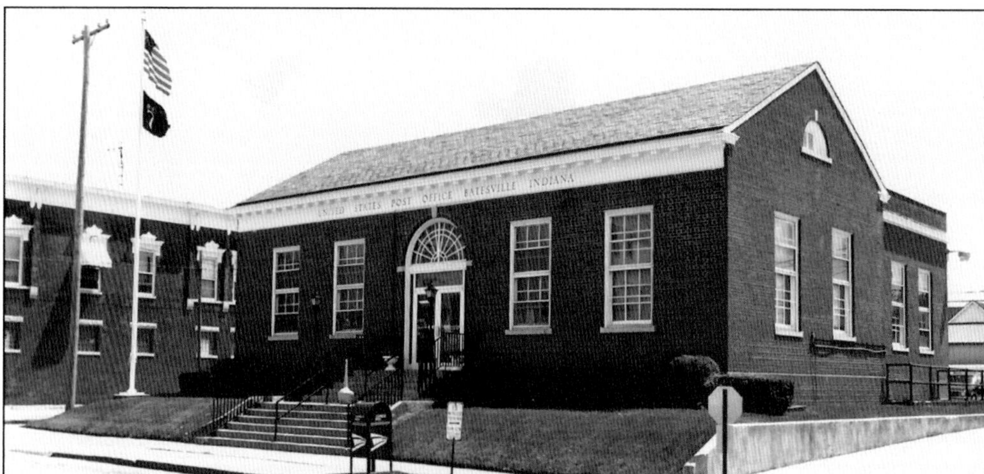

This photograph shows the current post office on the southwest corner of George and Walnut Streets. Before the town was laid out in November 1852, mail was carried over the Napoleon-Brookville road. Rural free delivery was established in 1901 marking the beginning of the system in the United States. Parcel post service was established in 1913. Free city mail delivery began in 1917. (Jean Struewing.)

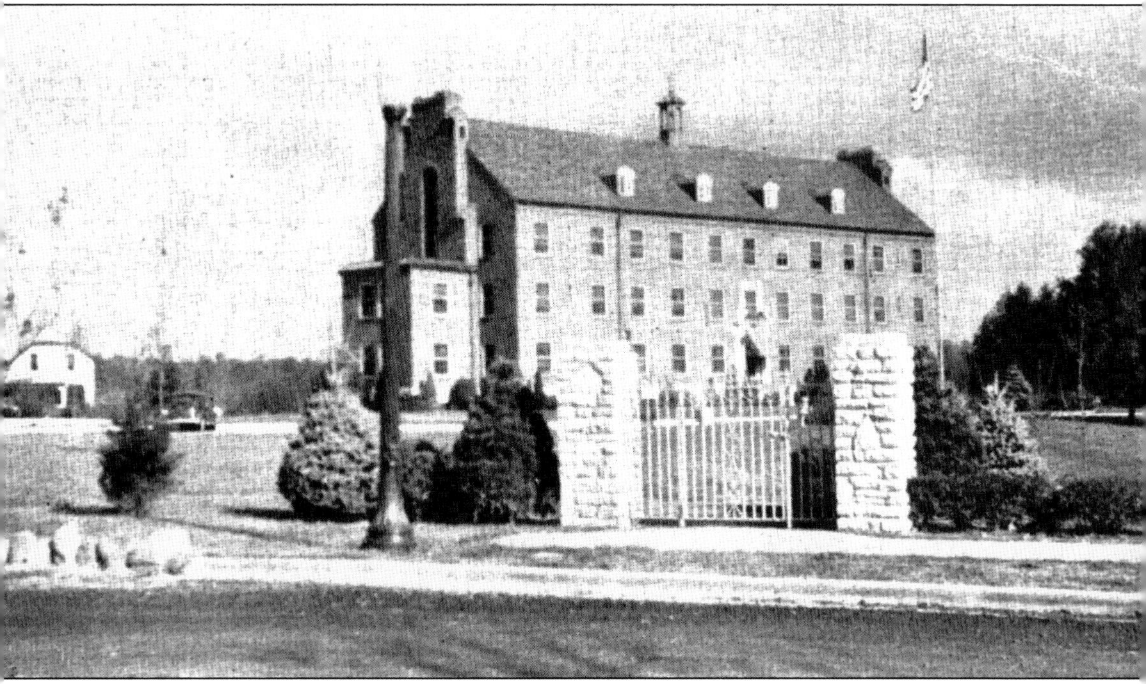

The first hospital was made possible through the bequest of Margaret Hillenbrand and her daughter Mary A. Mitchell. The site was donated by George M. Hillenbrand. The cornerstone was laid on February 1, 1932. The building dedication and open house were held October 29, 1932. It was a joyous occurrence to the area residents who were experiencing an end to the Great Depression. The Little Sisters of the Poor were contacted to take charge of the institution, oversee the construction, and to provide for its future management. Because of their unbounded generosity and unselfish love, the hospital flourished and effectively served the health needs of the community. History is made by time and change, but in the final analysis, it is the people that make a difference. To those people, all should be grateful. (Jean Struewing.)

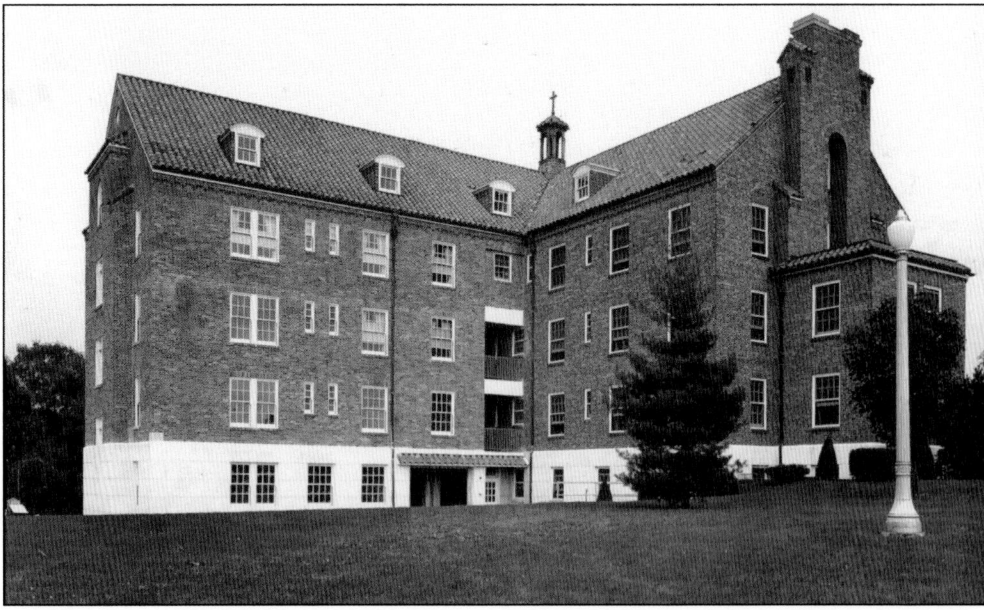

In 1941, there was already a need for expansion of the Margaret Mary Hospital, but due to government wartime restrictions, this did not become a reality until 1944. The north wing was completed on October 22, 1944. In spring of 1952, the entire hospital was redecorated. Through the ensuing years, Margaret Mary Hospital kept pace, progressing with the scientific and medical advances. (Women's Study Club.)

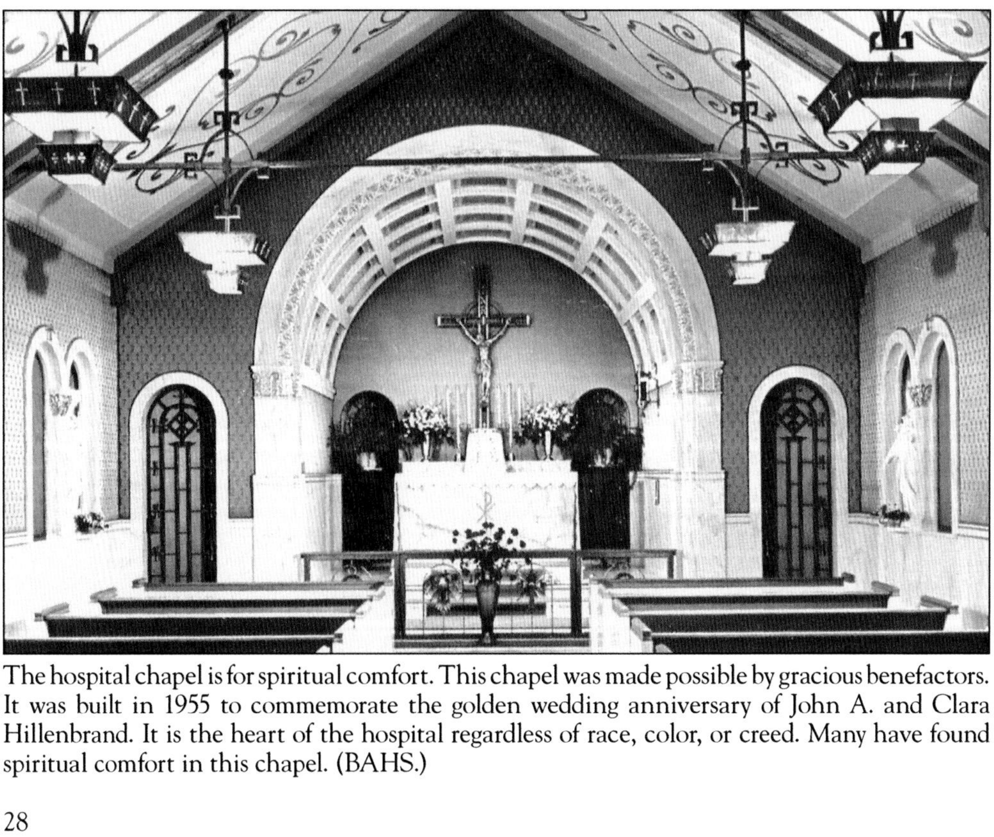

The hospital chapel is for spiritual comfort. This chapel was made possible by gracious benefactors. It was built in 1955 to commemorate the golden wedding anniversary of John A. and Clara Hillenbrand. It is the heart of the hospital regardless of race, color, or creed. Many have found spiritual comfort in this chapel. (BAHS.)

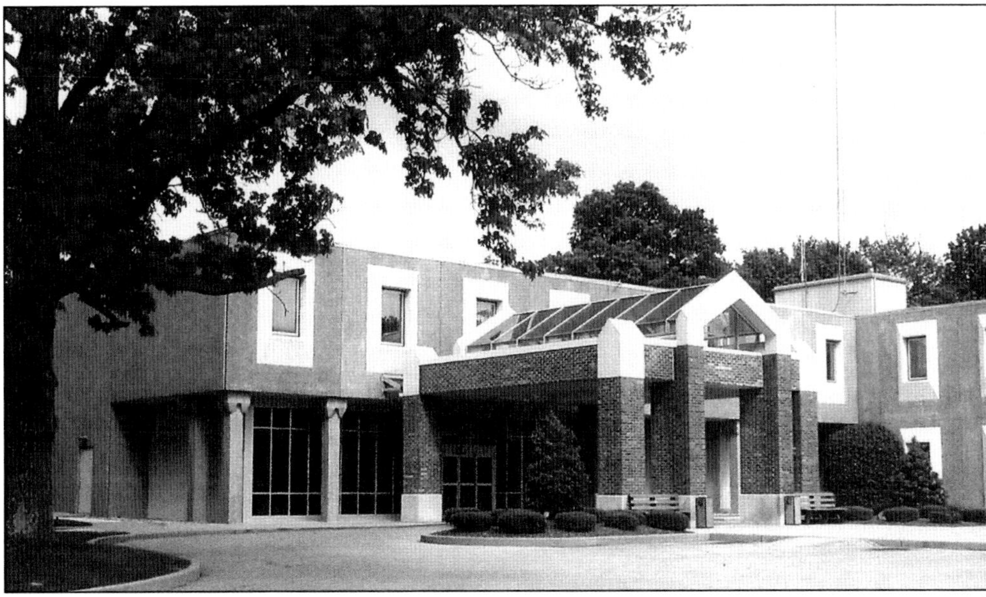

The present Margaret Mary Community Hospital's (MMCH) vision is to be the best health care provider for the communities, to be the place where people choose to come for services, the place where physicians choose to practice, and the place where people choose to work. The hospital boasts over 108 volunteers. The 2007 statistics show admissions at 2,065, outpatient volumes at 278,160, and the number of births at 352. (MMCH.)

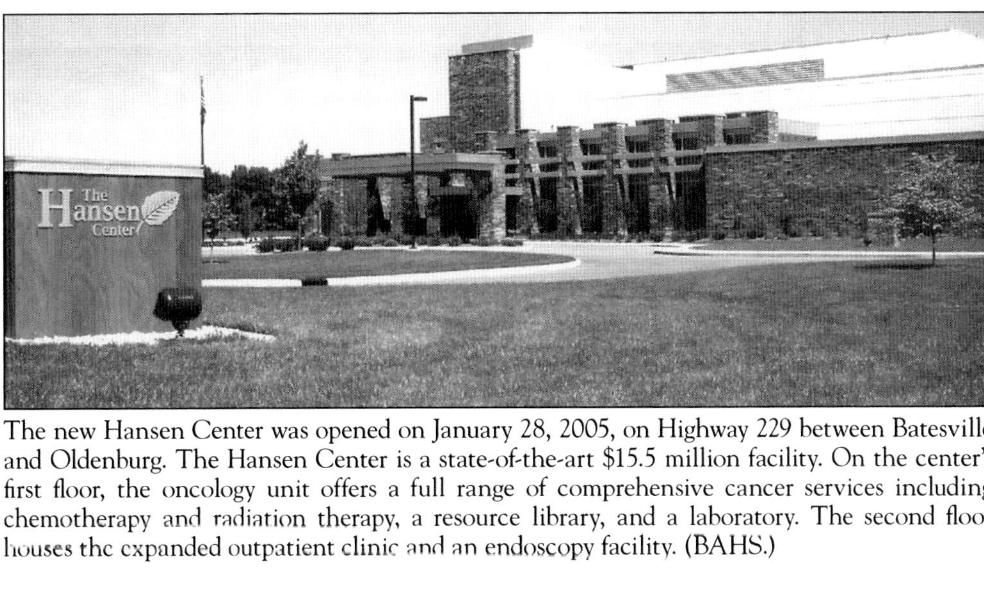

The new Hansen Center was opened on January 28, 2005, on Highway 229 between Batesville and Oldenburg. The Hansen Center is a state-of-the-art $15.5 million facility. On the center's first floor, the oncology unit offers a full range of comprehensive cancer services including chemotherapy and radiation therapy, a resource library, and a laboratory. The second floor houses the expanded outpatient clinic and an endoscopy facility. (BAHS.)

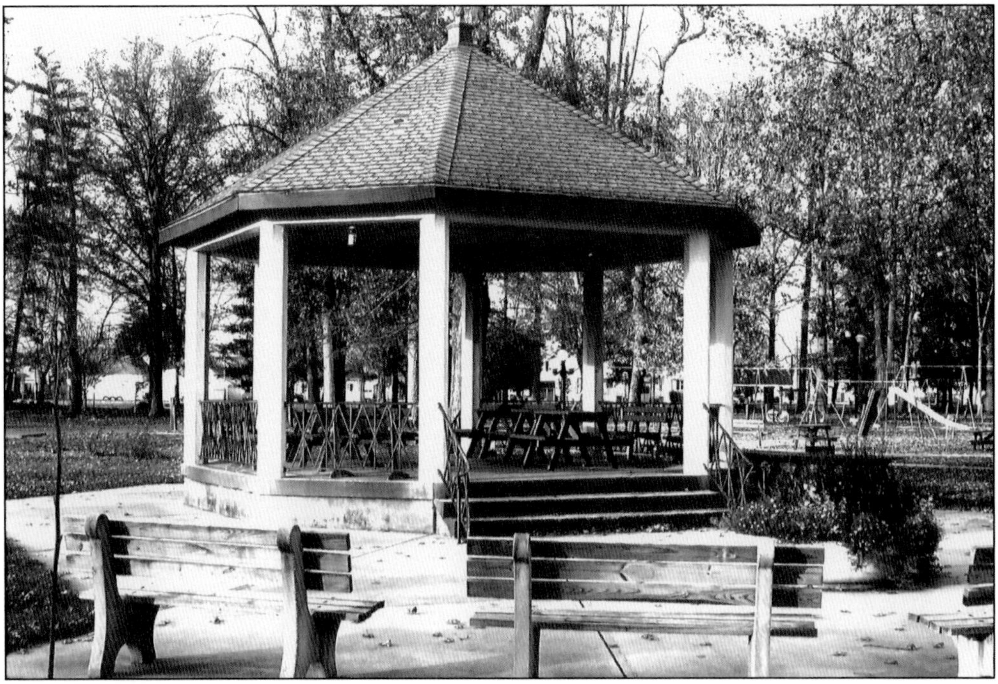

The dedication of the bandstand at Liberty Park took place in 1937. The bandstand was made possible through the generosity of G. M. Hillenbrand. The first piece played by the band at the dedication ceremonies was played in honor of his wife, Sophia Hillenbrand. (Jean Struewing.)

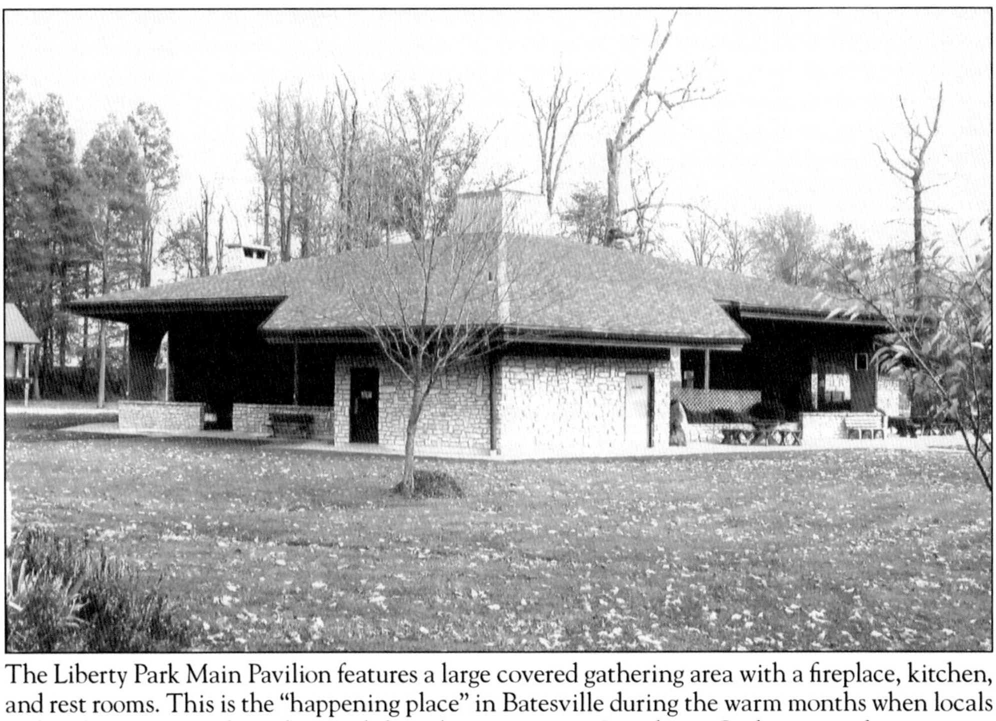

The Liberty Park Main Pavilion features a large covered gathering area with a fireplace, kitchen, and rest rooms. This is the "happening place" in Batesville during the warm months when locals gather for events, such as the Applefest, the Cincinnati Symphony Orchestra performance, or just to lounge during a summer musical performance. (Jean Struewing.)

Four

Churches and Schools

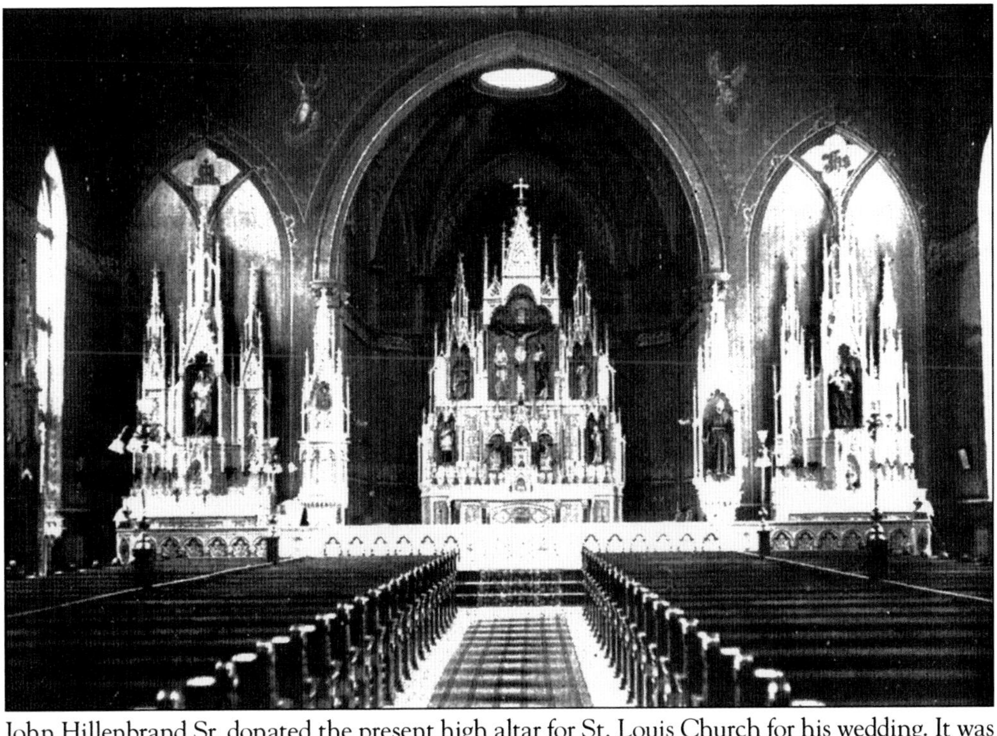

John Hillenbrand Sr. donated the present high altar for St. Louis Church for his wedding. It was made in Louisville. The altar was dedicated on March 3, 1903. In 1962, when the church was redecorated, some of the decorative pieces on the altar were removed. In 2008, a generous gift was made to St. Louis's parish by an anonymous individual, who had those pieces replaced and gold leafed. (Jean Struewing.)

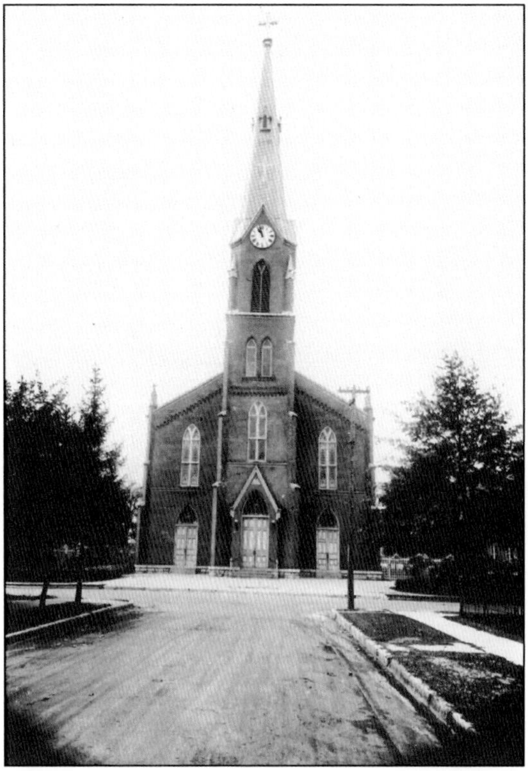

St. Louis Church was built during the early 1870s, with Walnut Street serving as an avenue of approach. The property where the church is built was deeded to St. Louis Church by Henry and Anna M. Boehringer and Herman and Adolphine Schrader for the purchase price of $5. Interestingly enough, all four were non-Catholics. (Pat Hare.)

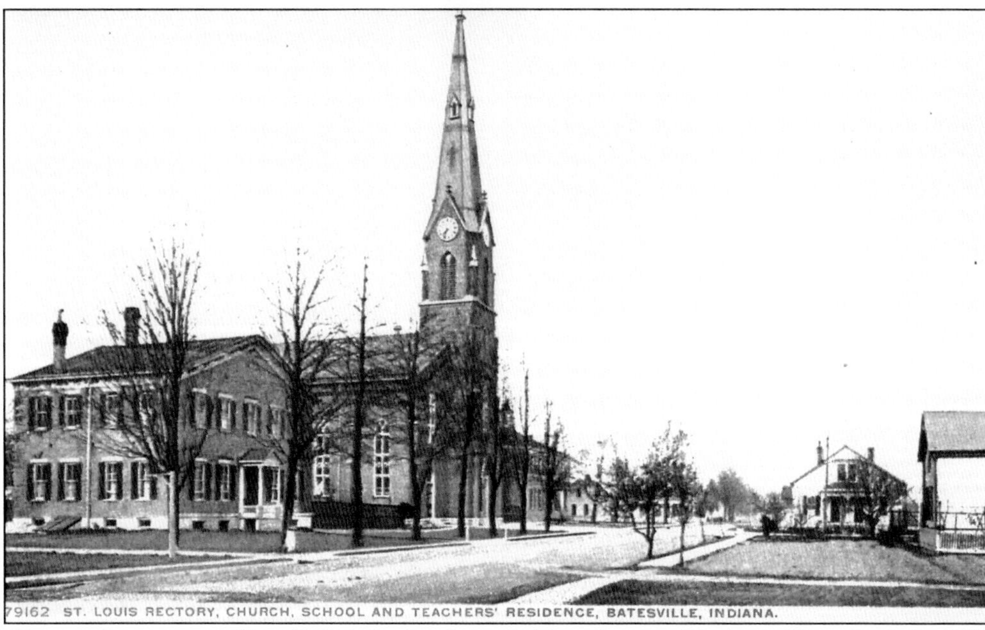

The parish was originally called St. Ludwig's, probably in honor of Fr. Louis Haverbeck. In 1871, Father Haverbeck built the first school, visible just beyond the church in this photograph, on the present site of the sisters' house. Its four classrooms were on the first floor and the sisters lived on the second floor. On the extreme left side of this photograph is the priest's rectory, built in 1876. (Jean Struewing.)

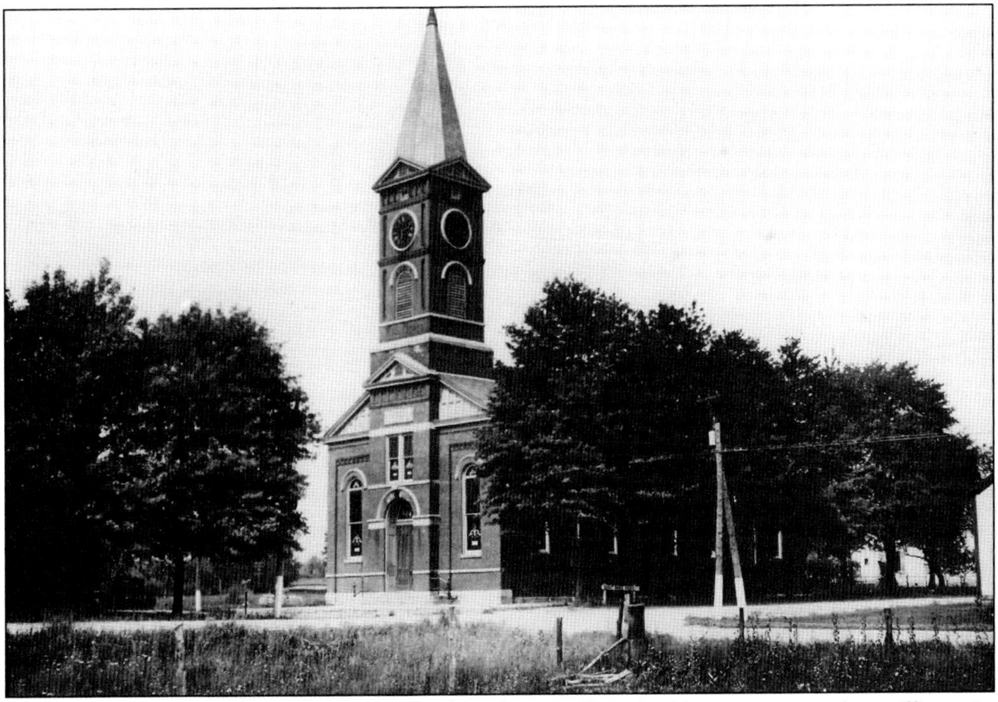

The story of the Huntersville Evangelical Lutheran Church, like so many other villages in America, begins in another land. The original immigrants to Huntersville, Indiana, came largely from Germany. Huntersville Evangelical Lutheran Church was organized in 1836. The first log church was constructed in 1840. This photograph shows the church built of brick as it is today. The town of Huntersville was laid out in 1841. (Pat Hare.)

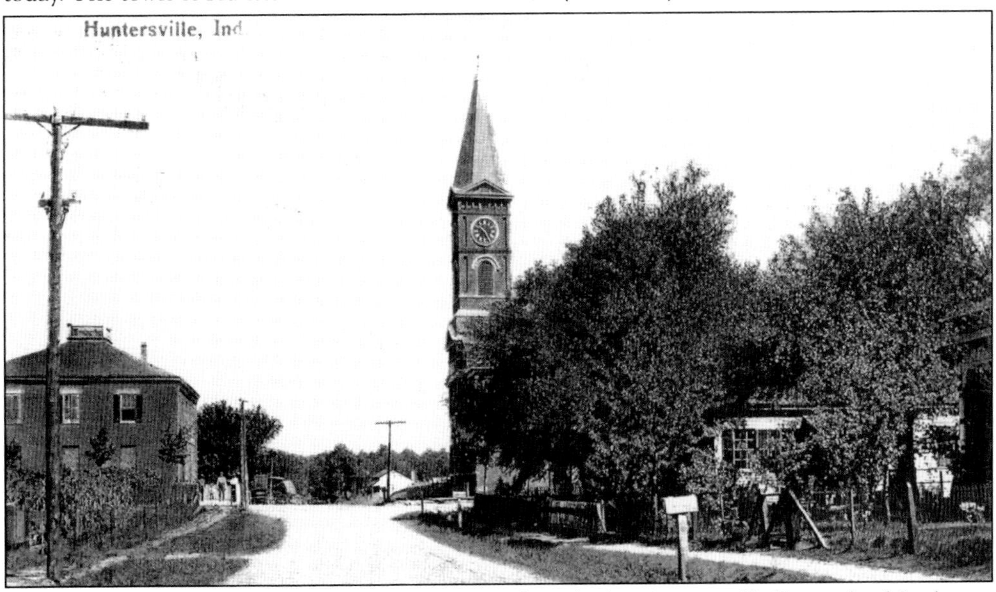

This postcard photograph was taken looking north with the Huntersville Evangelical Lutheran Church on the right. On the left is the D. H. Schrader Groceries and Hardware Store. This is now the home of Judy Tonges. Huntersville had been platted in July 1848 by the Lutheran pastor. The store was built in the 1850s (Jean Struewing.)

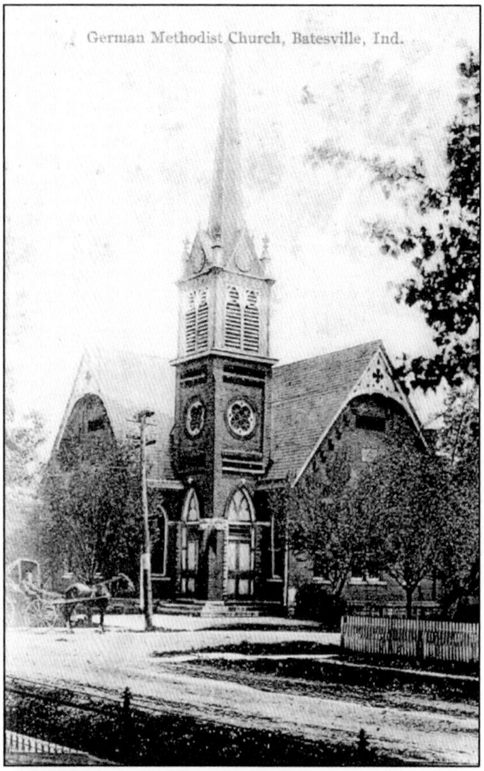

The German Methodist Church, located at the northeast corner of Park Avenue and South Streets, was built in 1889. Very few of the records of the business involved in its construction have been found, but it is known that much of the labor was donated by members. All services were originally conducted in the German language. Then in 1918, the official board resolved to discontinue the German services and conduct all services in English. (Pat Hare.)

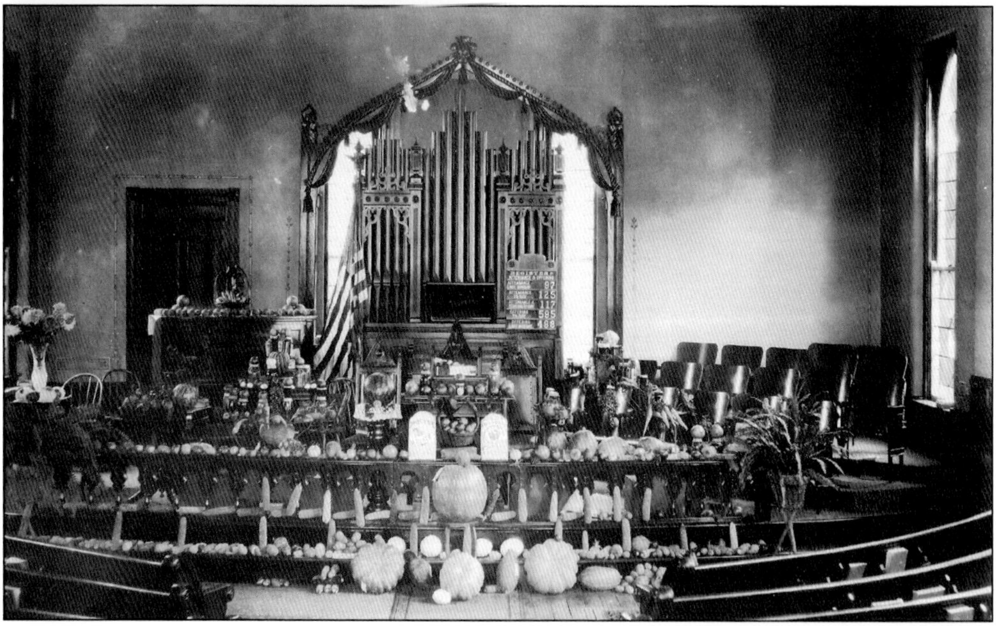

This picture shows the interior of the German Methodist Church, located on Park Avenue and South Street, with the altar decorated for Harvest Day. One can see pumpkins, ears of corn, gourds, and other produce displayed on the altar. The beautiful new Austin pipe organ was donated by Will J. and Elma Gelvin in memory of their mothers Lena Unnerwehr and Eliza Gelvin, on April 29, 1935. (Paul Wycoff.)

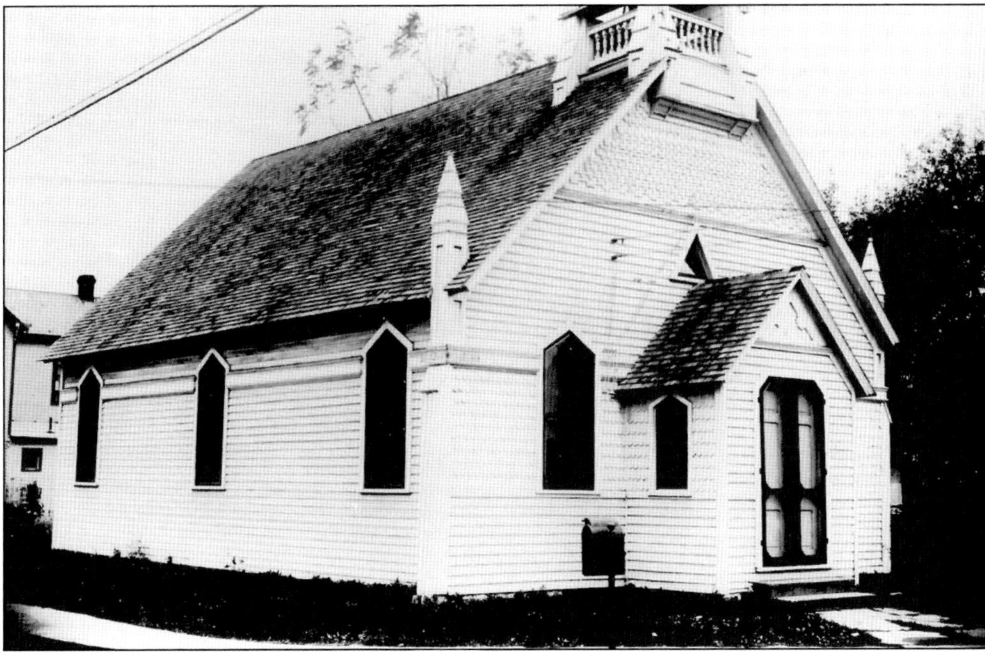

By February 1894, the new building for the English Methodists was built at the corner of Park Avenue and Catherine Street. The little church was of frame construction with wooden siding and was painted white. The new church was known as the English Methodist Episcopal Church until June 27, 1913, when the name was changed to the Wesley Chapel Methodist Episcopal Church. (Pat Hare.)

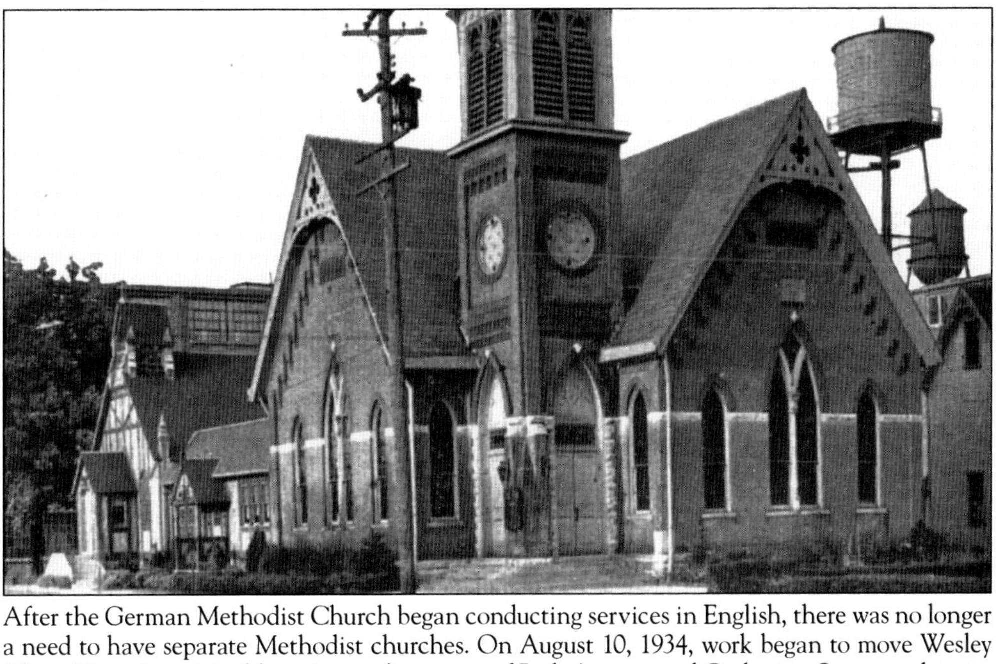

After the German Methodist Church began conducting services in English, there was no longer a need to have separate Methodist churches. On August 10, 1934, work began to move Wesley Chapel from its original location at the corner of Park Avenue and Catherine Street to this site as a unit of the First Methodist Church. The two church buildings were united, and can be seen attached in this postcard. (Jean Struewing)

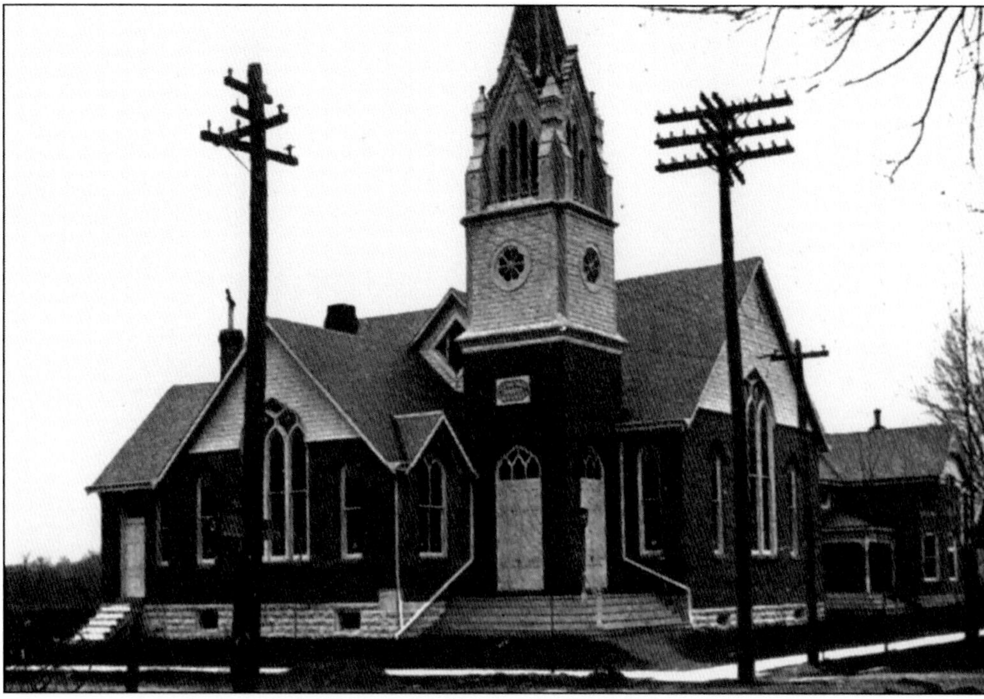

The cornerstone for St. Mark's Evangelical Lutheran Church building at West Pearl and Vine Streets was laid in August 15, 1897. Ward and Bohner erected the $7,000 structure, which was formally dedicated on March 20, 1898, by Dr. E. A. Severinghaus. The church bell bears an inscription in German that may be translated "St. Mark's bell, for the glory of God. Batesville, Indiana, December 8, 1899." (Pat Hare.)

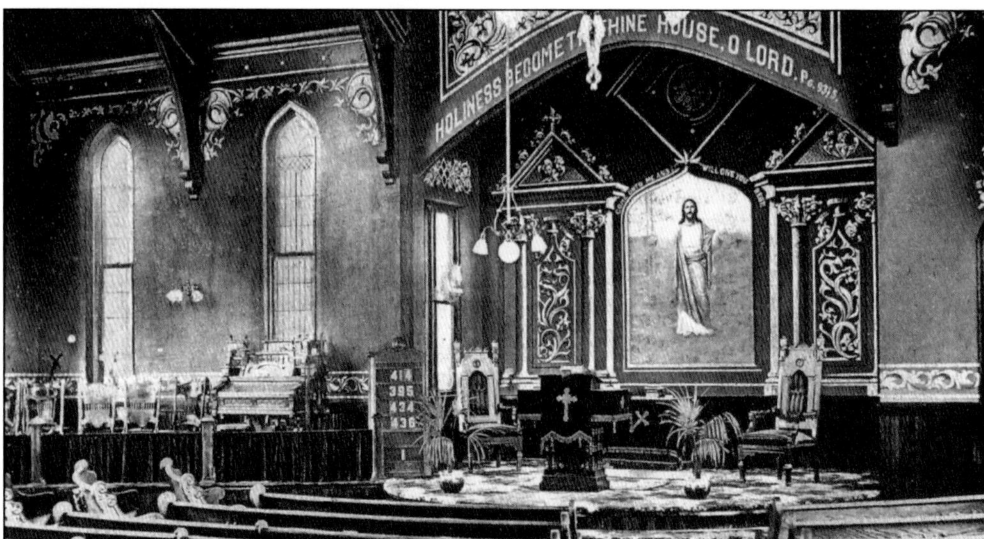

The sanctuary of St Mark's Lutheran Church, located at West Pearl and Vine Streets, is shown in this postcard. The first pipe organ was dedicated on June 11, 1911. The instrument was made by the Hinners Organ Company of Pekin, Illinois, and its $1,400 cost was shared equally by the congregation's Luther League and a special gift from philanthropist Andrew Carnegie. The Junior Luther League donated the marble baptismal font. (Pat Hare.)

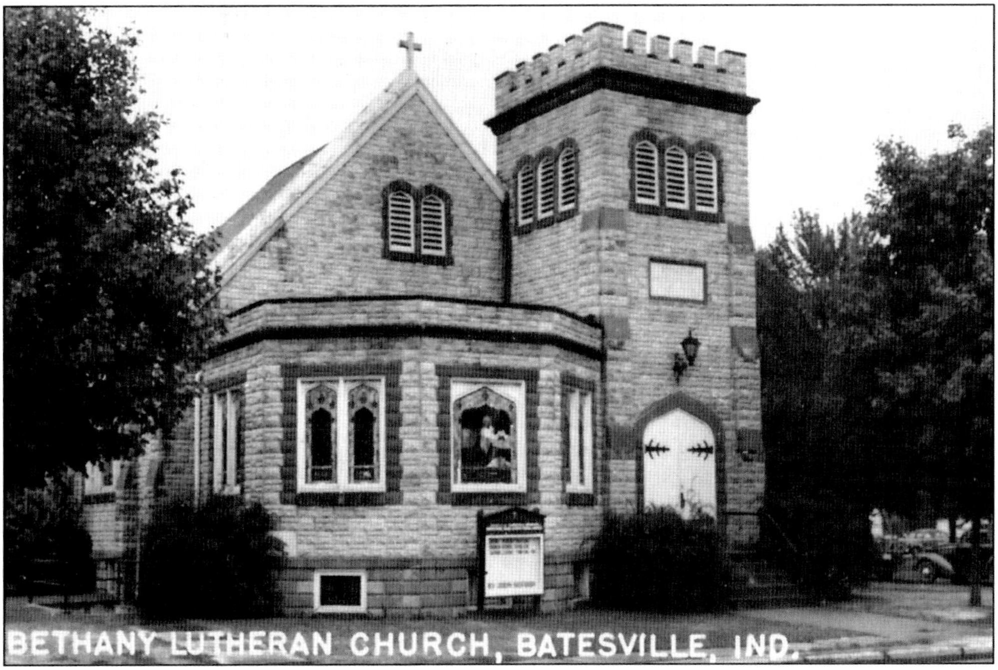

The Bethany Lutheran Church was built on the northwest corner of Catherine and Sycamore Streets, behind the Memorial Building, in 1909. It was christened Bethany Church and dedicated in 1913. The church was built in the Norman Style, with crenellated tower, stained glass, and square windows, an unusual type for a somewhat rural church. It was torn down around the year 2000. (Jean Struewing.)

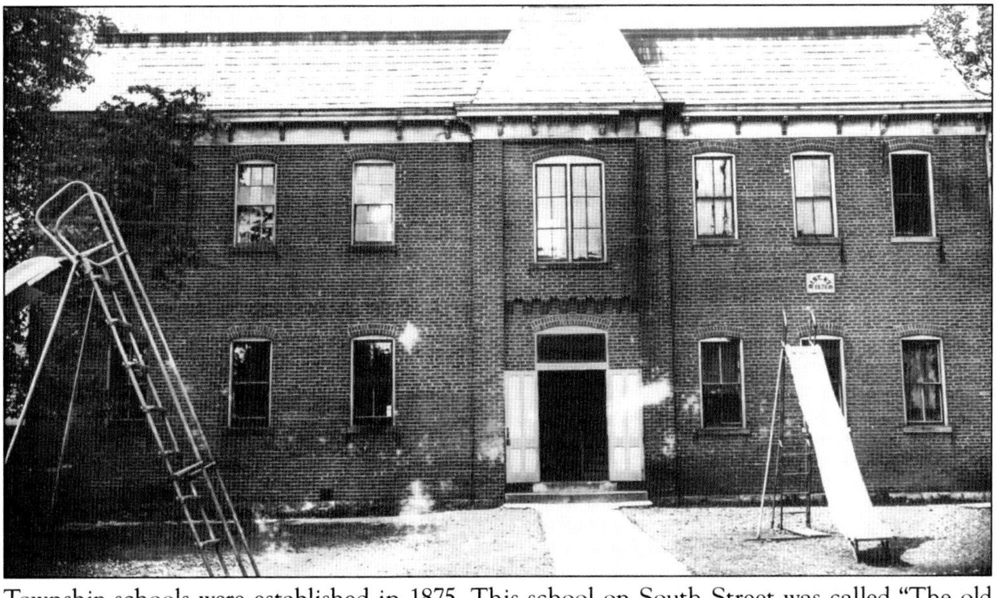

Township schools were established in 1875. This school on South Street was called "The old South Street School." This brick schoolhouse contained four rooms, two upstairs and two on the ground floor. A new high school building was constructed at the corner of Mulberry and Pearl Streets in 1895 and 1896. Since no better site was available, the two-story building was torn down, and a one-story grade school was built. (Paul Wycoff.)

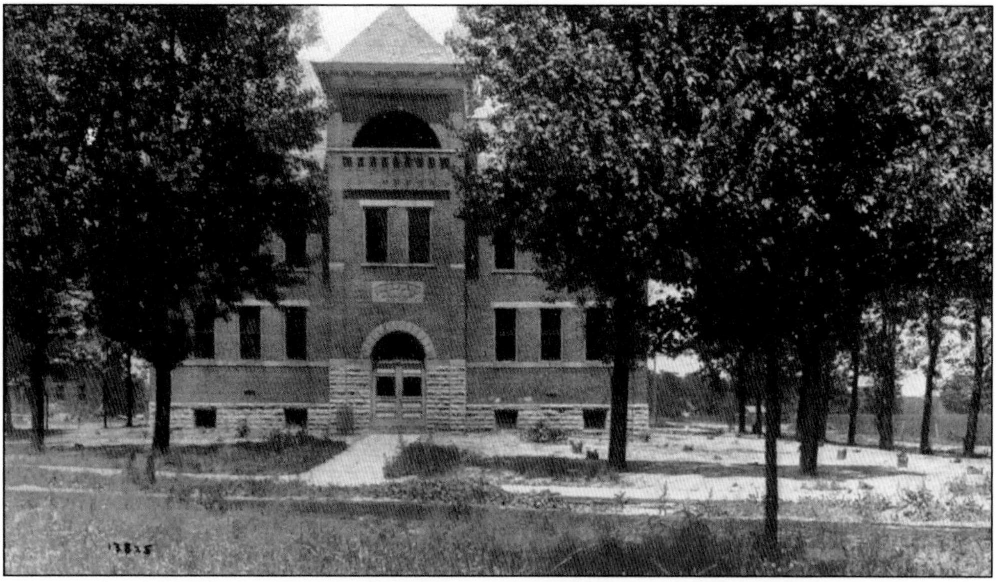

A new school building was erected at the corner of Mulberry and Pearl Street in 1895–1896. In 1910–1911, this building was remodeled to accommodate a four-year high school. As the enrollment increased a new high school was built in 1926–1927, and the building in the photograph was then used exclusively as a grade school. In 1938, a gymnasium was built on Mulberry Street behind this school. (Jean Struewing.)

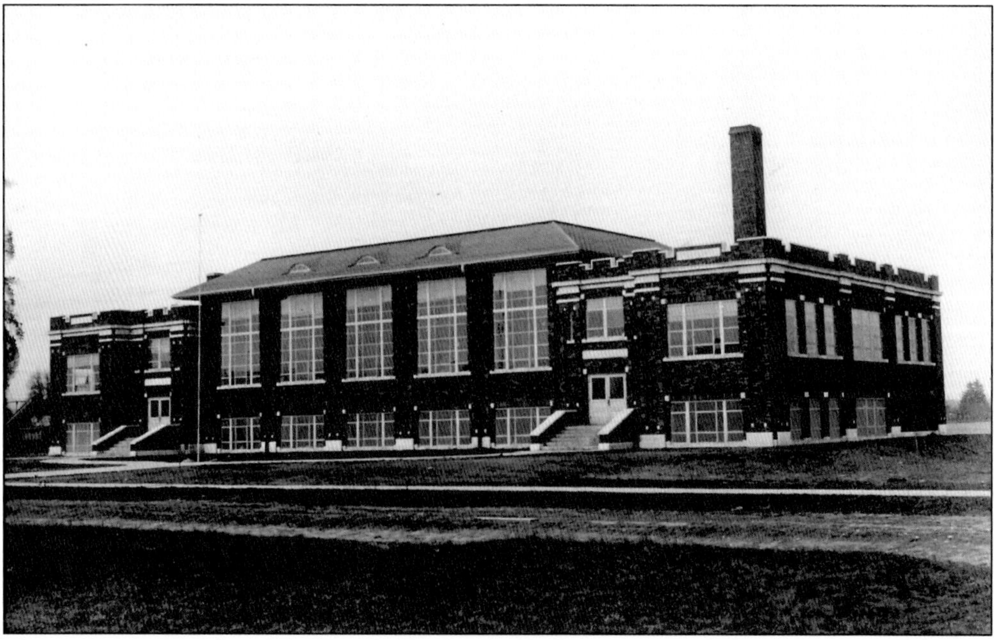

The year 1926–1927 found the Batesville school system with a new, separate high school building at the corner of Mulberry Street and Columbus Avenue. It was constructed at a cost of $56,000. The site for the new high school was given by the late George M. Hillenbrand and included enough ground for tennis courts, track, and a large playground. (Pat Hare.)

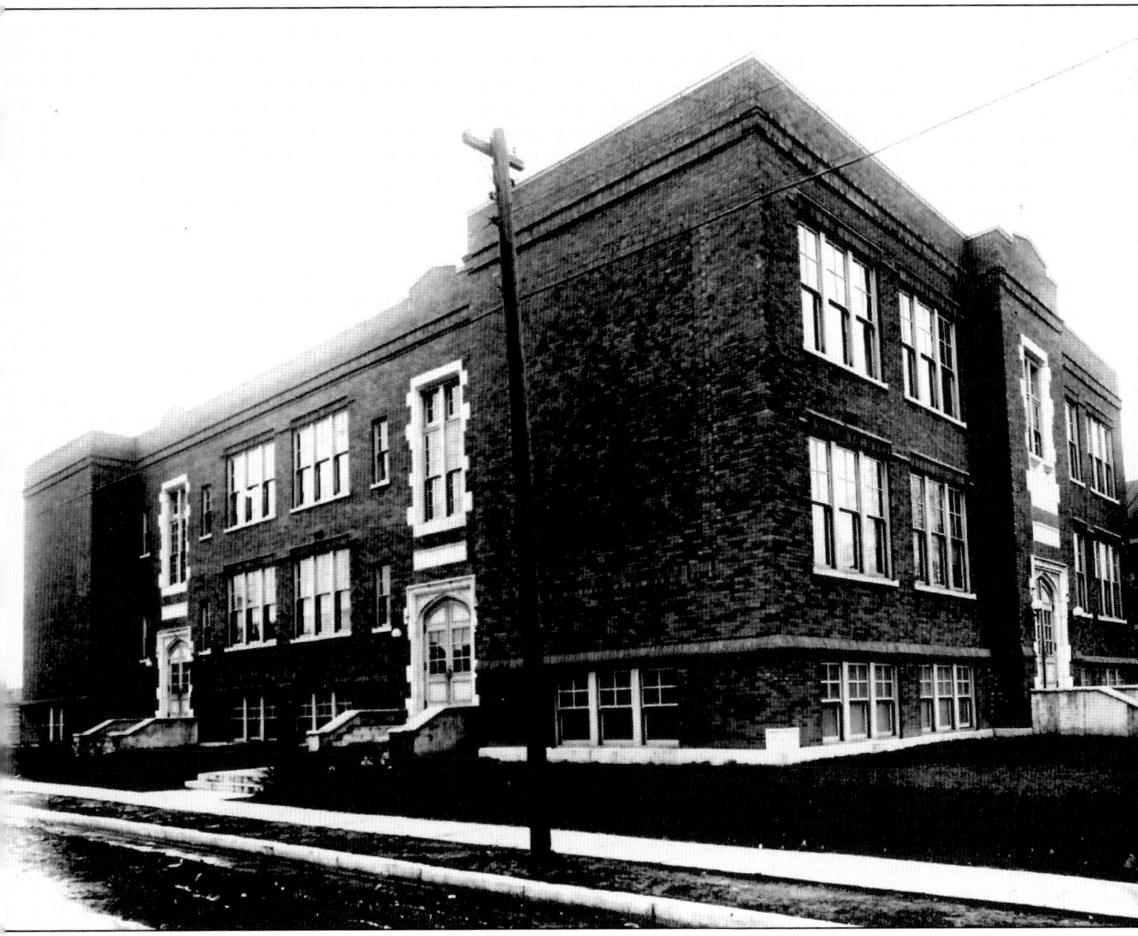

With but four classrooms and over 200 children, the original 1871 St. Louis Catholic School building was far too crowded, and it was evident that a bigger school was needed. The cornerstone for this school building was set in place September 10, 1922. Howard McClory of Cincinnati was the architect; W. A. Gutzwiller was the contractor. Dedication was November 25, 1923. The property where the school was built was a lumberyard owned by John Hillenbrand. Everyone knew that this was the ideal spot to erect the building and that the church wanted to buy the land. One Sunday night, the church representatives had a meeting, and Hillenbrand stood up and said that he was not going to sell the property to the church. A hush fell over the audience. "I am going to give it to the parish if the men will clean the place up!" said Hillenbrand. (Pat Hare.)

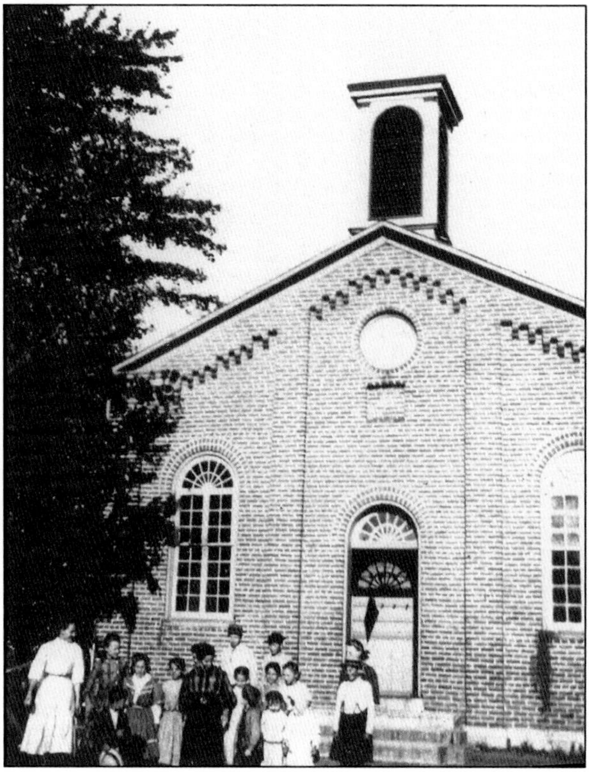

According to Huntersville Church records, the first Huntersville School classes were conducted in the parsonage in 1842. In 1870, this one-room brick school was built, which measured 58 feet by 28 feet, and was constructed at a cost of $2,300. It served the parish until the conclusion of the 1944–1945 school year. Education was a high priority amongst this group of immigrants. (Richard Flodder.)

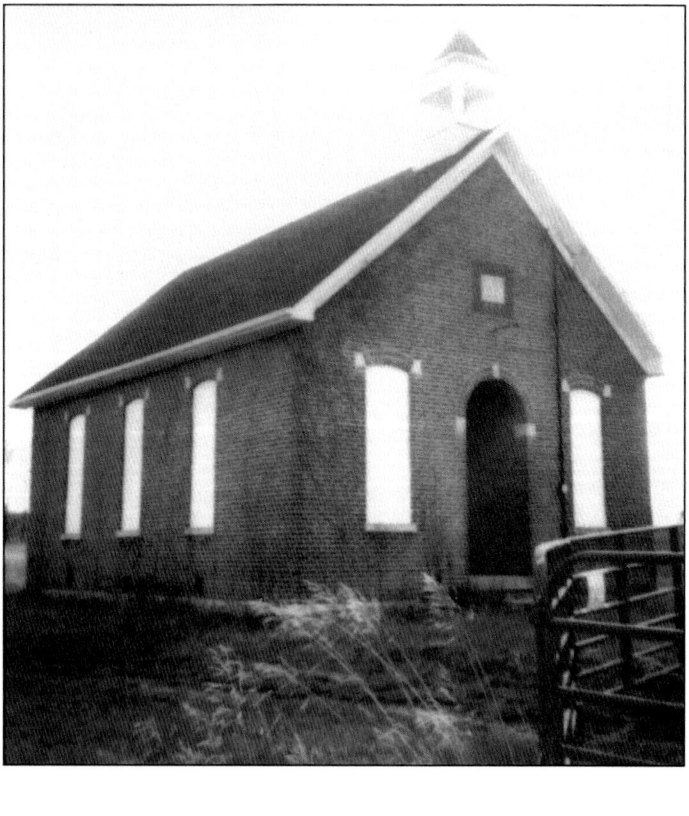

The one-room Hayti School was built in 1896, south of Batesville near the Ballstown Hill, on Everett Wilson's farm. Among the teachers who taught here were Mr. Newman, Howe Petti, Ella Showers, Mr. Shaddy, Carrie Thackery, Norma Heinlein, Cecil Caster, Jenny Ford, and Gladys (Windsor) Einhaus. This schoolhouse still stands on the Wilson Farm owned by Margaret Wilson on highway 229. (Richard Flodder.)

Five

FACTORIES

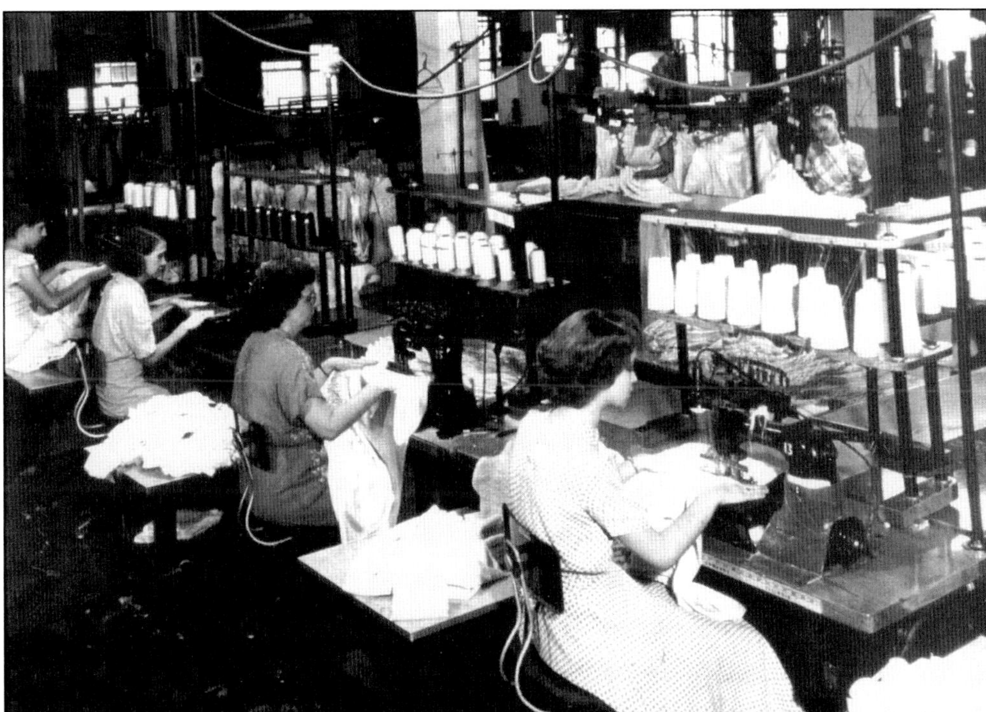

In the early years of the Batesville Coffin Company, the interiors of the caskets were sewn with hand-operated sewing machines. Each worker sewed a different part of the interior. Various types of interior cloths were used. Batesville Casket Company got its start in 1906, when John A. Hillenbrand rescued a small town coffin manufacturing company from insolvency. (Batesville Casket Company.)

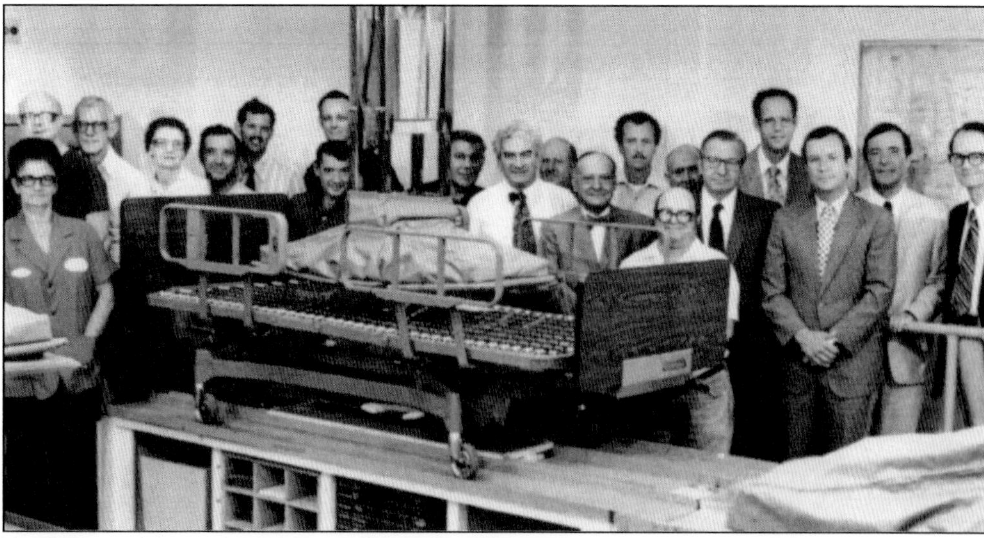

Employees celebrate the occasion of the 500,000th Hill-Rom bed rolling off the factory assembly line. The bed in the photograph was the all-electric bed. From left to right are Barb Good, Gerald McClain, Tim Weigel, Ruth Stirn, Sylvester Bedel, possibly Jim Drockelman, Virgil Hensley, Leo Merkel, Leo "Beesy" Wetterding, Frank Holtel, Alphonse "Butch" Mollaun, Bill Hillenbrand, possibly Dale Foster, Hugo Voegele, Jim Hornberger, Fran Burst, Dave Sunderman, Gus Hillenbrand, Bill Kelley, and Jack Clawson. (Tom Steinkamp.)

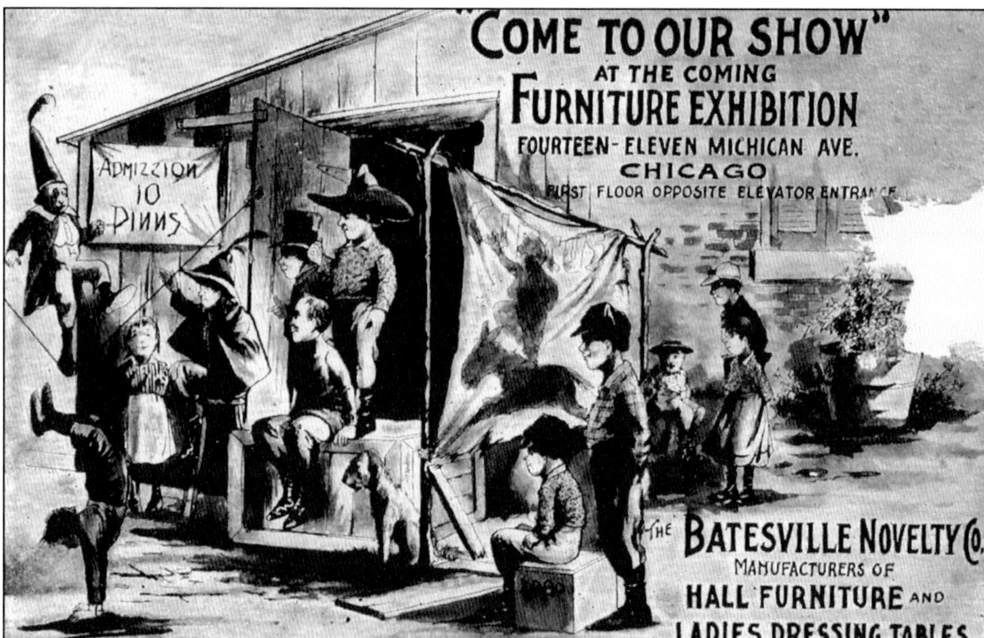

The Batesville Novelty Company was located at the corner of North Vine Street and Hillenbrand Avenue. The building was a two-story frame structure previously owned by a small furniture manufacturer known as the Jacob Blank Jr. Company. The Batesville Novelty Company continued business until 1911, when they went into receivers' hands, and the business was dissolved. (BAHS.)

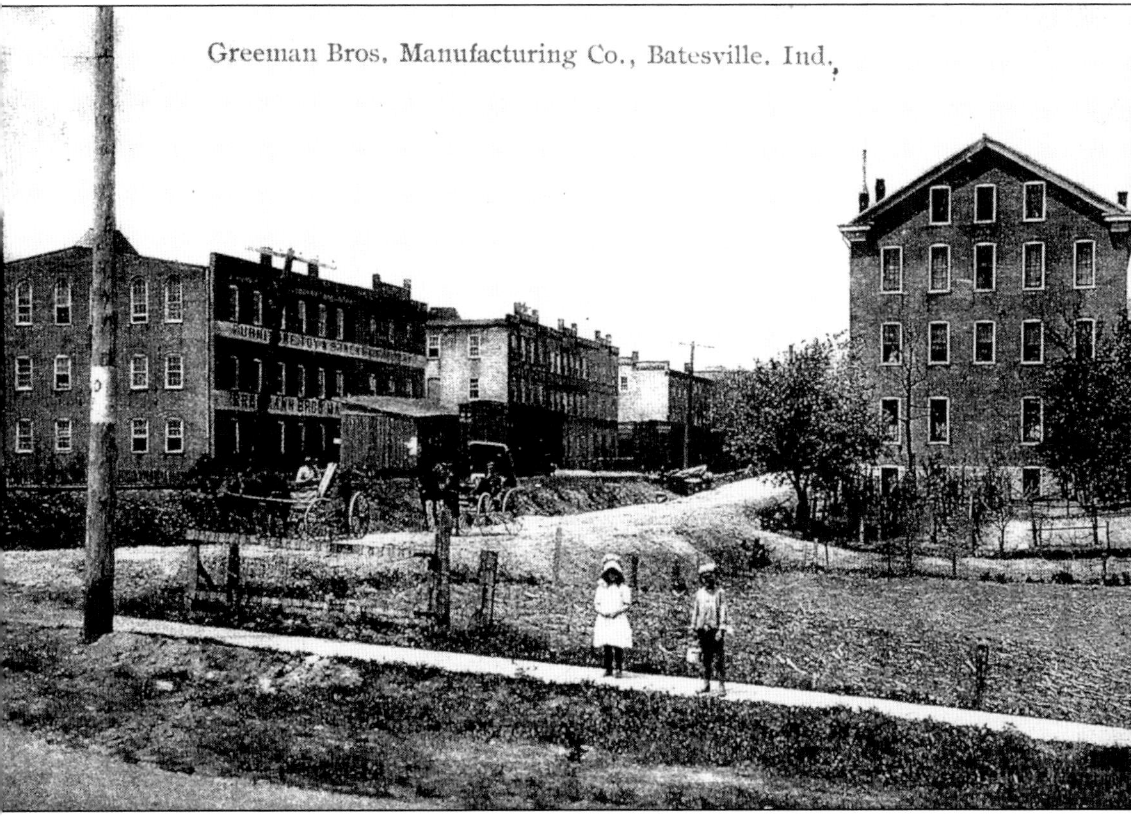

The Greeman Brothers Manufacturing Company was organized in 1876 as the Batesville Carving Company with capital of $5,000. Many workers learned the trades of carving, cabinetmaking, and varnishing during their employment at the Greeman factory. The starting wage was $1.50 per week for a workweek of six days, 10 hours each day. The company failed after the death of William T. Greeman, oldest son of Frederick Greeman. After a number of efforts to regain prosperity, the company was sold to the Hillenbrand Company in March 1913. (Jean Struewing.)

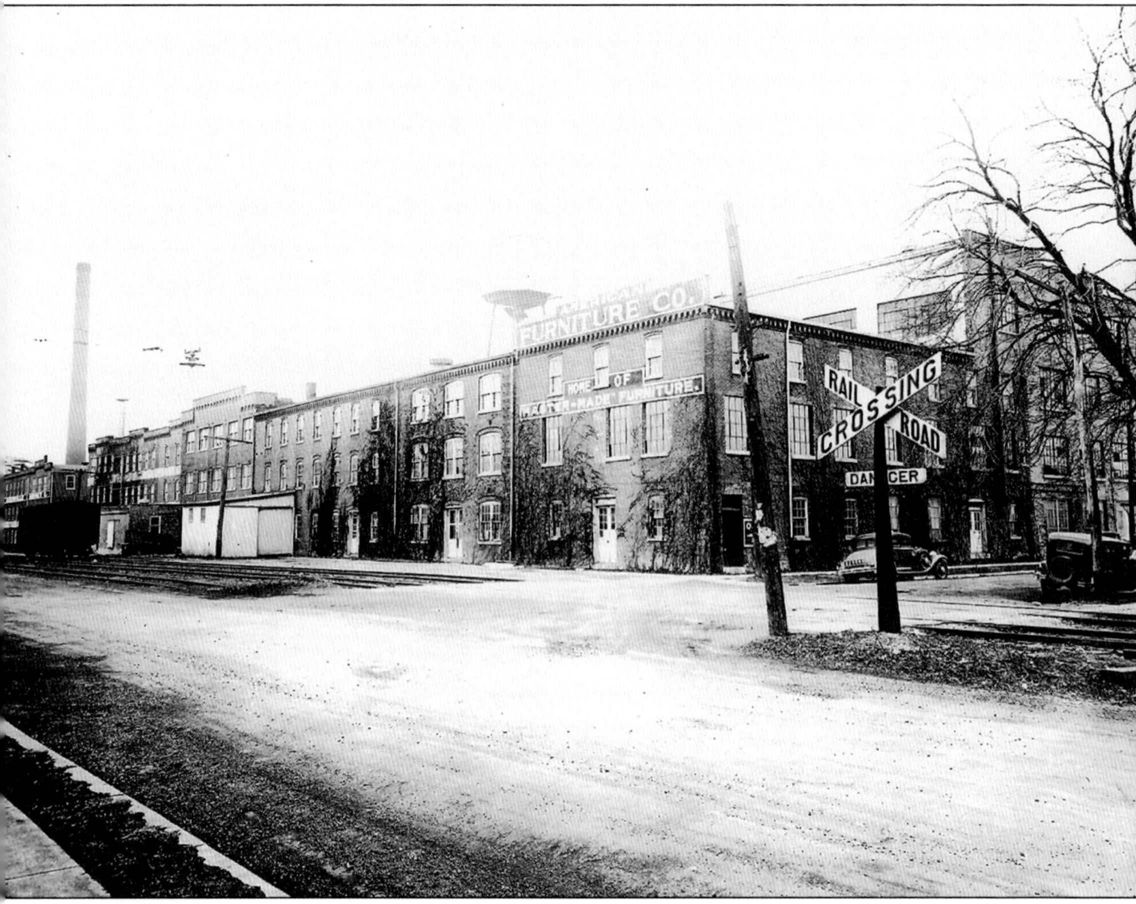

The American Furniture Company was organized as a stock company after the dissolution of the Hillenbrand brothers partnership in 1886. It had succeeded the Schrader Furniture Company after the death of Herman Schrader in 1882. The American Furniture Company's office building was built in 1909 at Main and East Pearl Streets, facing Main Street and extending west to Walnut Street. Eventually the American Furniture Company merged with the Romweber Company, their main product being Viking Oak furniture. (Paul Wycoff.)

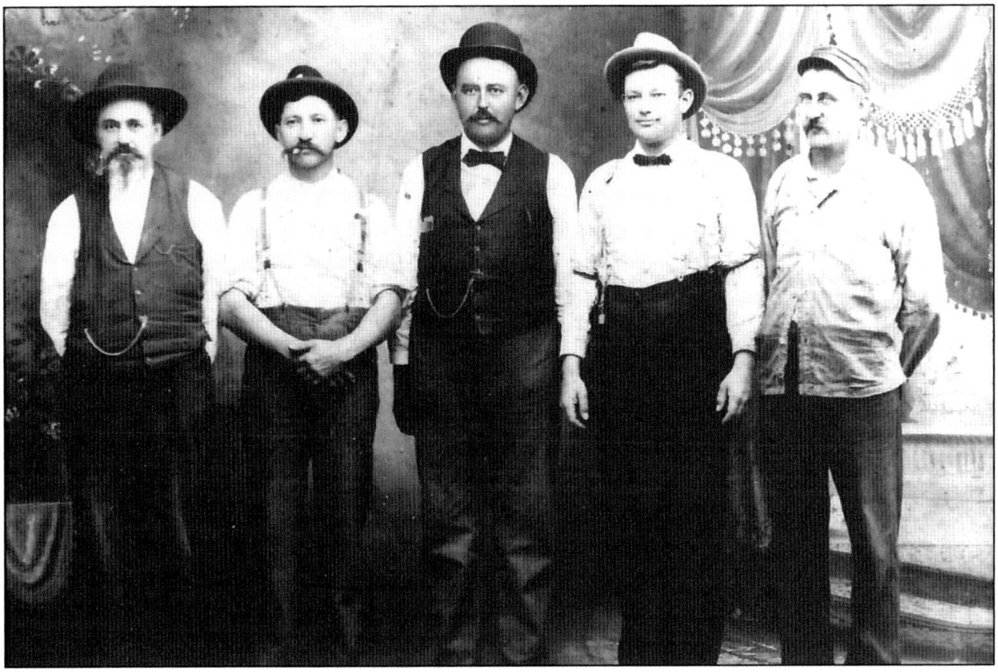

This is a photograph of the "Anti Trust Group" of the 1890s. From left to right are Dr. Ernest Timmerman, the town doctor; Jacob Engel, a saloon keeper; Edward C. Timmerman, their bookkeeper; Fred Morgan, owner of Enterprise Casket Company; and Charles Schein, factory foreman of Enterprise Casket. (Jean Struewing.)

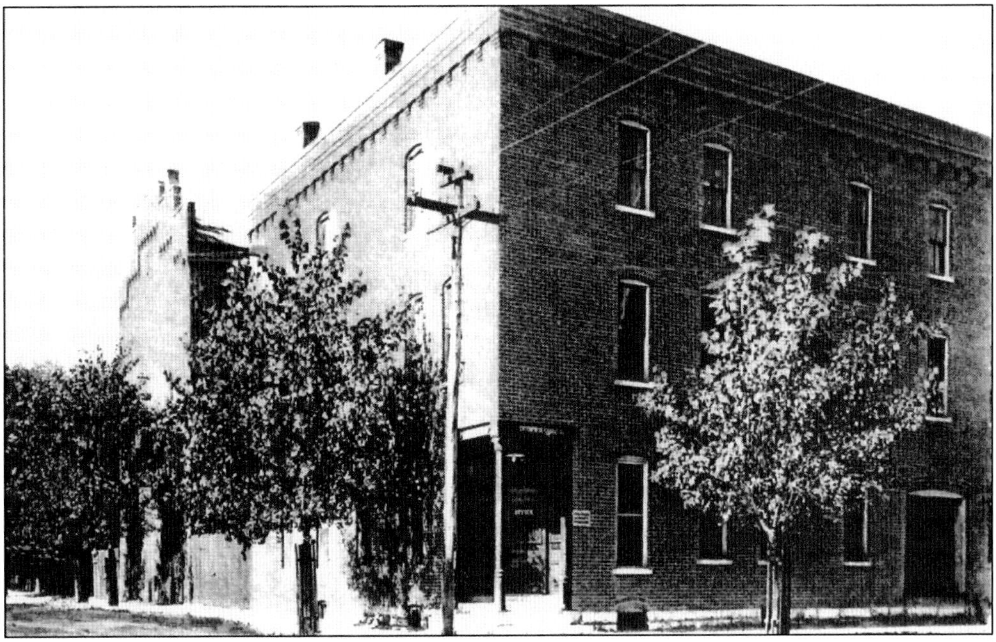

Enterprise Casket Company was located on the southwest corner of Walnut and West Pearl Streets, the current site of Hill-Rom Architectural Products office. The factory was operated by R. N. Papet. Charles Schein invented a casket hinge that revolutionized the casket industry. (BAHS.)

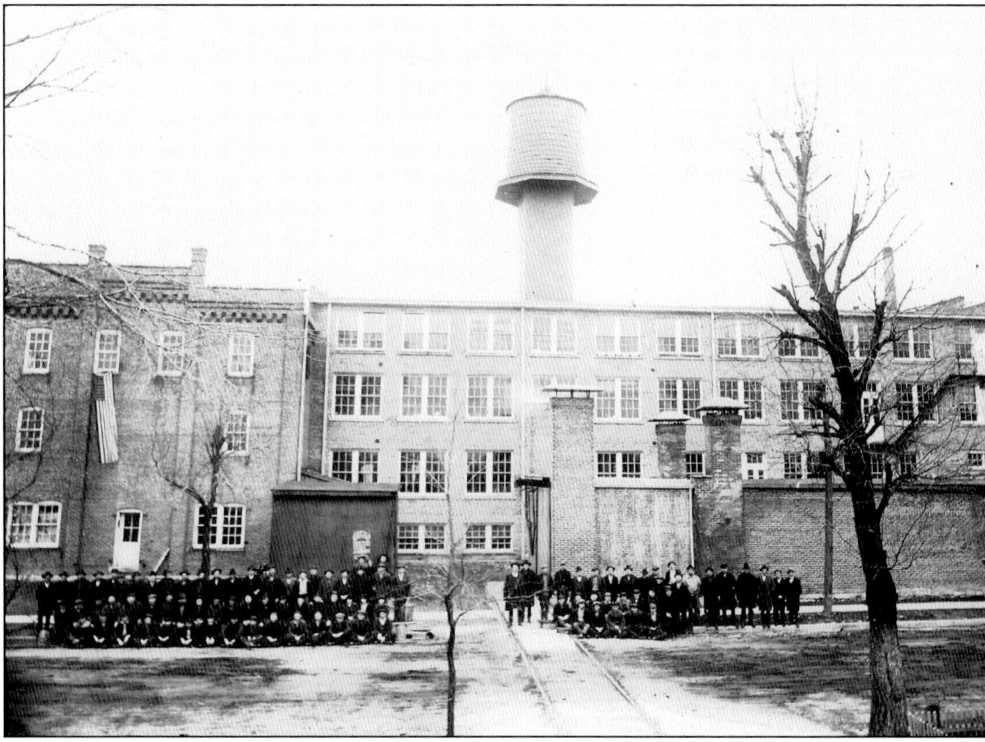

The Union Furniture Company is shown during its prime manufacturing years when it was Batesville's oldest continuously-operating company. It was organized by George, Frederick, and William Schultz as a mutual stock company. The employees owned a large portion of the stock company. This picture shows many of its employees and stockholders. The Union Furniture Company was a subsidiary of Jamestown Sterling Company at the time it ceased production. (Paul Wycoff.)

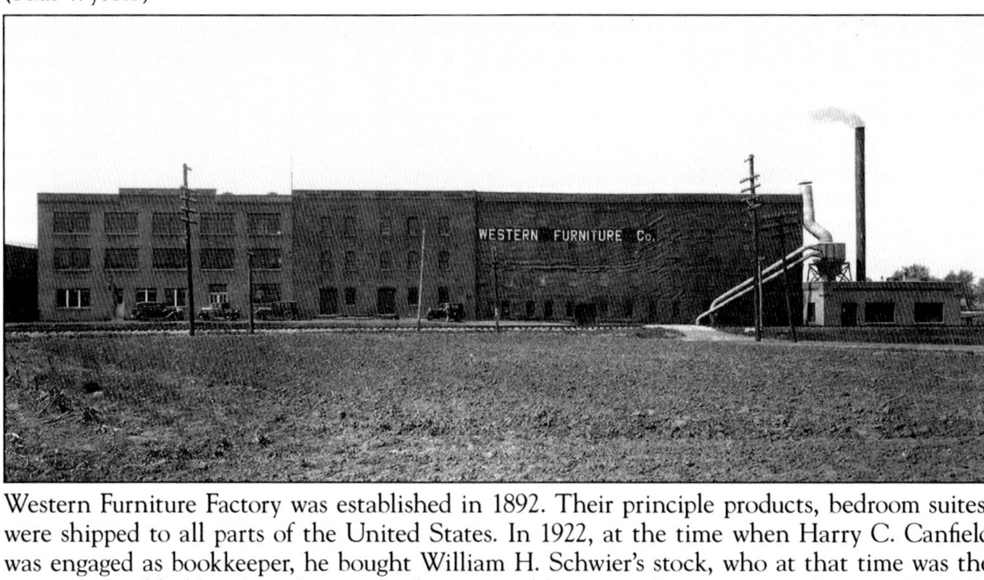

Western Furniture Factory was established in 1892. Their principle products, bedroom suites, were shipped to all parts of the United States. In 1922, at the time when Harry C. Canfield was engaged as bookkeeper, he bought William H. Schwier's stock, who at that time was the principle stockholder. As a furniture salesman and later as a furniture manufacturer, Canfield became widely known throughout the whole country. (Paul Wycoff.)

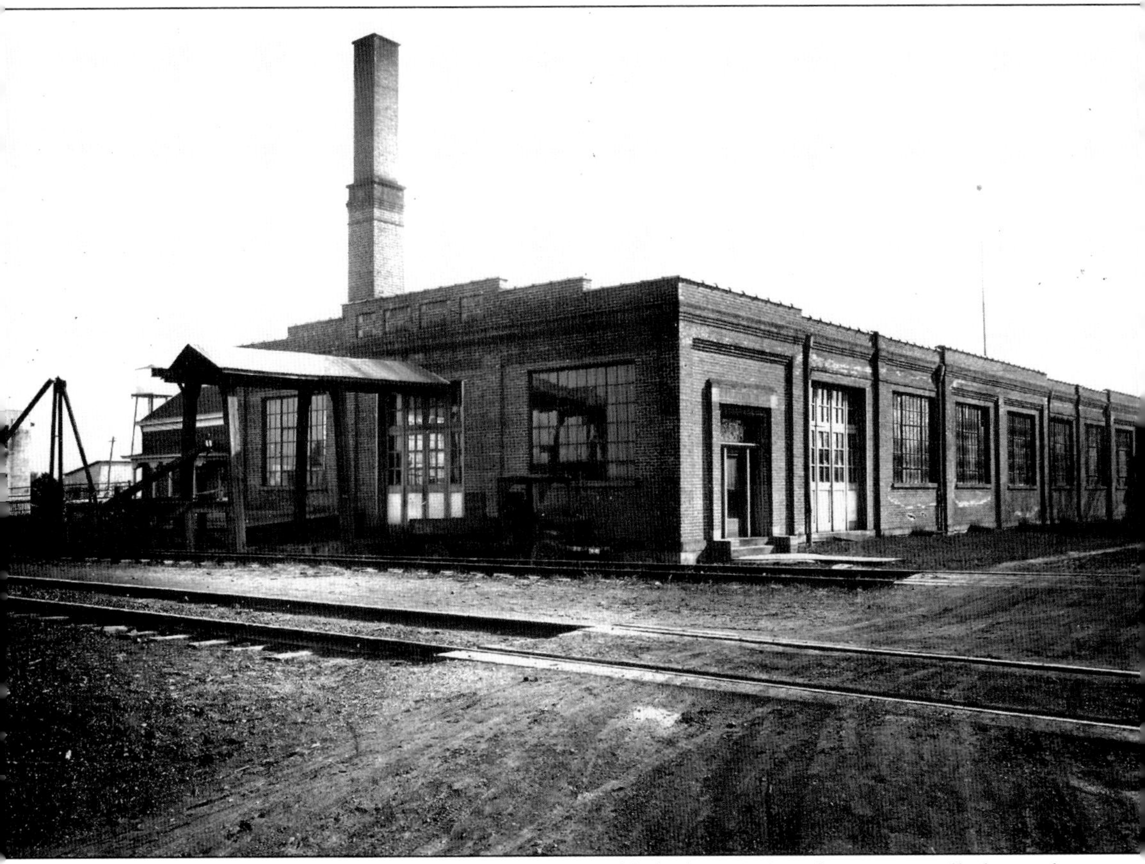

The Hageman Mirror-Plate Glass Company was established in 1912 and was originally located on land owned by Christian Schwier on the site of the early flour mills of Batesville. But as business increased, they enlarged their factory and in 1917 moved to this site facing the railway freight tracks on the southeast side of East Pearl Street and Eastern Avenue. (Paul Wycoff.)

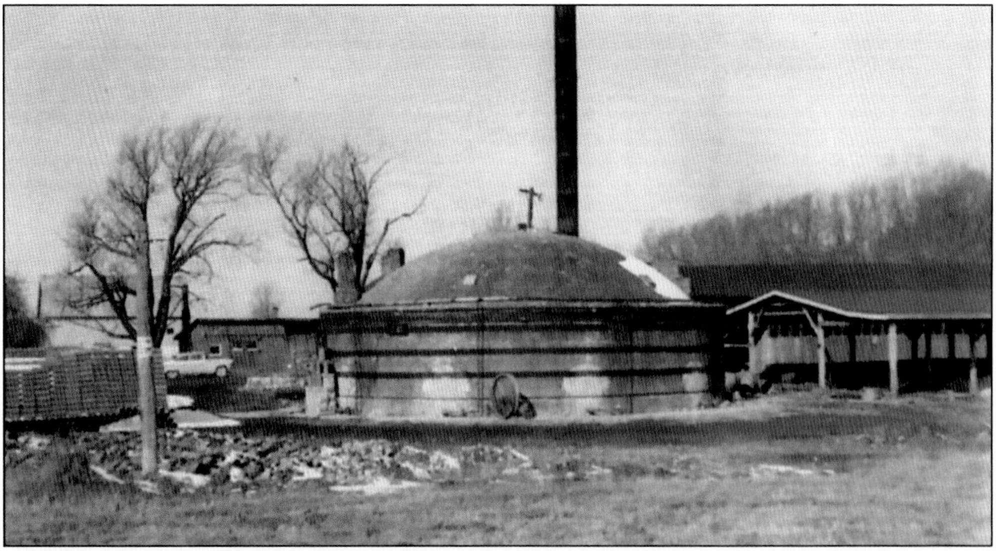

This is a view of the kiln built in 1960 by the Huntersville Brick and Tile Company. It was intended to be coal fired; however, the Batesville Water and Gas Company desired to balance out their annual gas consumption and convinced the Huntersville Brick and Tile Company to fire their kiln with natural gas. This was a step forward for the tile manufacturing process. (Bill Swain.)

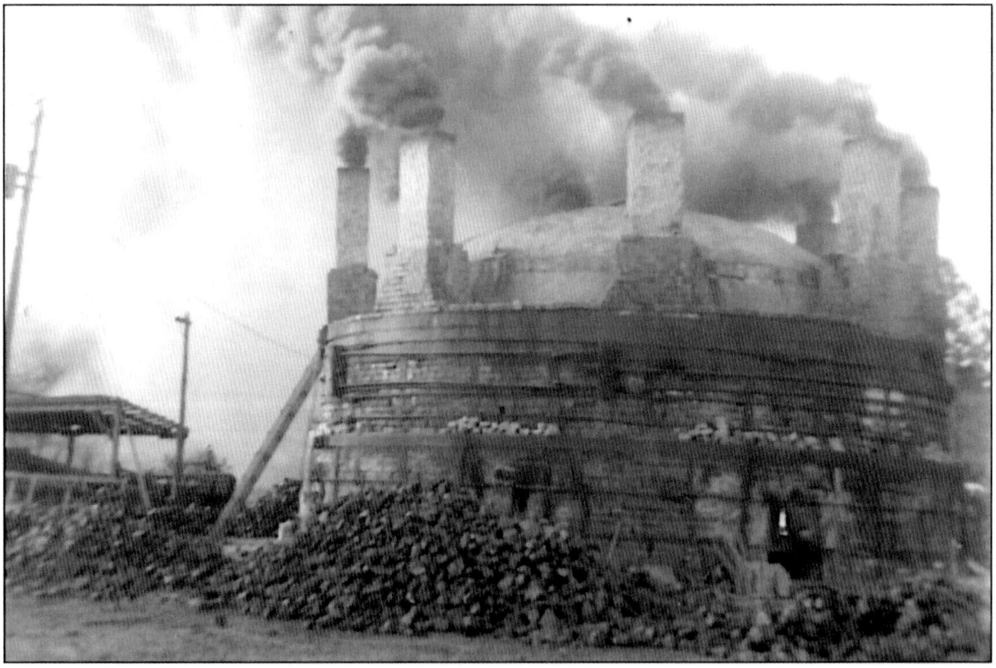

Henry Wessel established a brickyard on his own farm just north of Huntersville adjacent to the Ripley County line. He operated it in connection with his farm work throughout his life, and his sons continued the same industry. The Wessel brickyard proved a long-standing institution enduring in the Wessel family. This picture shows Wessel's coal-fired kiln of approximately 22 feet inside diameter with 32-inch-thick walls. Huntersville owned the tile plant from 1958 until June 1963. Bill Swain bought the brick and tile company in the 1960s. (Bill Swain.)

Six

Entertainment

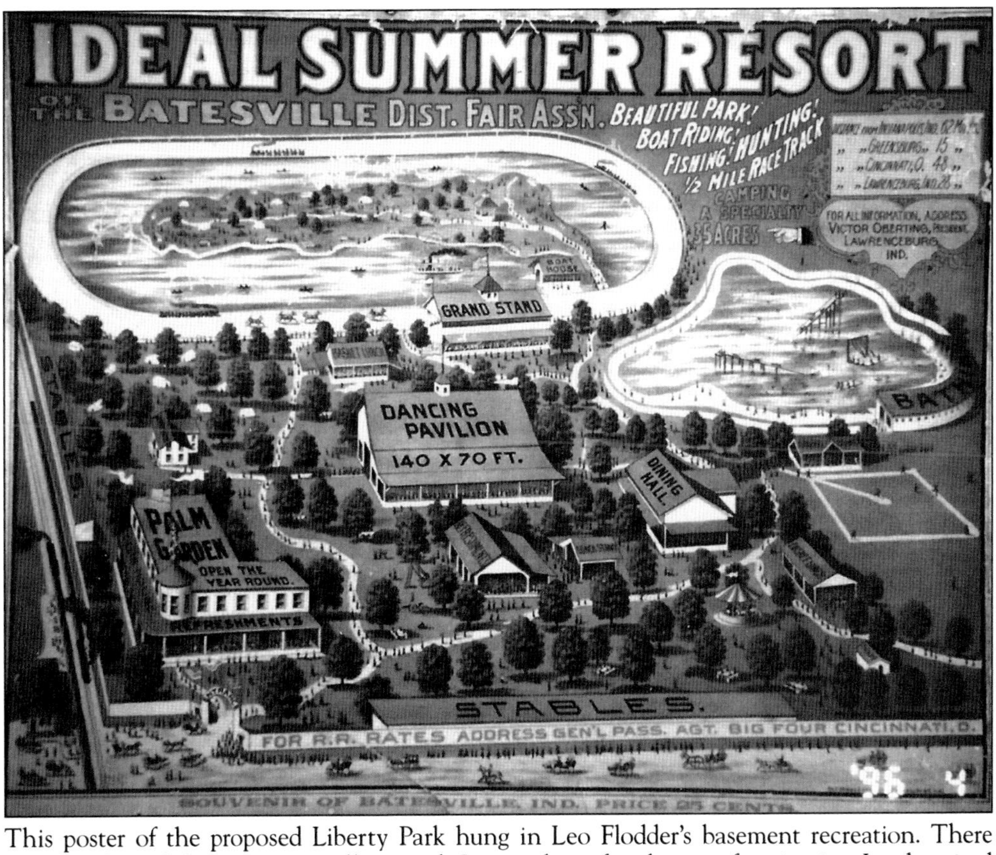

This poster of the proposed Liberty Park hung in Leo Flodder's basement recreation. There are very few of these posters still around. It was three feet by two feet in size. It advertised Liberty Park as an "Ideal Summer Resort." Some of the features, such as the swimming pool and bathhouse, did not materialize. The half-mile racetrack was a reality. (Leo Flodder.)

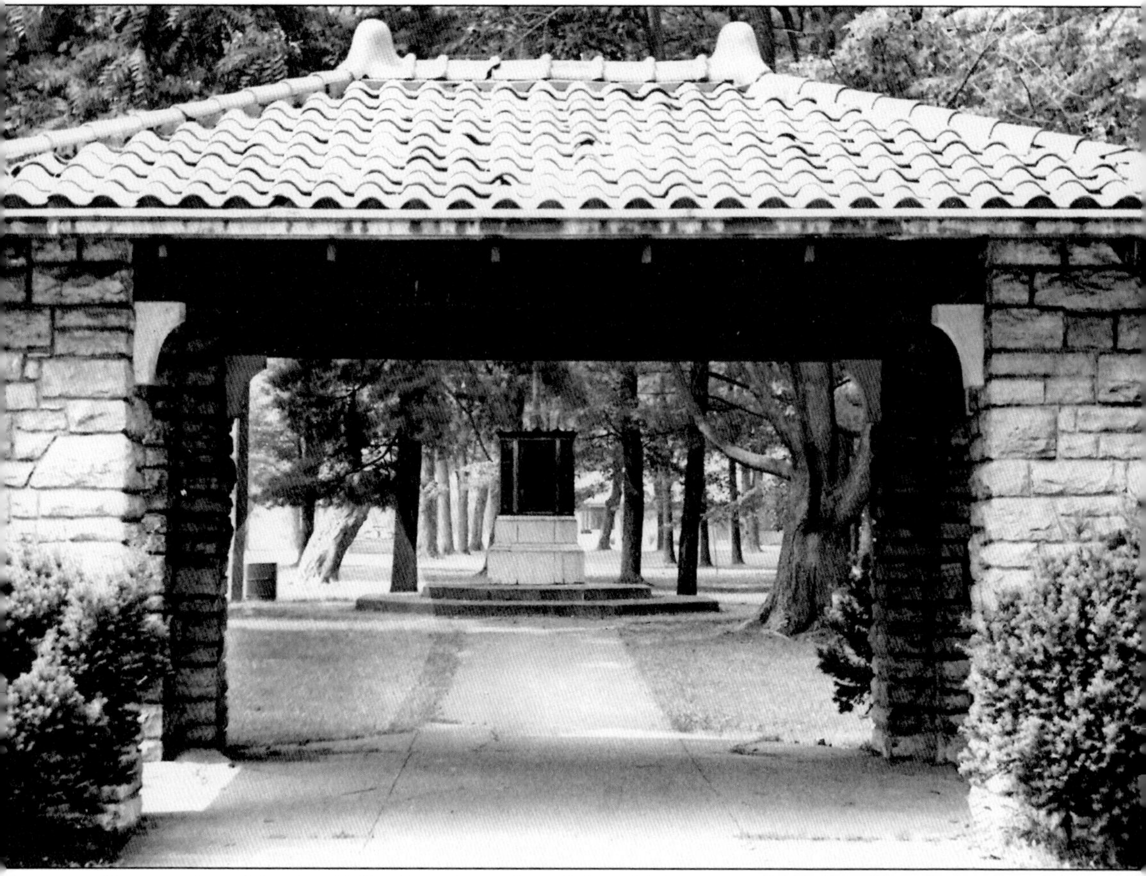

George M. and Sophia Hillenbrand purchased the old fair grounds in the 1920s and presented it to the City of Batesville as a gift. It was to be called "Liberty Park." An Armistice Day program in 1929 dedicated the entrance gateway and flagpole. The entrance leads through a beautiful arch of Bedford stone with connecting walls and pillars. Just past the entrance gateway, the flagpole rises from a foursquare base with bronze tablets bearing the names of World War I servicemen from Batesville and six nearby townships. They had sulky races around the canal. There was a bridge that led to the island in the center of the canal. Verda Blank told of lovers going out on the island to have some privacy. The hall was used for big celebrations along with many dances. (Women's Study Club.)

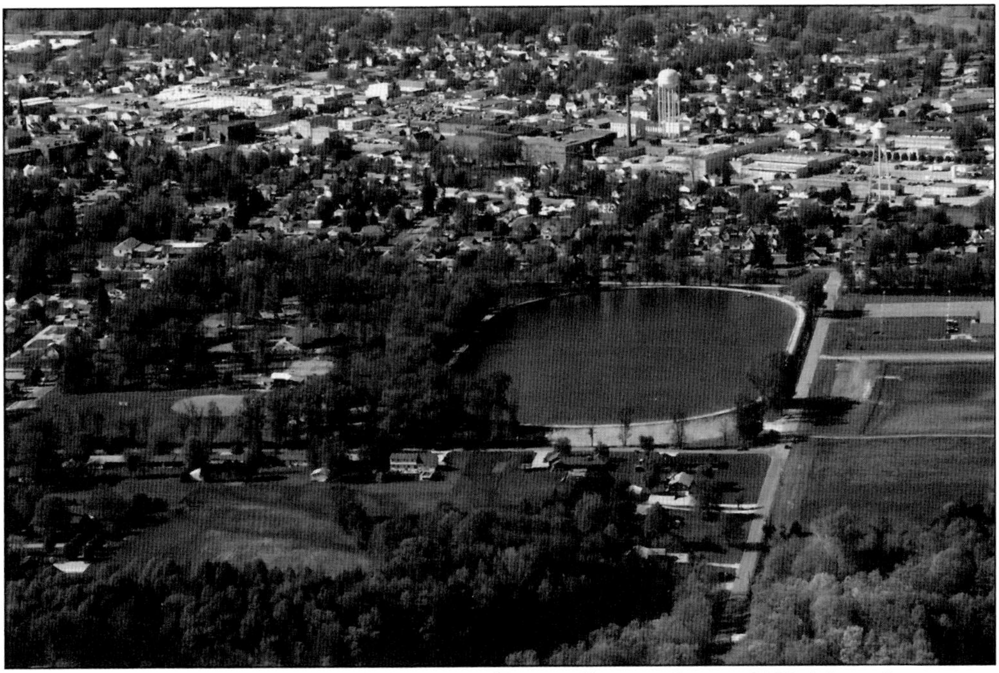

This aerial view of Liberty Park and the town of Batesville was taken in 2002. Many changes are noted since the beginning of the park. In January 1921, C. L. Burkholder of Purdue University laid out a tree nursery, walks, and drives at the park. The baseball team built a new grandstand there in April 1921. The park opened for the first time in March 1925. (Dave Engelking.)

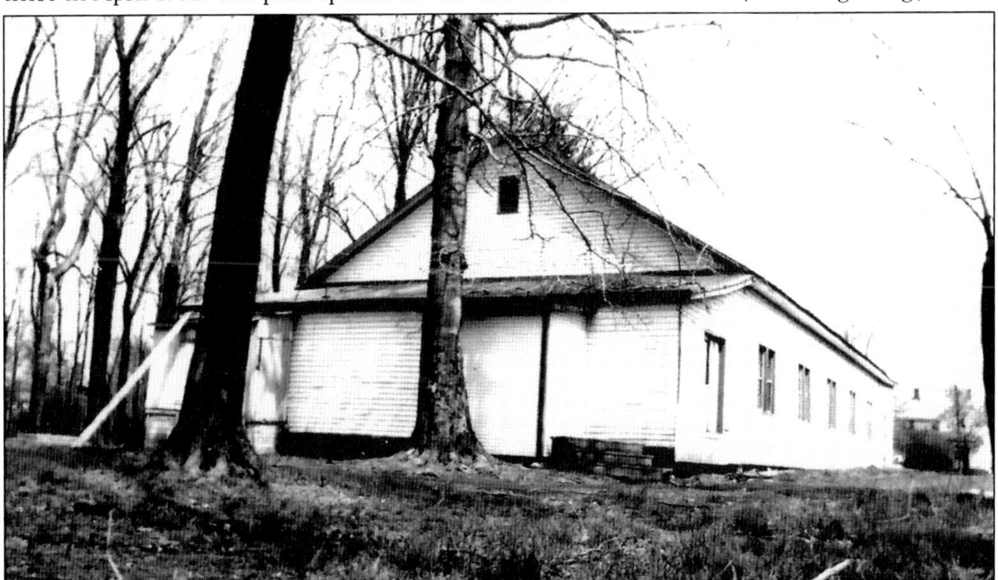

Charles and William H. St. Clair built the famous dance hall and amusement park known as St. Clair's Hall and St. Clair's Park. Located along Second Street west of town, this pavilion and park served as Batesville's principal amusement center from its establishment in the early 1980s until after World War I. With the donation of Liberty Park to the city, the use of St. Clair's Hall and St. Clair's Park substantially declined. (Jewelnita Luhring.)

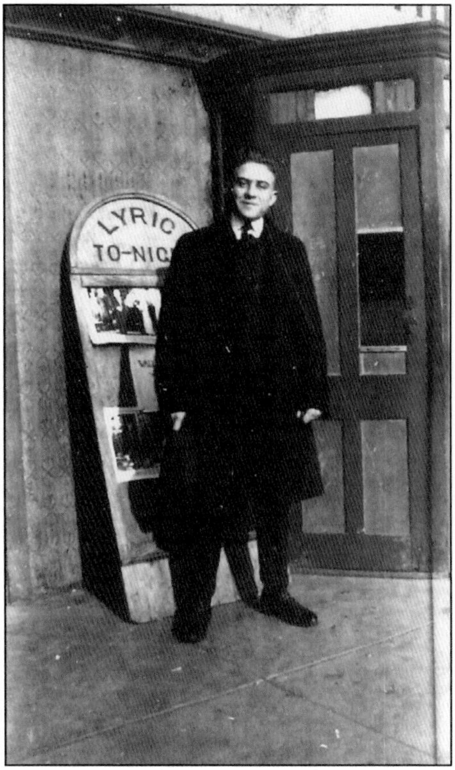

The Lyric Theatre, located on East Pearl Street next to the railroad tracks, was founded by John Wintz and opened on November 24, 1911. It was a family operation. George Wintz helped run the theater, Susie (Wintz) Canfield sold tickets, and Paul J. "Pete" Wintz, as a youngster, played the player piano to provide background music for the silent movies. This theater was the first building to be dedicated solely to theatrical purposes in Batesville. (Mary Carolyn Wintz.)

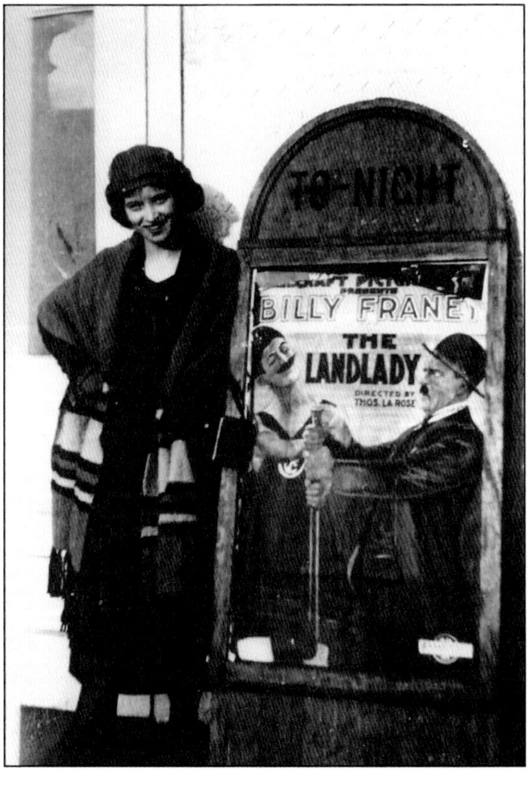

This picture was taken in front of the Lyric Theatre on East Pearl Street around 1920. Lucylle (Wachsmann) Fuson is the lady in front of the theater. Lucylle's mother is Anna Nickel. The building had been remodeled and enlarged to accommodate 200 seats, an orchestra pit and stage, ticket booth, elevated floor, and double-entrance doors. All these improvements brought the little theater up to standards. (Nioma Nickel.)

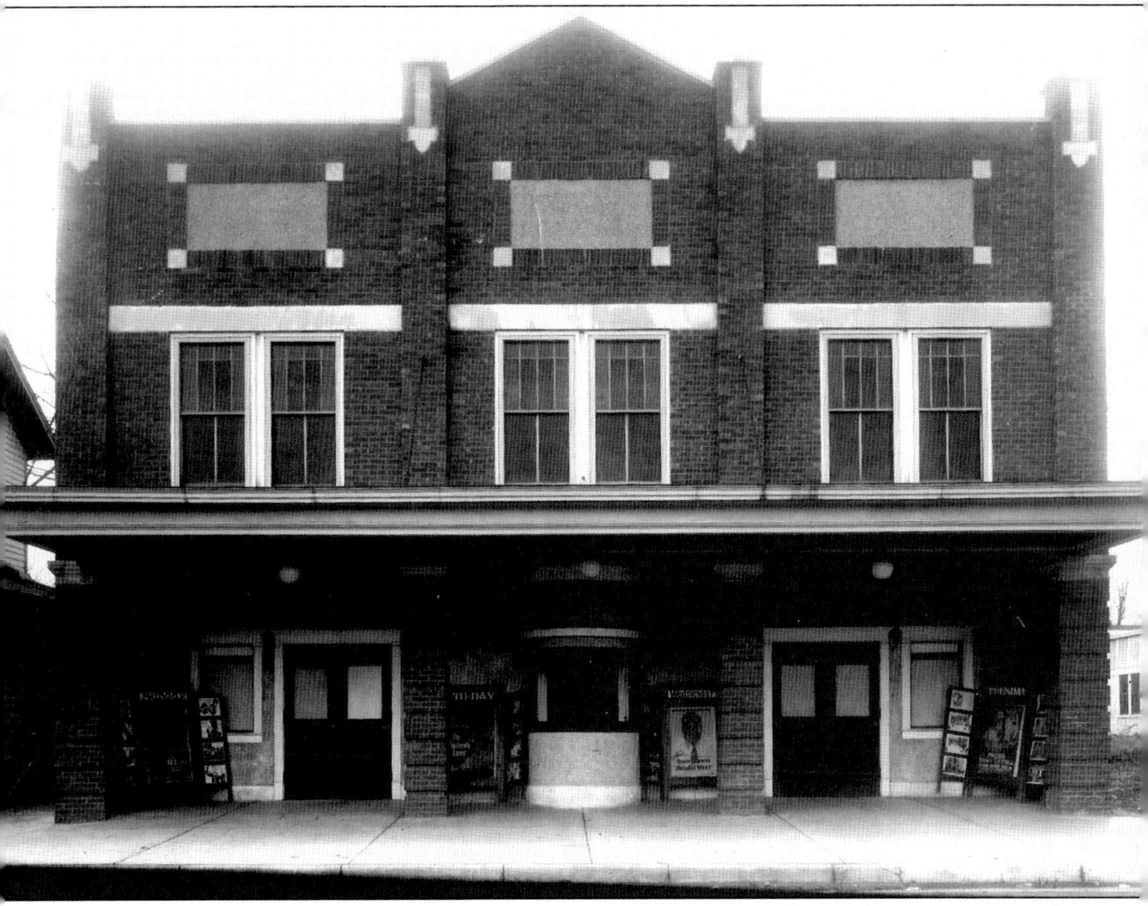

Dr. Charles W. Gibson was a builder of new industries, and the Gibson Theatre was one of his endeavors. He built the new theater on Main Street just north of Boehringer Street with up-to-date plans for regular theatrical plays as well as moving pictures. He began bringing in the most celebrated screenplays in production in 1922. "Talking pictures" were introduced in 1929. Electronic pianos, live pianists, player pianos, and local orchestras were all replaced by pictures with sound. Dr. Gibson also built the Gibson Garage on Boehringer Street just east of Main Street. His sons and sons-in-law operated these enterprises while he continued in his medical practice. (Paul Wycoff.)

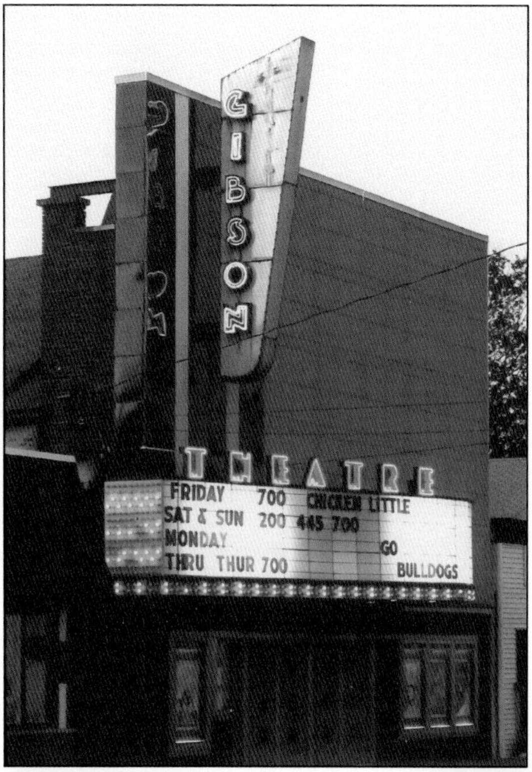

Many changes have been made to the Gibson Theatre, but the name has stayed the same all these years. The ticket booth has been moved to the left side of the front. All new interior decorations and seats have been installed and a concession stand is right inside the front doors. Wolf Theatres owned it for a long time, and in 2007, Kim Powell purchased it. (Jean Struewing.)

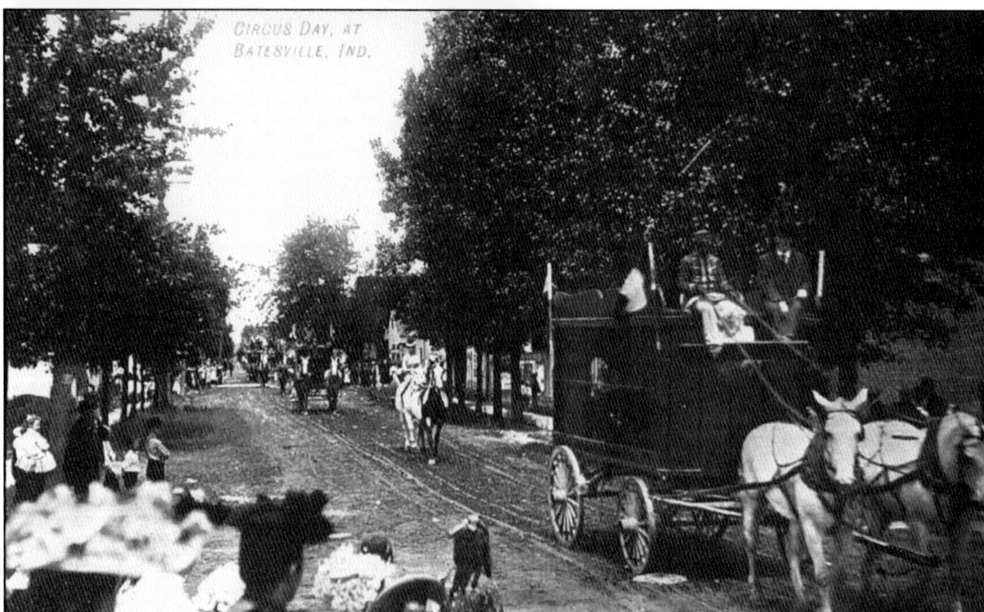

Circus day in Batesville Indiana was an exciting time. The circus would perform on the John Wonning Property on the northeast corner of West Pearl and Mulberry Streets, where the swimming pool now stands. As a boy, Henry Walsman recalls his greatest days were those on which a circus came to town and almost without exception he worked for them carrying water for the animals. (Jean Struewing.)

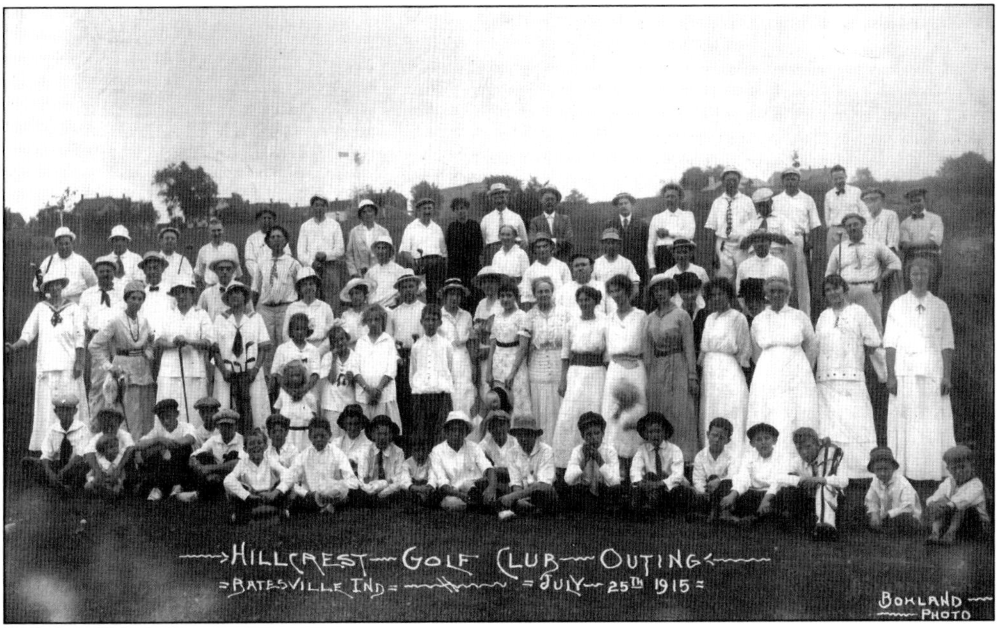

Pictured here is the Hillcrest Golf Club Outing in Batesville on July 25, 1915. Men and women alike enjoyed the golf course. Even the children would bring their golf clubs to play. Notice the third boy from the right in the first row with his golf clubs. Dr. Robertson Smith (not in the photograph) served as architect and designer of the Hillcrest Golf Course in 1912. (Mary Ollier.)

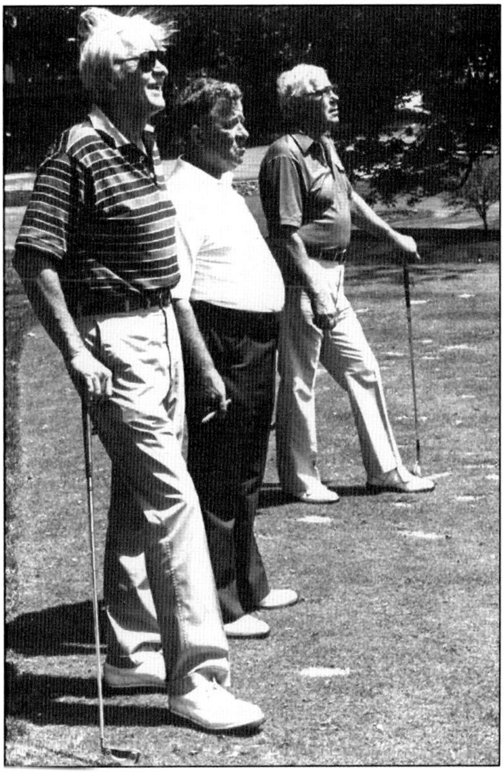
Golfing has long been a favorite pastime for Batesville. Here one sees three guys who could be found on the golf course most any sunny summer day. From left to right are Don Weigel, Don Dickey, and Luther "Lute" Lindemann. Notice the divots and consider how many of them might have been made by these three. (Women's Study Club.)

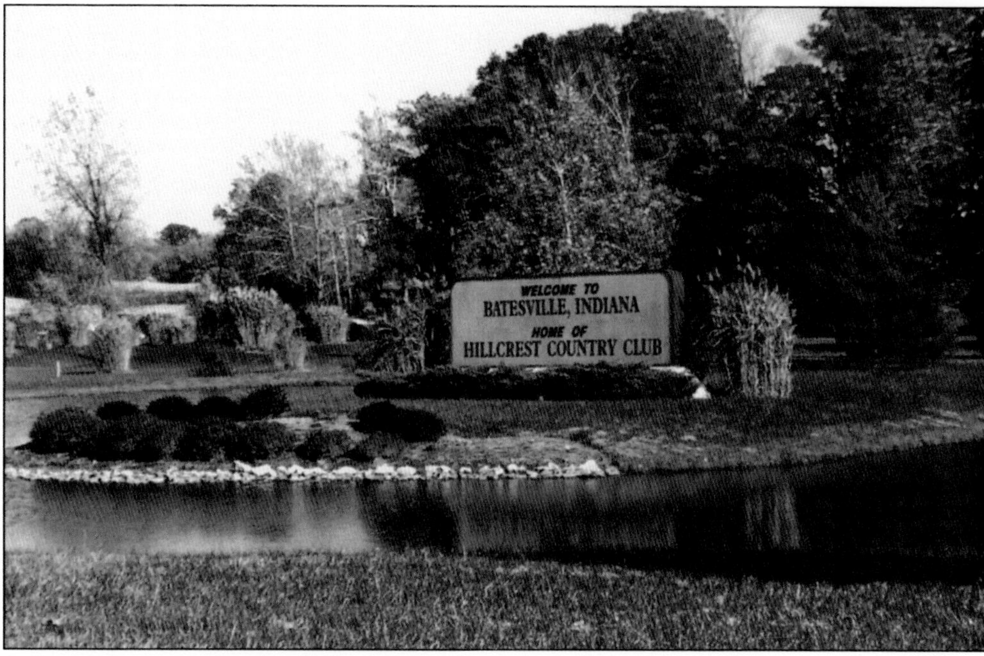

Only members can play the challenging, well maintained, and very well known 18-hole Hillcrest Country Club golf course. The club has a PGA professional on staff. The club also boasts a pro shop, full-service restaurant and bar, swimming pool, tennis courts, and snack bar. (Lowell Yorn.)

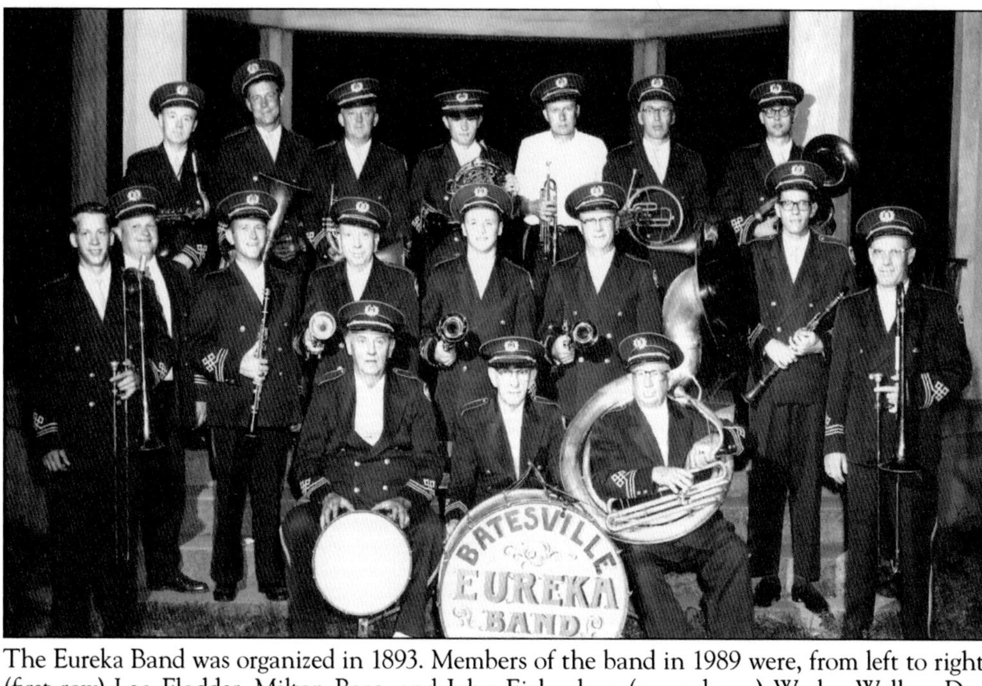

The Eureka Band was organized in 1893. Members of the band in 1989 were, from left to right, (first row) Leo Flodder, Milton Baas, and John Eichocher; (second row) Wesley Walker, Don Becker, Bill Schein, George Baas, Earl Bruning Jr., Bess Bartling, Jim Mergenthal, and Owen Schumacher; (third row) Earl Bruning Sr., Mark Prickel, Clyde Flodder, Ray Gibson, Fritz Turner, Ray Lamping, and Ron Wachsmann. (Leo Flodder.)

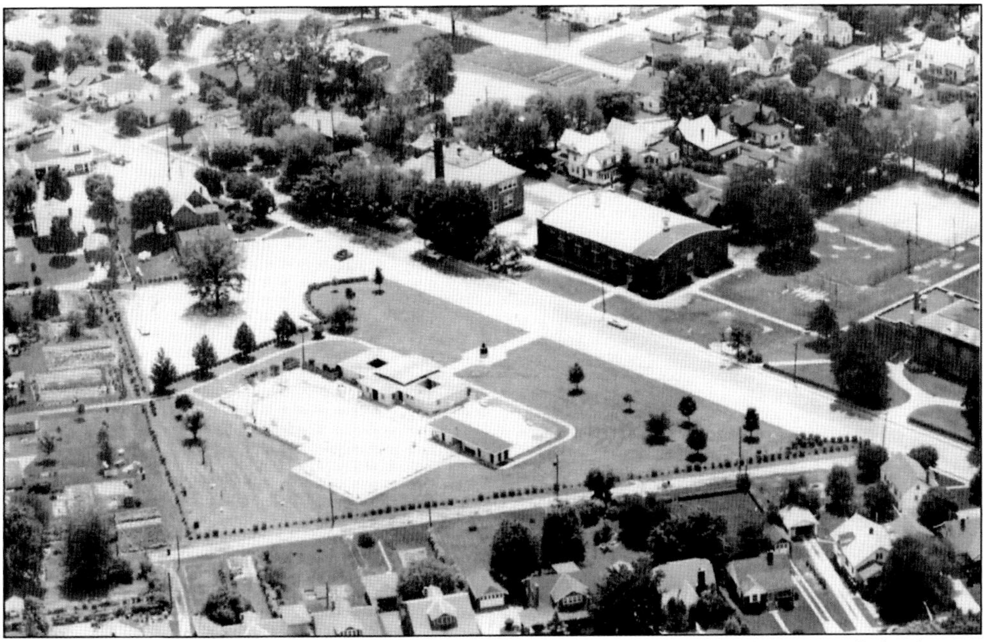

On July 9, 1945, the City Council of Batesville received a deed for several lots as a gift for the use and benefit of the citizens of Batesville to be used for the furtherance of physical education and recreation. Presented by John A. and Clara Hillenbrand, the War Memorial Swimming Pool was dedicated to the men and women of World War II. This bird-eye view of the swimming pool was taken in 1962. (Bob Brokamp.)

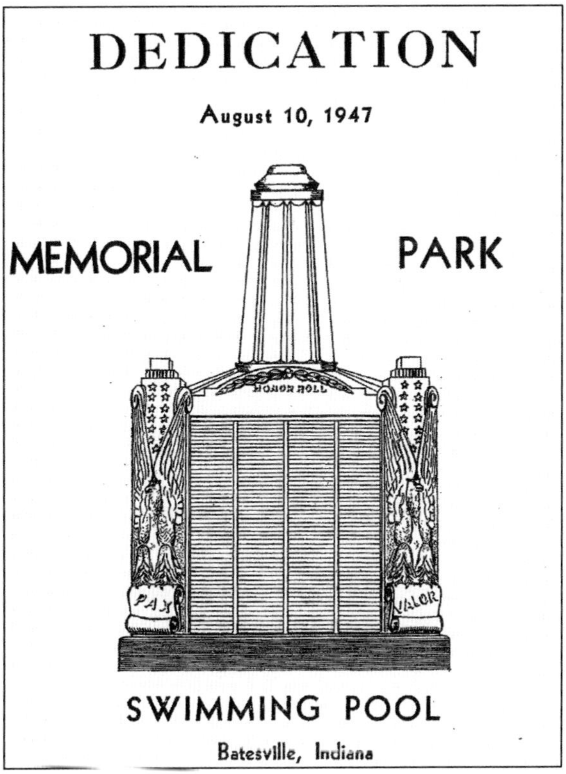

The dedication of the Batesville Memorial Park and Swimming Pool was held Sunday, August 10, 1947, with a complete program that culminated with the opening of the swimming pool to the public for the first time. The dedicatory speaker was the Honorable Henry F. Schricker, governor of Indiana from 1941 to 1945 and 1949 to 1953. (BAHS.)

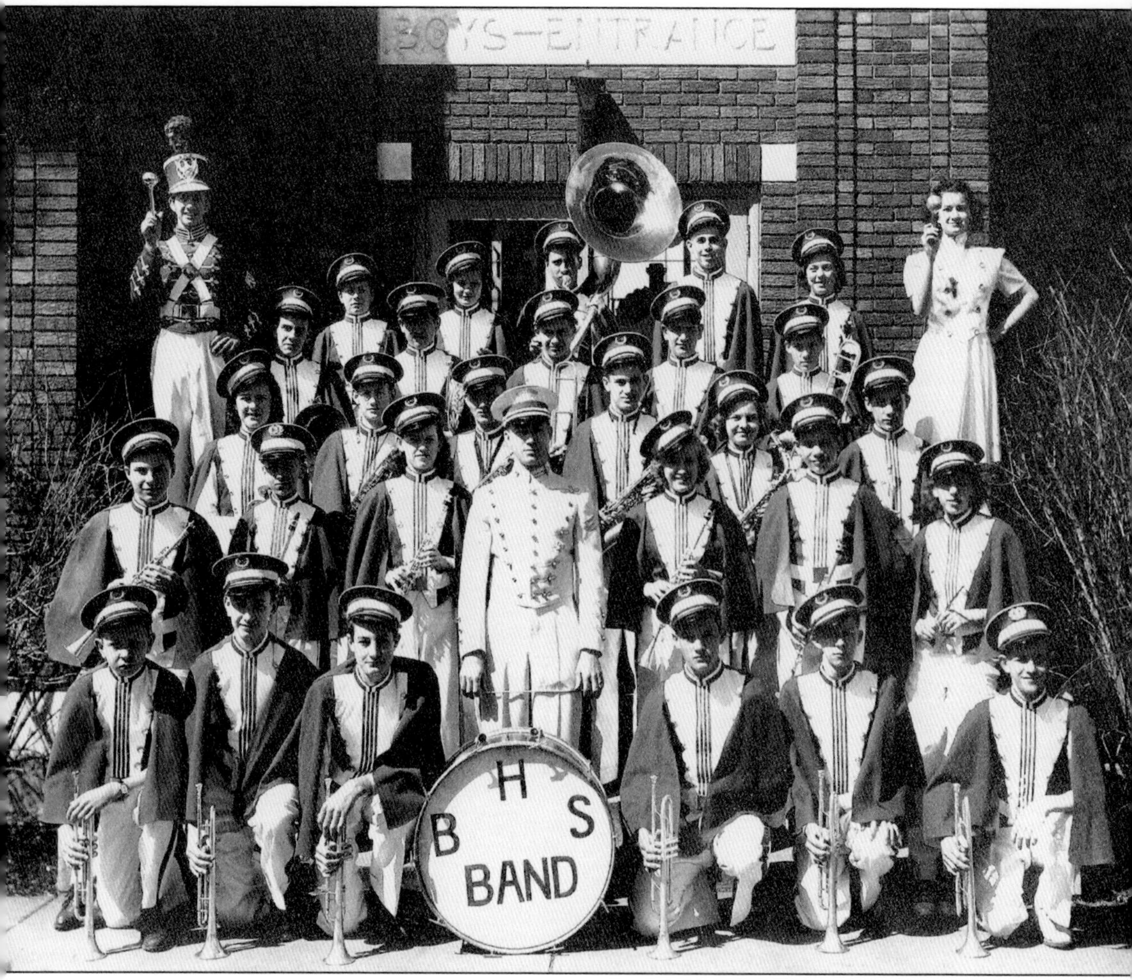

Sylvester "Bess" Bartling was band director for many years at the local high school and always had a good band that entertained at football games, basketball games, and parades. Here is the high school band from 1940. Members are, from left to right, (first row) John Baas, Bob Harder, Francis Firsich, Elmer Narwold, Harold "Fritz" Turner, and Andy Irrgang; (second row) John Strohlein, Marion Wessler, Viola Westerman, Sylvester "Bess" Bartling (director), Ann Nedderman, John Westerfeld, and Janet Baas; (third row) Juanita "Neetz" Lindeman, Harry Zimmerman, Raymond Thie, Herschel Borchelt, Jean Sitterding, and Leonard Sieg; (fourth row) Myron Gehring, Victor Fullenkamp, Oscar Fischmer, Irvin Placke, and Lawrence Sieg; (fifth row) drum major Paul Walsman, Johnny Ray, Dottie Buckhave, Ray Lamping, Paul Heitzman, Viola Gander, and drum majorette Mary Ann Meyer. (Andy Irrgang.)

This is Harold "Fritz" Turner in 1948 when he was playing with different dance bands. The Fritz Turner Orchestra dominated the big band scene in Indiana for over 50 years. (Harold "Fritz" Turner.)

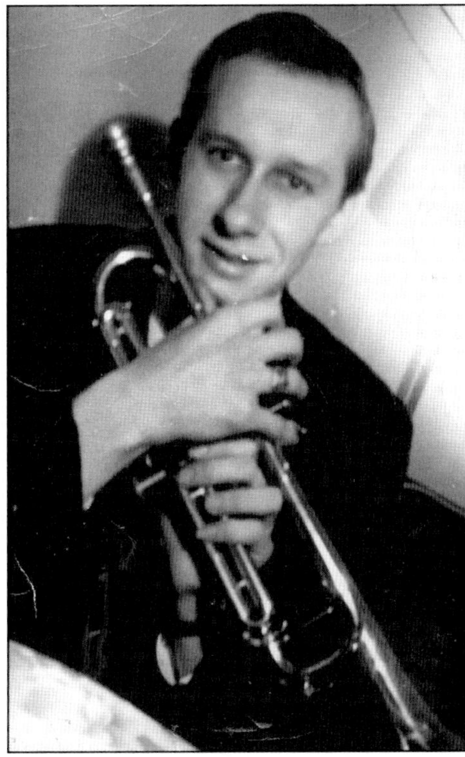

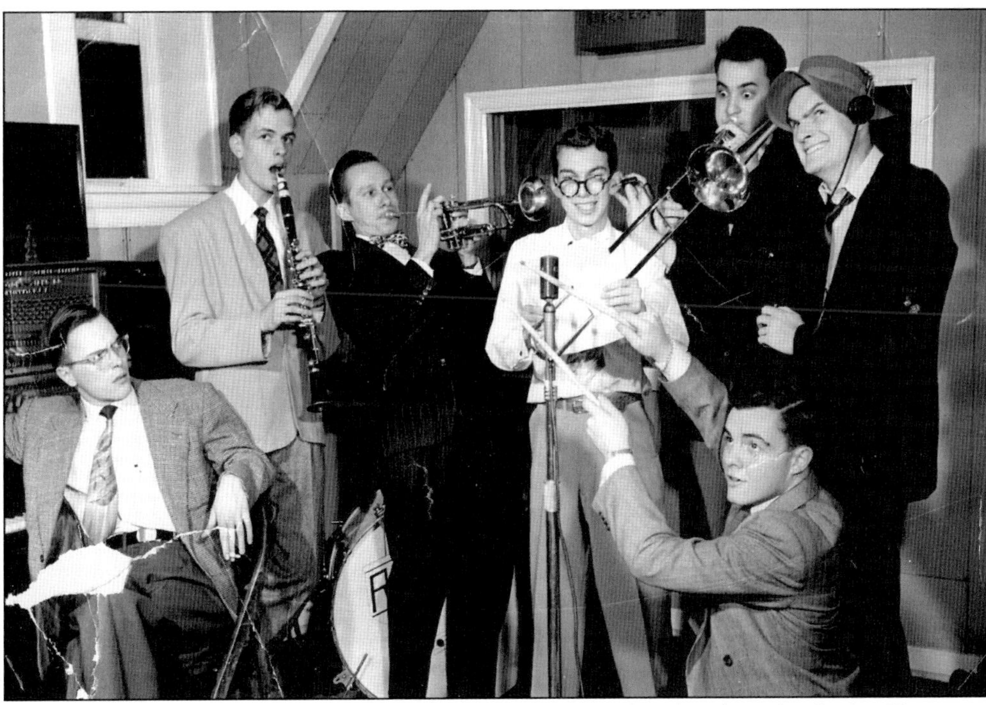

When Turner went to Butler University in 1951 to 1954, he played in the Butler University Dixieland Band. He is the person in the center of the picture, playing the trumpet. (Harold "Fritz" Turner.)

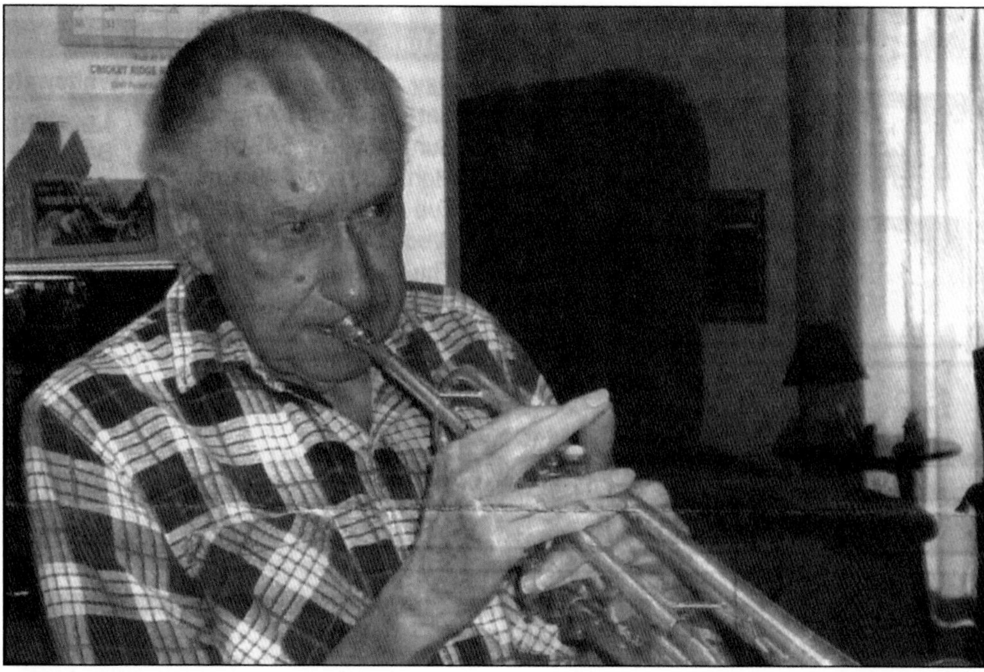

Harold "Fritz" Turner gets some beautiful sounds out of his custom-made trumpet after playing big band tunes for over 50 years. Starting his own band was something that he always wanted to do. He admits to having music in his blood. He excelled in his craft so quickly that he was able to join his first musical group, Carl Moeller's Band, at the age of 14. (Harold "Fritz" Turner.)

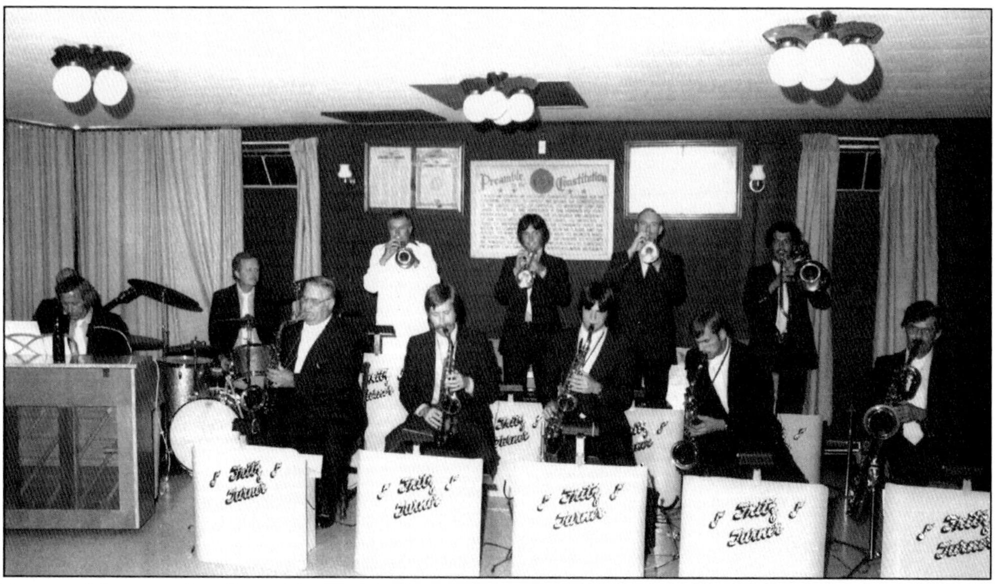

Pictured here is the Fritz Turner Orchestra in 1970. Seen here are, from left to right, (first row) at the piano, Bill Schein; sax, Pete Howard; sax, Greg Johnson; sax, Mark Records; sax, unidentified; and sax, Tim Rothler; (second row) drums, Don Ebling; trumpet, Fritz Turner; trumpet, Greg Meyers; trumpet, Tom Polley; and trombone, Rick Nickelson. They played songs from popular artists like Glenn Miller, Benny Goodman, Duke Ellington, Harry James, and the Dorseys, among many others. (Harold "Fritz" Turner.)

Seven

RETAIL BUSINESS

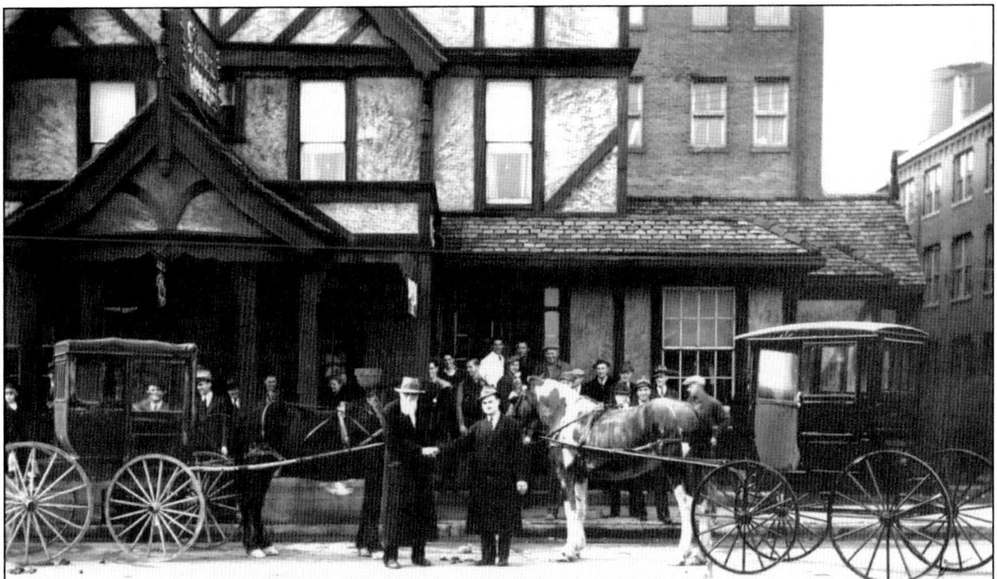

One of the oldest businesses in Batesville is the Sherman House. John F. Brinkman built the original Sherman House beginning in April 1865. Brinkman happily chose the name Sherman House in honor of Gen. William Tecumseh Sherman. The two men in the foreground of this 1938 photograph are George Carl Hillenbrand (right) and Carl Martin (left), director of purchases for Hillenbrand Industries and a very good friend of Hillenbrand's. (Nick Stewart.)

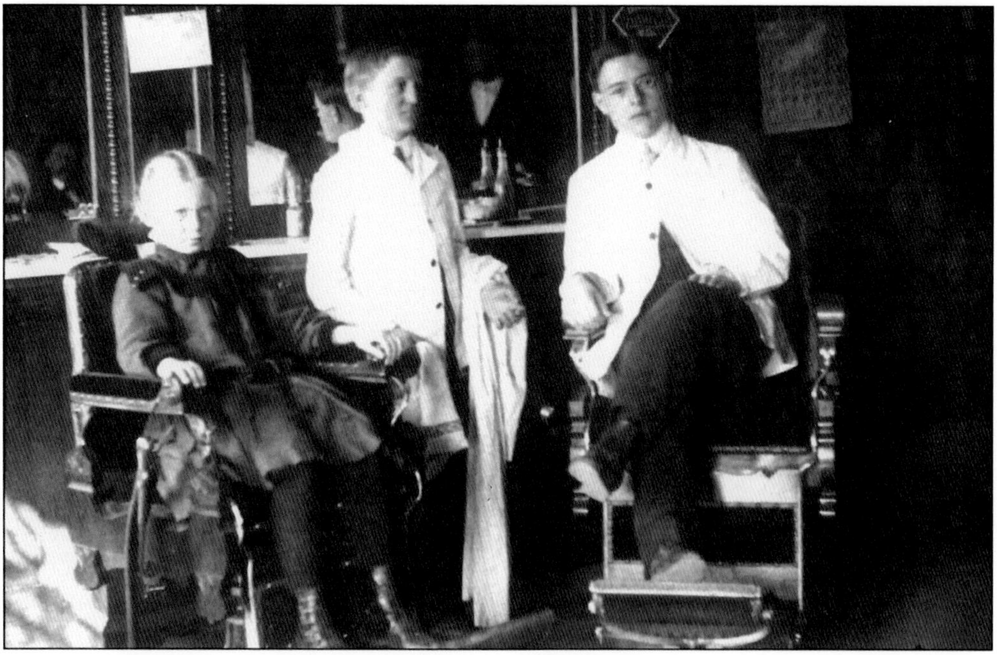

In 1905, the place to get a hair cut was the Jake Telles Barbershop. He started cutting hair in Germany in 1898, moved to Cincinnati in 1903, and to Batesville in 1905. He once gave a 20¢ haircut to William Howard Taft before he became the 26th U.S. president. People in the picture are, from left to right, Adeline Telles, John Telles, and Jake Telles. (Women's Study Club.)

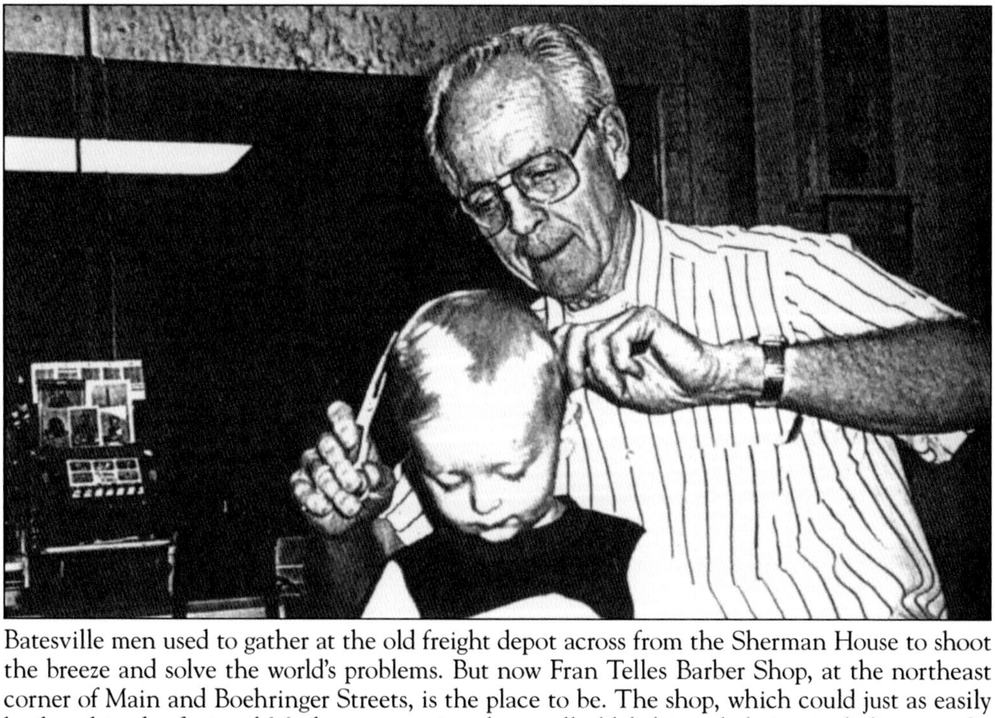

Batesville men used to gather at the old freight depot across from the Sherman House to shoot the breeze and solve the world's problems. But now Fran Telles Barber Shop, at the northeast corner of Main and Boehringer Streets, is the place to be. The shop, which could just as easily be found in the fictional Mayberry, contains three tall old-fashioned chairs, including one for toddlers. (Herald Tribune.)

The Batesville Bank was organized October 7, 1889. The capital stock rose to $50,000 by 1892, and to $55,000 by 1900. Pictured in front of the Batesville Bank are, from left to right, George Johanning, Harry Sitterding, Eddie Reibel, Pete Schorr, Irvin Schein, and Charles Johnson. (Paul Wycoff.)

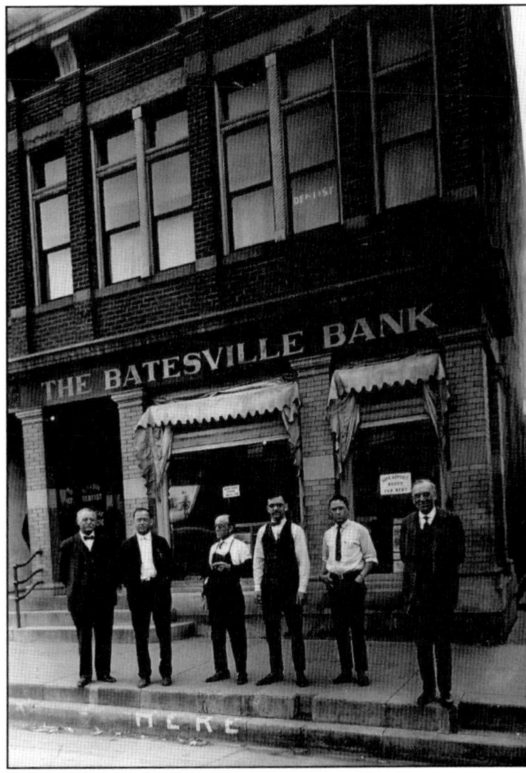

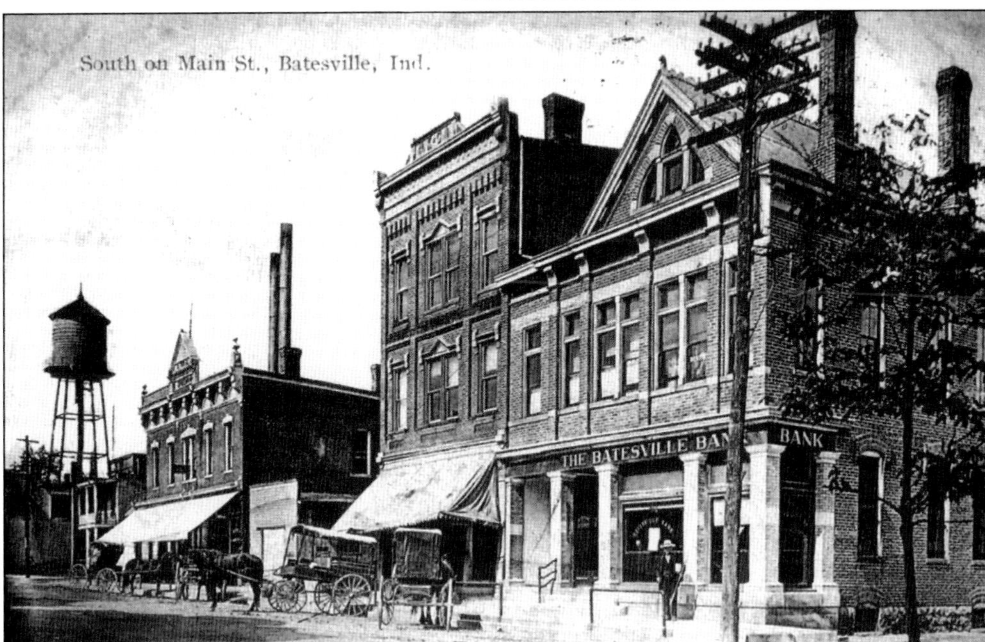

The Batesville Bank built an addition to its building that connected the bank building with the drug store building in the spring of 1922. In 1929, the Batesville Bank opened under a new charter as the Batesville State Bank, a change in name to identify the bank as a part of the Indiana State banking system. (Jean Strewing.)

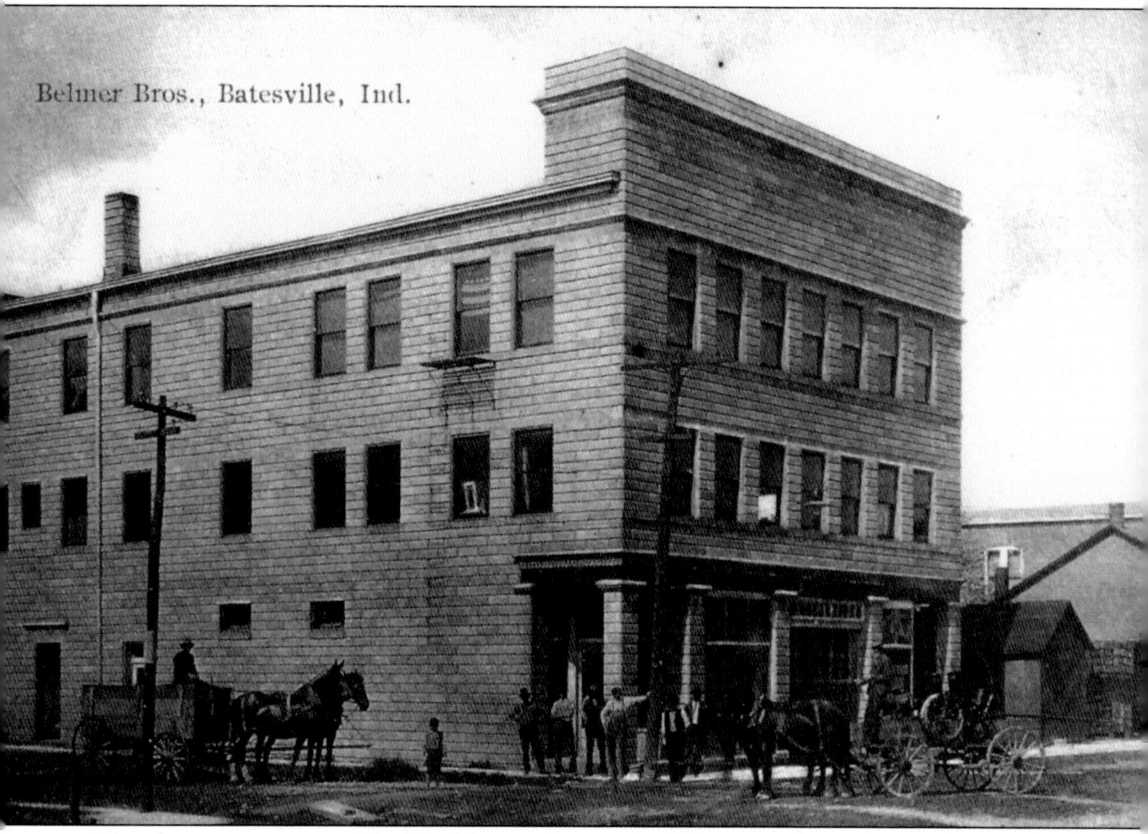

This three-story concrete block building at the corner of George and Sycamore Streets was built by the Behlmer Brothers in April 1911 on the former site of a livery-barn. Behlmer Brothers, contractors and builders, occupied the lower floor, using it as a planning mill, storeroom, and offices space for their building products and supplies business. The Behlmer Brothers opened a new business on the second floor of their building in June 1914, under the name of the Behlmer Shirt Company. Power sewing and cutting machines were installed there for making men's shirts. The third floor was rented to fraternal organizations. The Masonic and Eastern Star Orders, the Knights of Pythias, Phytian Sisters, and Red Men and Pocahantas Orders all rented the third floor at various times. The Kroger Company moved in this building from the Lehmkuehler building in the 1940s. (Jean Struewing.)

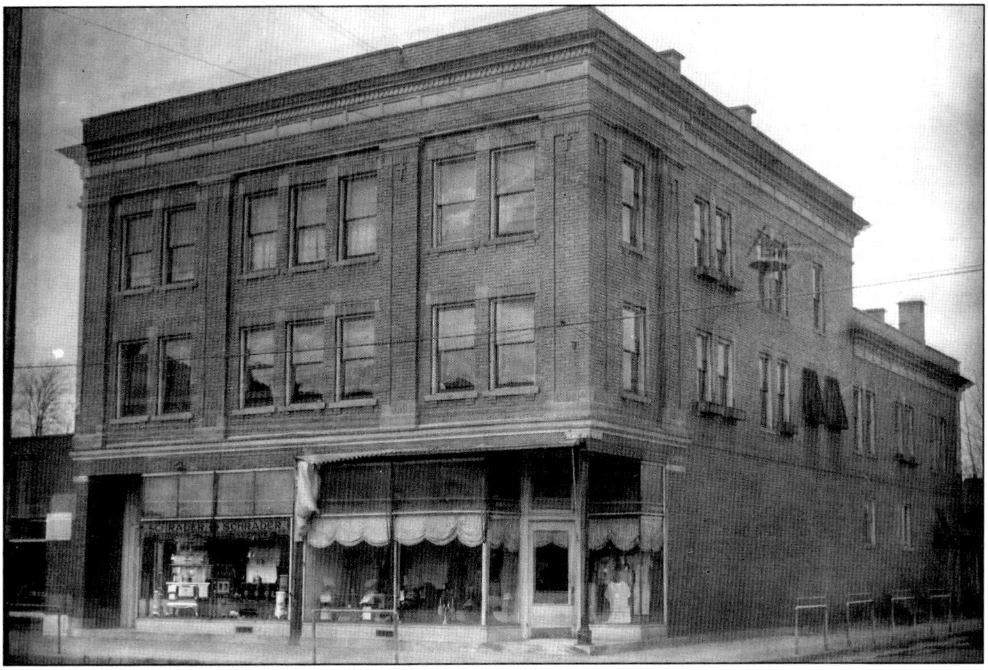

Henry F. E. Schrader built this three-story apartment building with extensive retail space on the first floor and modern apartments on the second and third floors. He and his sons, Elmer Schrader and Reuben Schrader, operated a tinning and roofing business out of the back of this building. He rented the corner store to Tom Telles of Telles Ready-To-Wear Store. (Paul Wycoff.)

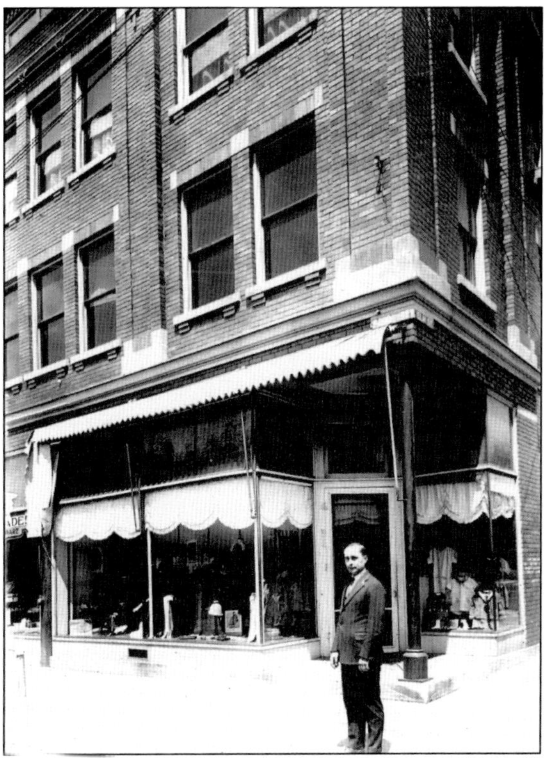

Tom Telles stands before his new ready-to-wear store in the Schrader Building, which today is occupied by the Eagles lodge, on West Pearl Street. Telles started the business here in 1923 and later moved to Main Street across from the Memorial Building. After being burglarized several times at that location on Main Street, Telles moved to the north side of George Street, behind the Sherman House. (Marg Reverman.)

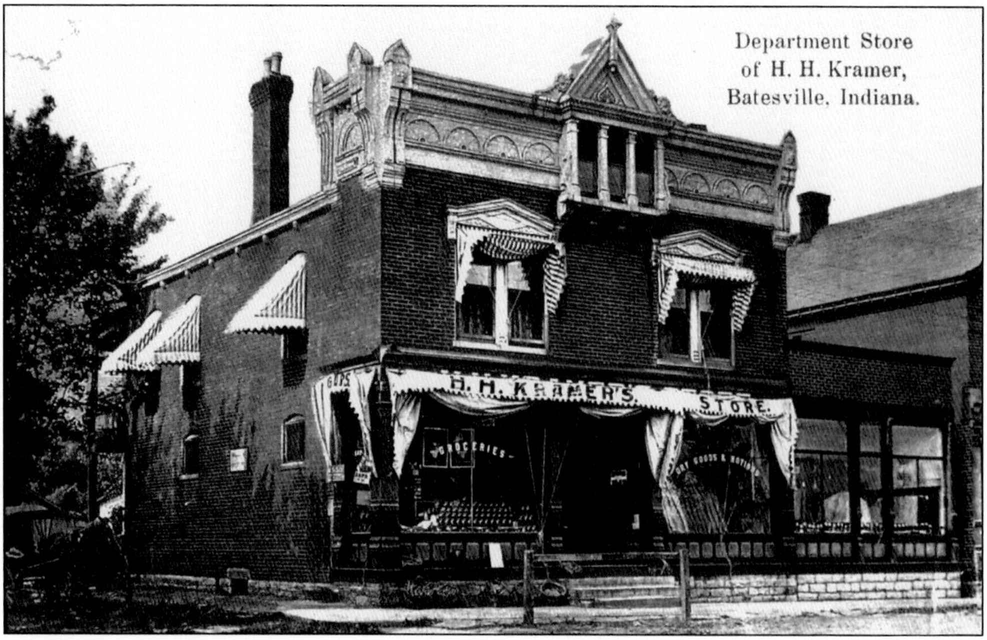

The H. H. Kramer Department Store was started by Henry H. Kramer in 1891, when he married his competitor's daughter, Anna Bertram, whose father, Benjamin Bertram, owned the former John H. Bosse store on West Pearl Street. The Kramers operated the store for over 57 years. (Jean Struewing.)

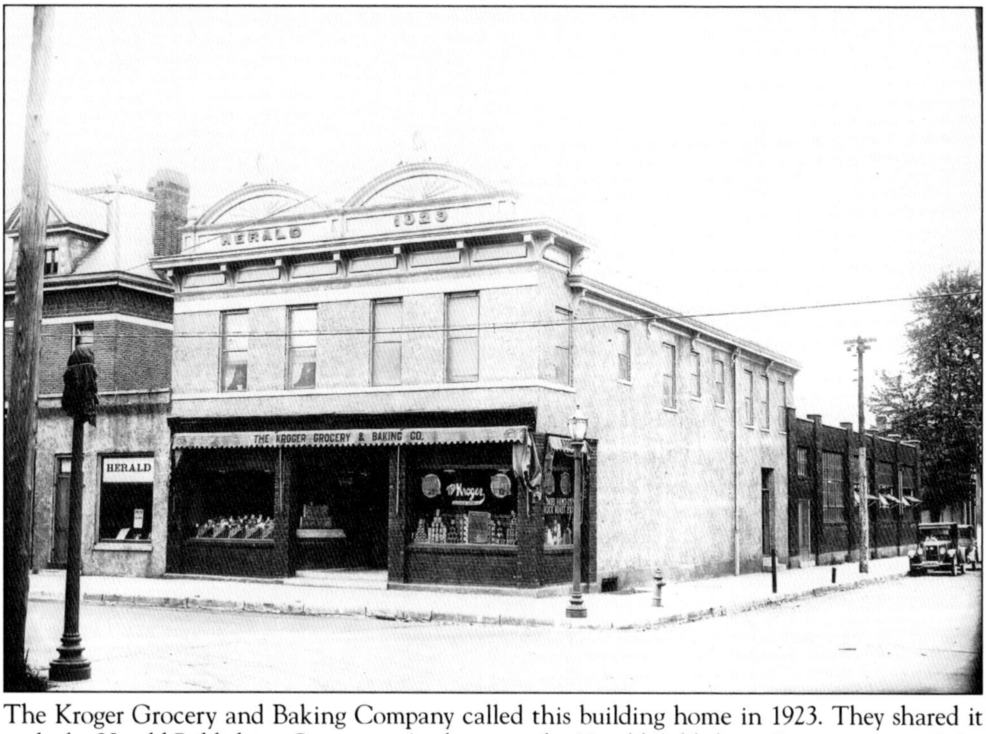

The Kroger Grocery and Baking Company called this building home in 1923. They shared it with the Herald Publishing Company. At the time, the Herald Publishing Company owned the building. It was located on the northwest side of Walnut and West Pearl Streets. (Paul Wycoff.)

Janet Baas, daughter of Milton and Clara Baas, stands in front of their faithful Model T, which they used when they made their grocery delivery rounds in Batesville. The store featured a line of staple and fancy groceries and dry goods. White Villa Brand products were their most popular line. (John Baas and Milt Baas.)

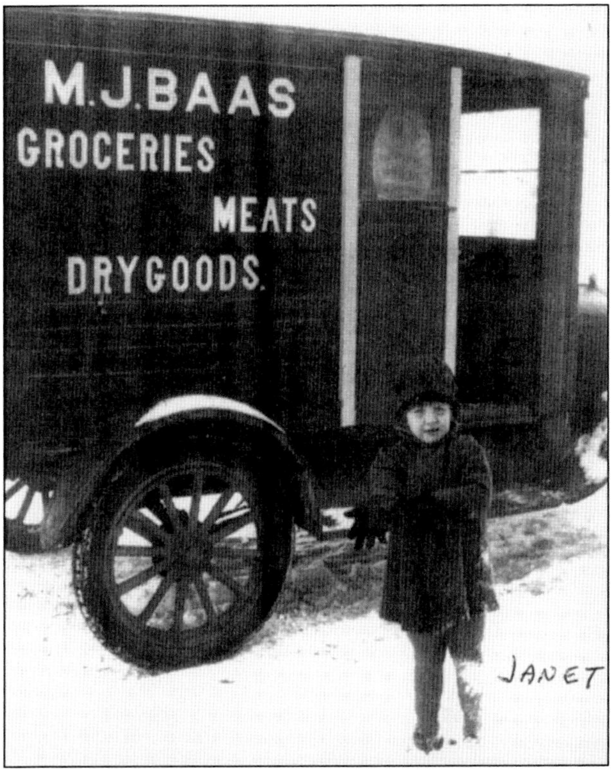

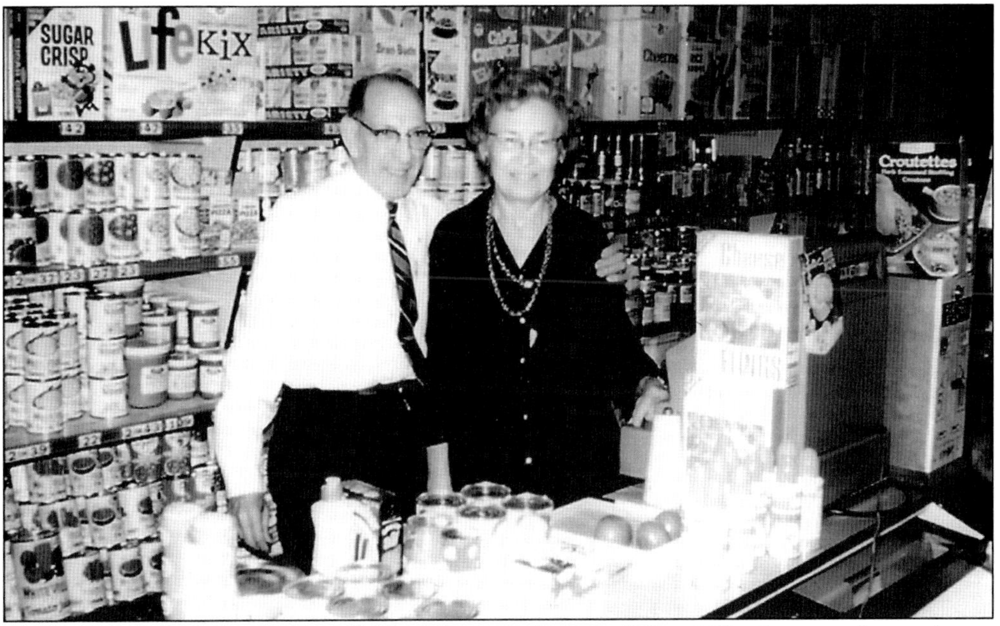

This is Milton J. Baas and Clara (Huber) Baas in the Baas White Villa Store on the southwest corner of Western and Liberty Streets. They bought the store from Ed Fischer in 1923 and owned and operated it for 43 years. Previously, the store was owned by Andrew Tekulve and Albert Tekulve and was located across Western Avenue from its present location. (John Baas and Milt Baas.)

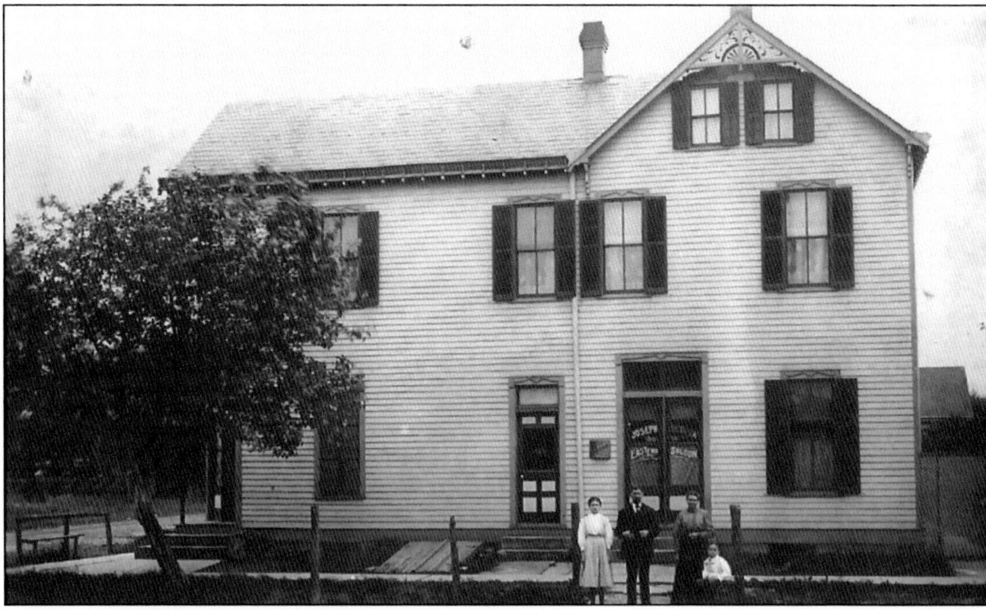

The East End Saloon was located at the southwest corner of Eastern Avenue and South Street. This same building is now Harmeyer's Corner Grocery Store, operated by Ron and Steve Harmeyer. It is one of the few corner grocery stores still in business. Home delivery remains one of their specialties. (Margie and Ron Harmeyer.)

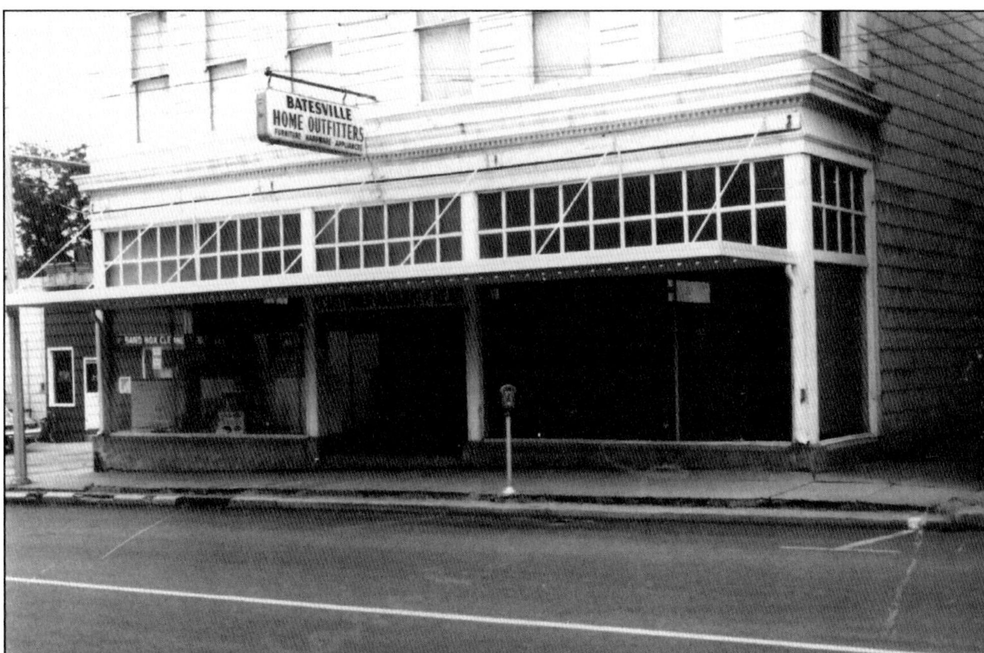

Batesville Home Outfitters, with a long reputation for fine furniture at affordable prices, was the oldest retail furniture store in Ripley County in the 1970s. Joe Schroeder began the business in 1918. The business became known as the Batesville Home Outfitters because of a contest to name the store. It operated under that same name for 40 years. (Women's Study Club.)

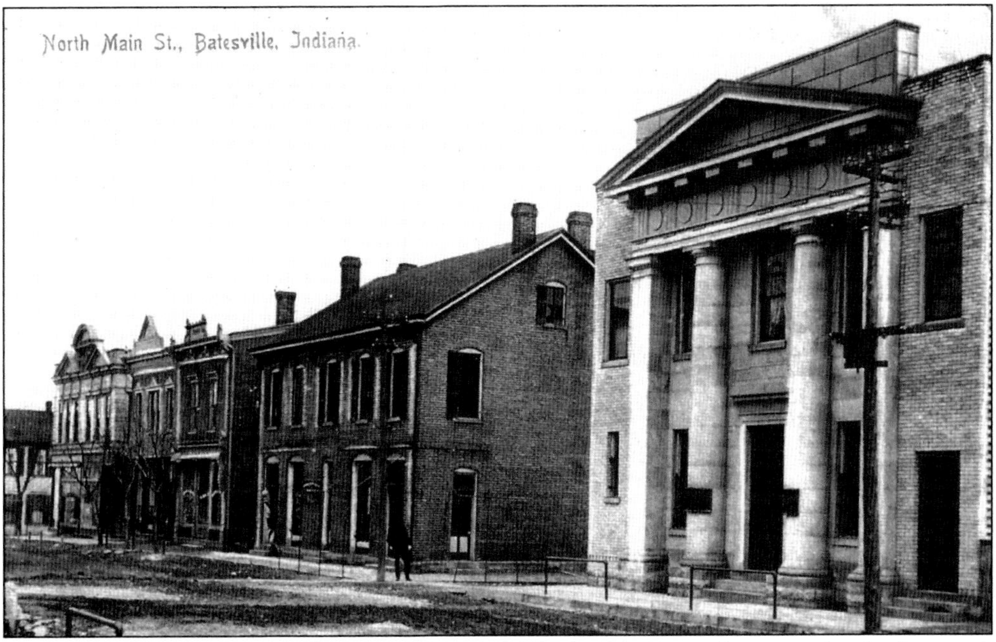

This is North Main Street looking north in 1912. The buildings are, foreground to background, the First National Bank, Benz's Meat Market, Brockman Shoe Store, the Gehring Bakery, and the last building is Star Hardware Company. (Women's Study Club.)

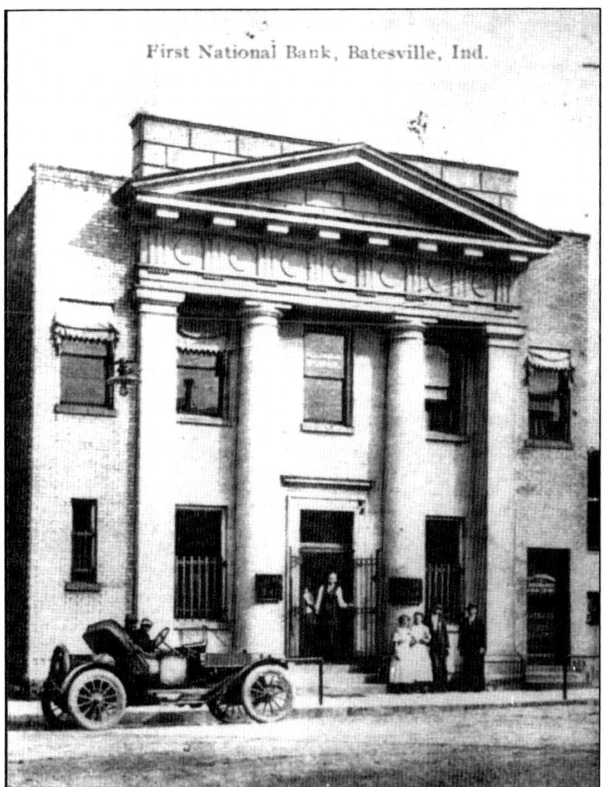

The First National Bank of Batesville opened on July 15, 1905, with a capital stock of $30,000. In 1907, this building was built on Main Street facing East Pearl Street. It was robbed on March 15, 1907, by seven men who used three charges of nitro-glycerin to blow off the outer door of the safe. In the 1960s, it was a part of the urban renewal plan for downtown Batesville. (Jean Struewing.)

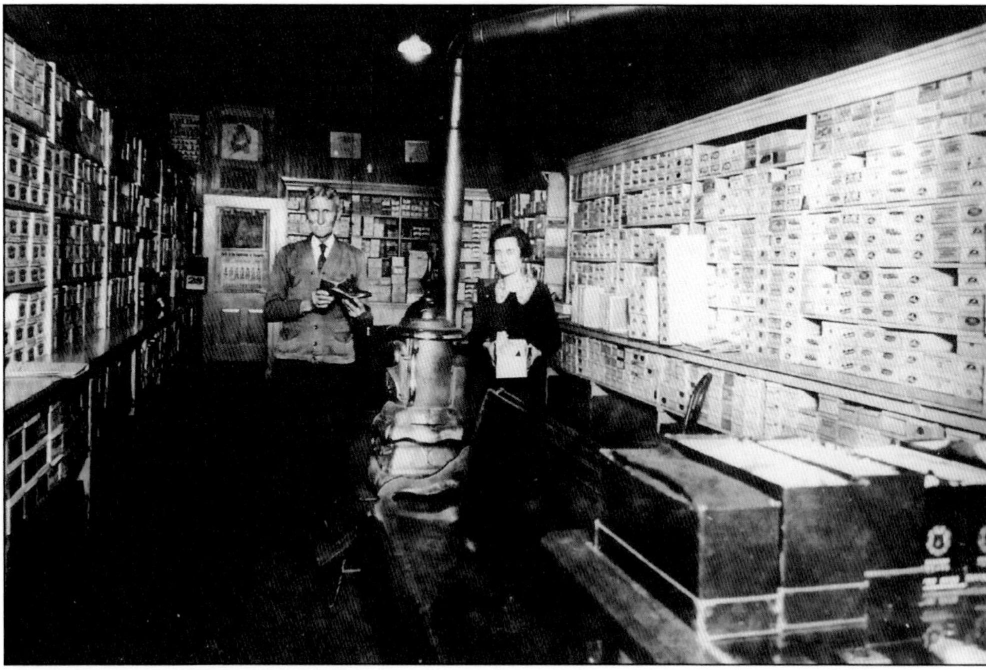

The Dieckmann Shoe Store opened in December 1903 on West Pearl Street. They advertised that they sold Peters Weatherbird Shoes made of solid leather. This picture of Fred Dieckmann and Catherine Goldsmith was taken inside the shoe store after the business moved to the building now occupied by Fullenkamp's Sporting Store on George Street. (BAHS.)

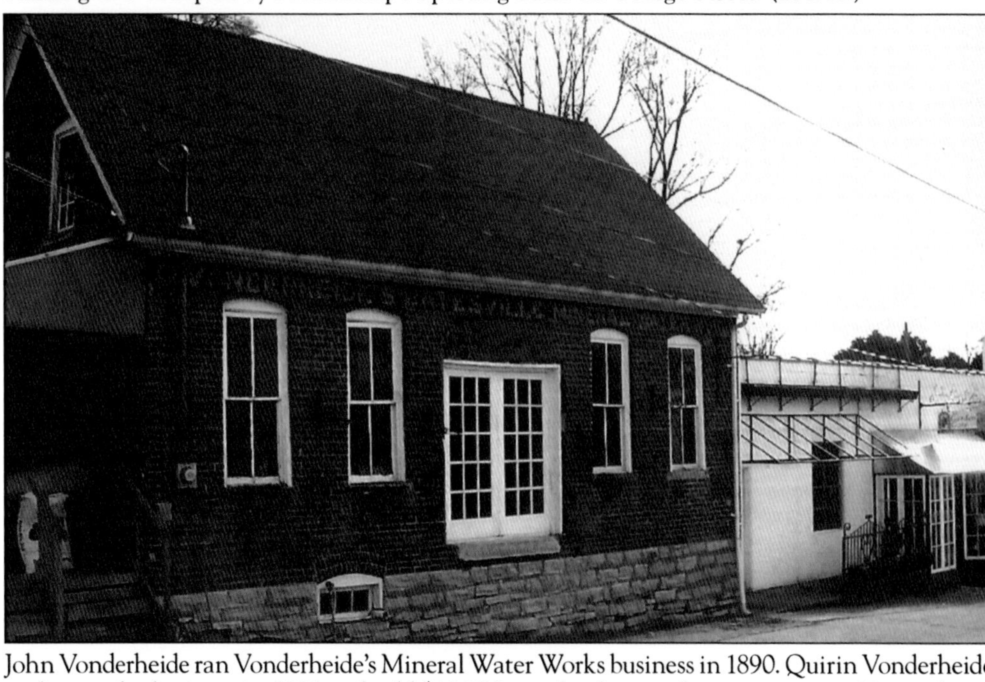

John Vonderheide ran Vonderheide's Mineral Water Works business in 1890. Quirin Vonderheide took over the business in 1896 and sold $10,000 worth of mineral water per year. He employed four people. His "pop wagon" with its team of well-kept horses was a feature of Batesville life for many years. He sold the business in 1932 to Joseph Luesse. (Jean Struewing.)

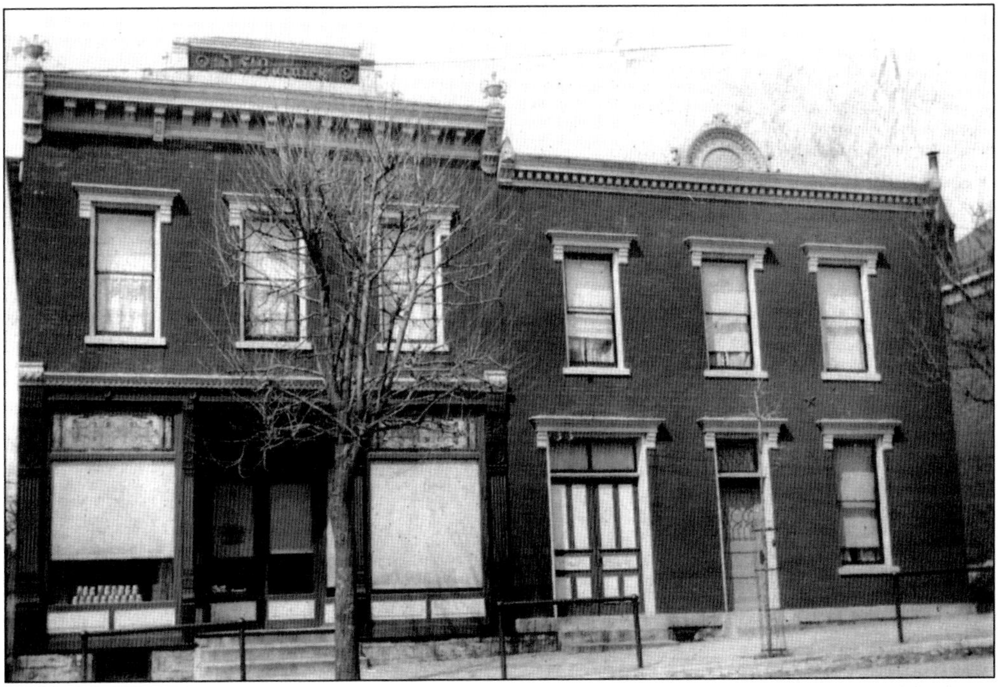

The name J. S. Burdick is embossed at the top of this building on Main Street in Oldenburg. The Harry Burdick family operated a general merchandise store in the building years ago. The Helen and Ralph Wagner family now operate Wagner's Village Inn in this location. (BAHS.)

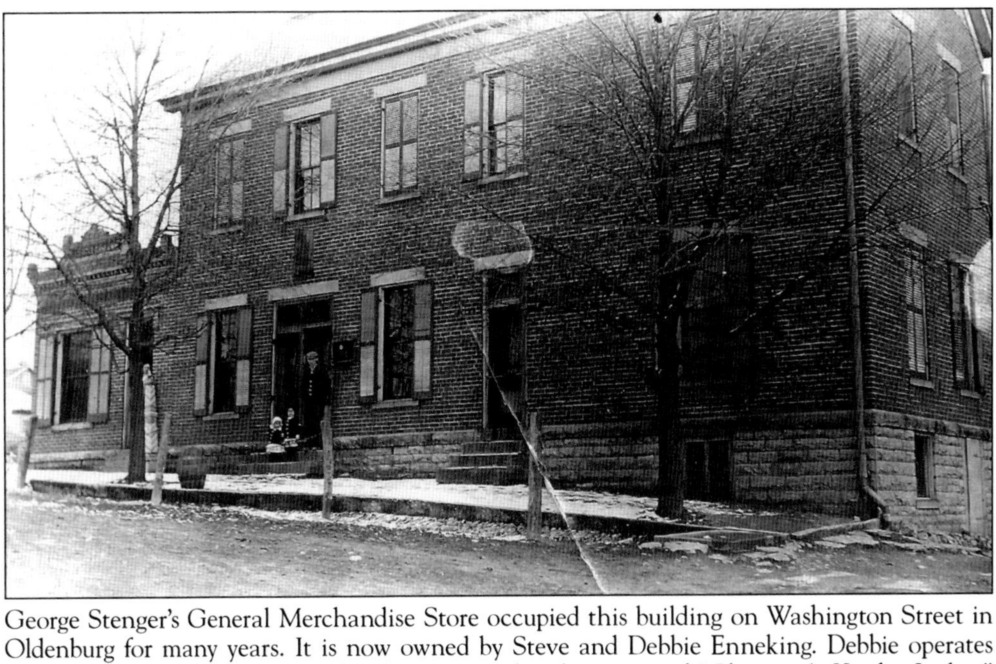

George Stenger's General Merchandise Store occupied this building on Washington Street in Oldenburg for many years. It is now owned by Steve and Debbie Enneking. Debbie operates a children's clothing store in this location under the name of "Christian's Kinder Laden." (Jean Struewing.)

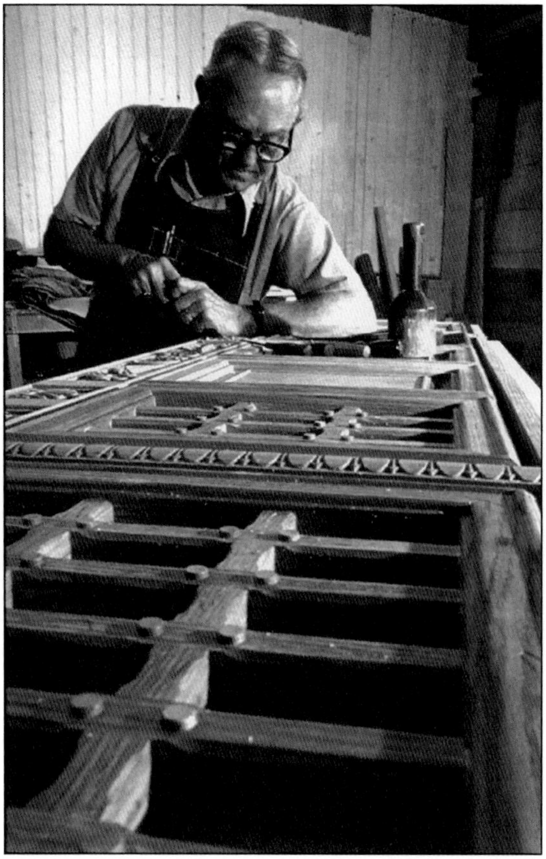

William J. Weberding began carving around the age of six years old. His father gave him some chisels and wood while William was recuperating from an appendectomy and pneumonia. He needed something to keep him busy, and apparently he found the right solution. His dad had no idea this would turn into his son's life occupation. He continued carving and honing his skills on his own, and mostly for pleasure, until the age of 16, when he was hired as an apprentice at Romweber Furniture Company in Batesville. He worked at Romweber Furniture Company for 9 or 10 years, but always had the desire to open his own business. To accomplish this, he carved religious statues in the evenings at home. In his spare time, he visited different parishes to show the priests his carvings and let them know what he could do for them. He eventually started getting orders, and his dream started to become a reality. In 1942, at the age of 25, he opened his own carving shop. (Bill Weberding.)

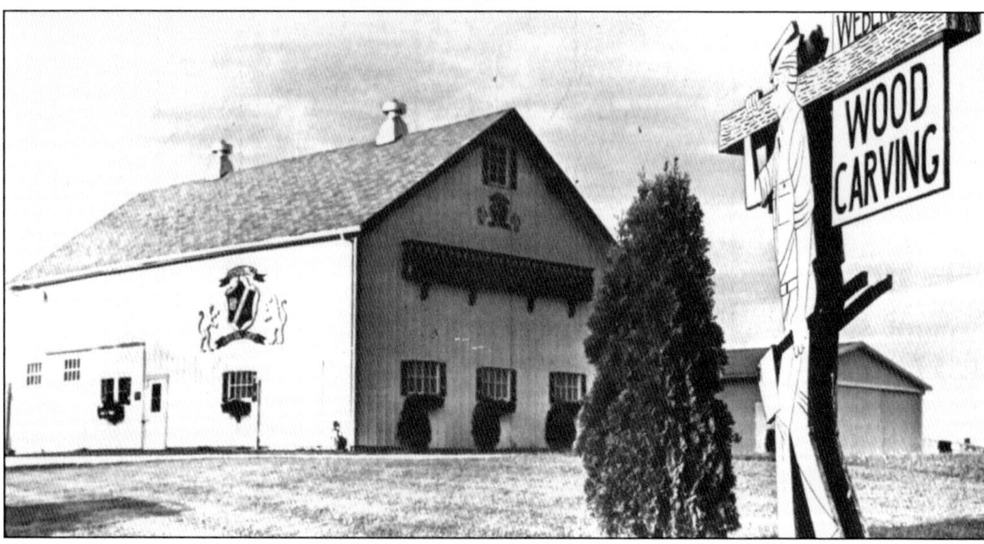

Weberding's Carving Shop is a business involved in a variety of projects including custom furniture, cabinetry, fireplace mantles, and entertainment centers for the home. William established his shop in a small building 10 by 12 feet in size. William retired in 1981. William's sons William G. Weberding, Terry Weberding, and Tim Weberding are currently head of operations. (BAHS.)

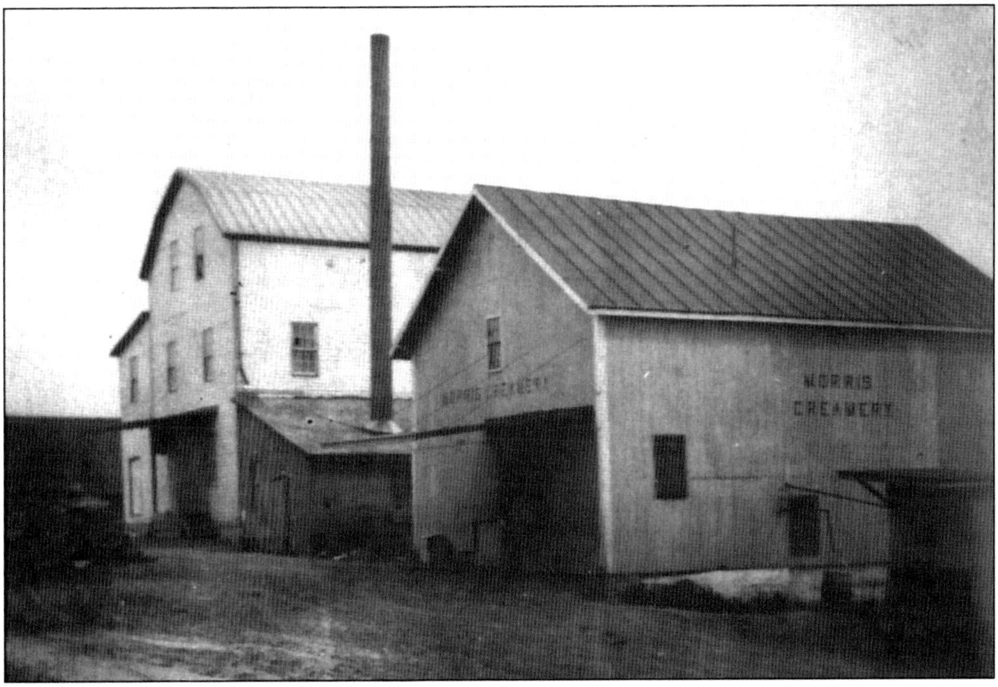

The Morris Creamery buildings were located on the present site of the Morris Feed Mill. The Morris Feed Mill was operated by John A. Nordmeyer and William L. Nordmeyer back in 1921. Today it is still operated by the Nordmeyer family. (BAHS.)

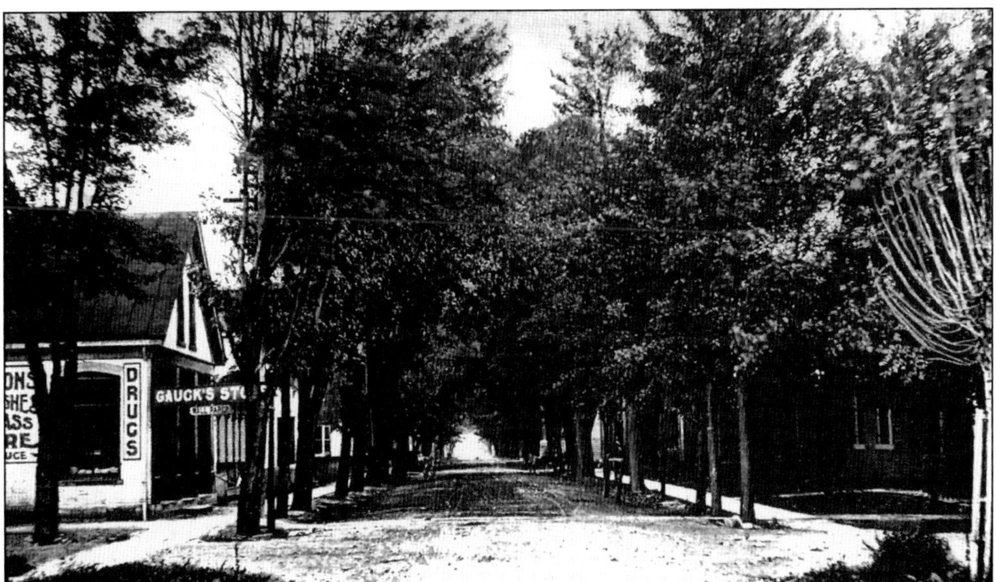

The Gauck Drug Store was located in the building where the Bookshelf is today. In December 1897, the Gauck Drug Store opened a prescription department with T. E. Cain as the new pharmacist. Many types of businesses have been located in this building, from drug store, to grocery store, to teen canteen, to the Bookshelf. (Jean Struewing.)

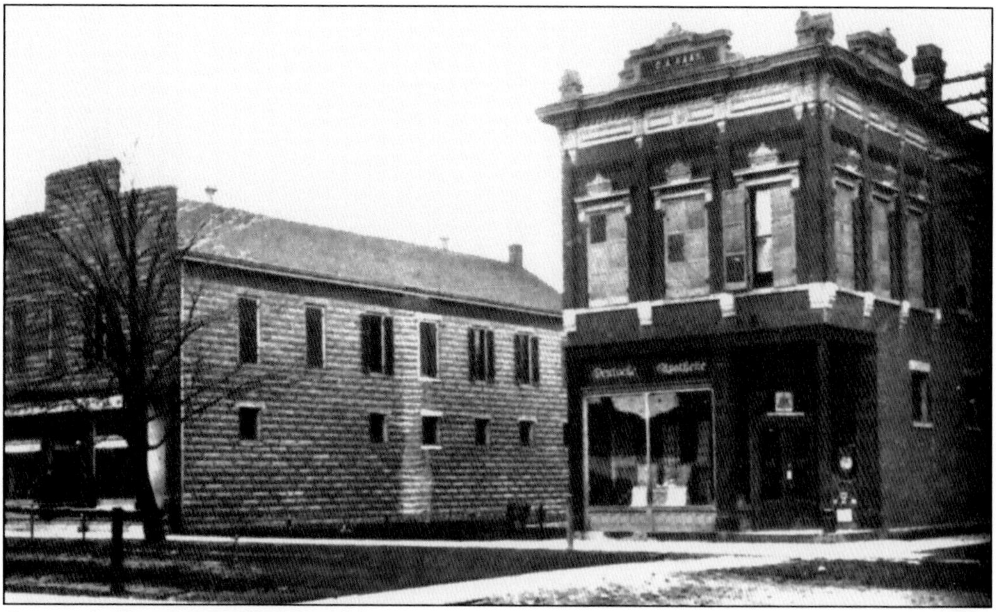

George A. Baas originally named his drug store the City Drug Store. The first Baas Drug Store was built in 1888, at the northeast corner of Walnut and George Streets, diagonally across from the post office. In this photograph, one can see where Baas built a new drug store at its present site on George Street in 1892. The telephone exchange was located in the rear room of the drug store until 1903. (Pat Hare.)

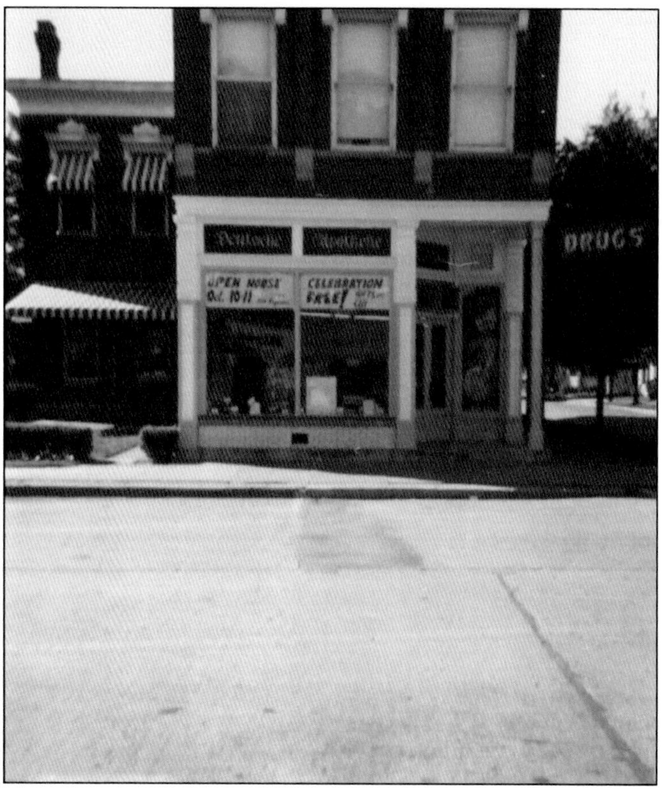

When Clinton Nolte bought the drug store in 1958, he and his family lived on the first floor of the building seen to the left of the store. They had five rooms, a bath, an attached garage, and even a nice yard. Upstairs above the store was a five-room apartment. Later the Noltes vacated their home on the first floor and used the space to enlarge the drug store. (Clinton Nolte.)

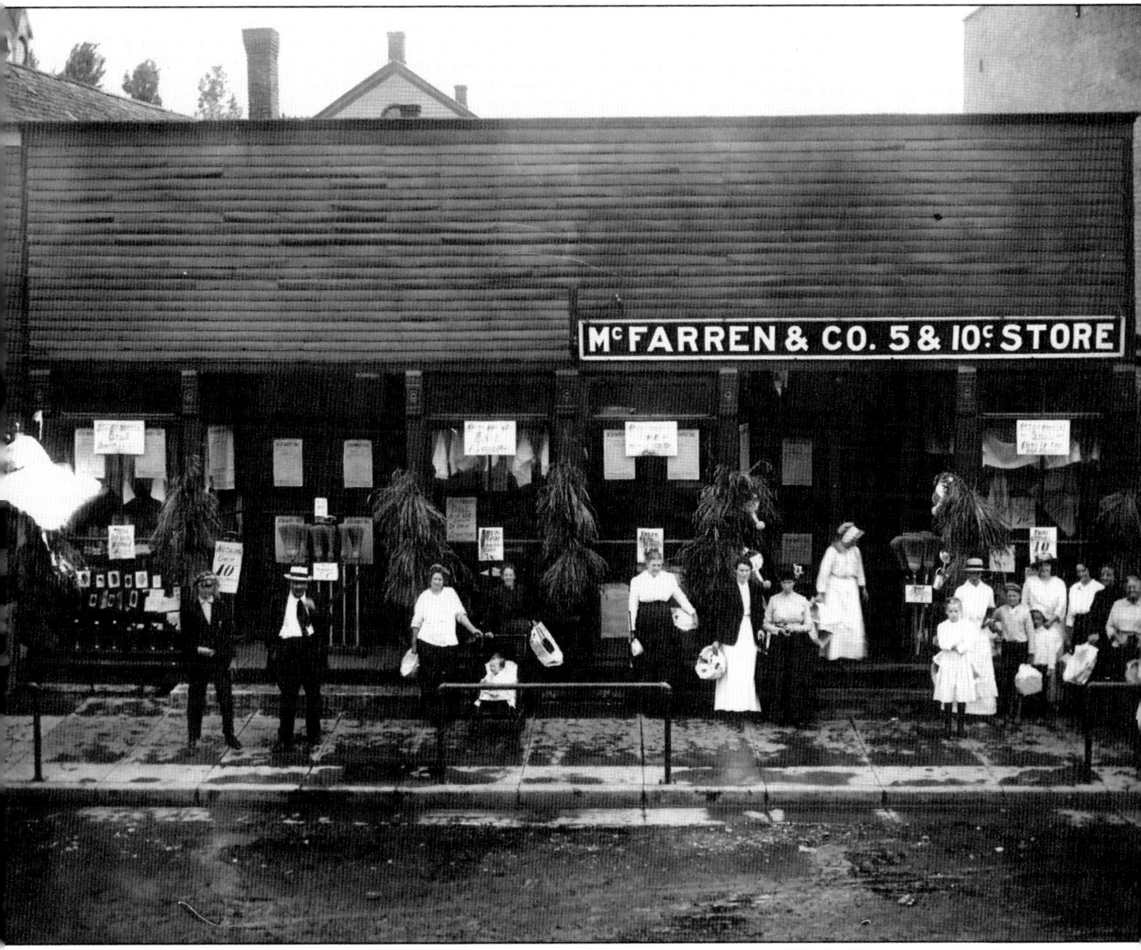

McFarren and Company 5 and 10¢ Store opened in Batesville in one of H. J. Walsman's buildings on George Street on September 12, 1914. The business was renamed the Lockwood 5 and 10¢ Store when it moved from the Walsman frame building seen in the photograph into the brick building, owned by Walsman, one door further west on George Street. The brick building had been formerly occupied by the Star Hardware Company. (Paul Wycoff.)

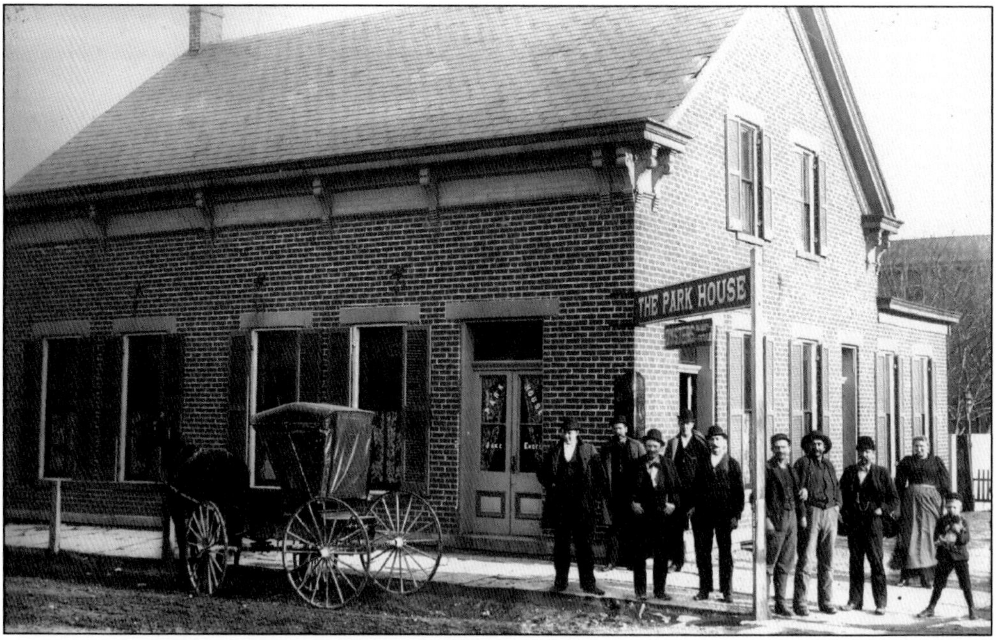

The Park House hotel and restaurant was built in 1896 and opened for business in 1897. The Batesville Yachting Club's headquarters was at the Park House. Its meetings were held in the Park House garden. Jacob Engel, not pictured in the photograph, was proprietor of this pleasure resort and was an active member of the yacht club. (Alma Miller and Georgann Flory.)

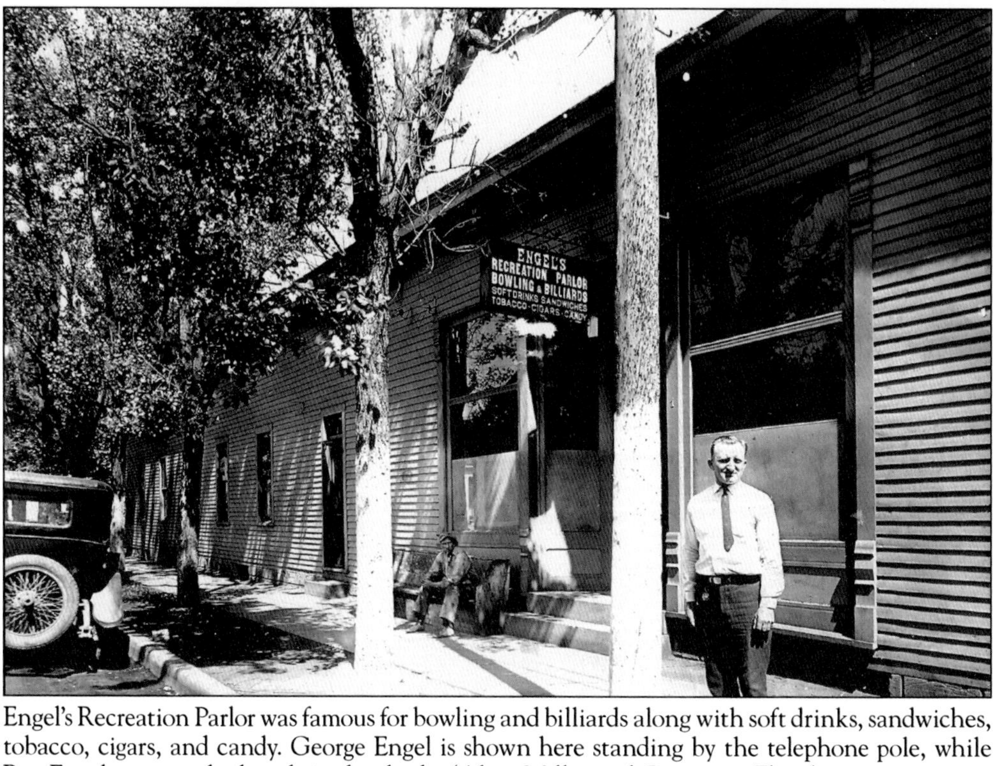

Engel's Recreation Parlor was famous for bowling and billiards along with soft drinks, sandwiches, tobacco, cigars, and candy. George Engel is shown here standing by the telephone pole, while Ray Engel rests on the bench in the shade. (Alma Miller and Georgann Flory.)

The Kaiser Brothers' Livery and Feed Stable, shown here in the days of horse-drawn vehicles, became a taxi and motor-drayage business as motor vehicles took the place of horses. Adolph Kaiser continued the business after his brother Herman's death. Another important business change occurred in May 1929, when John Kappes bought the business from the Kaisers. (Paul Wycoff.)

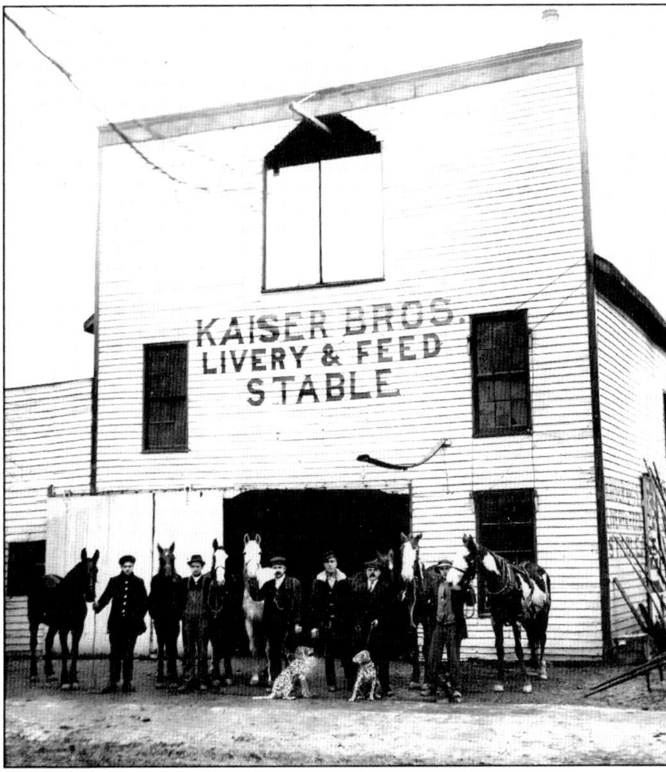

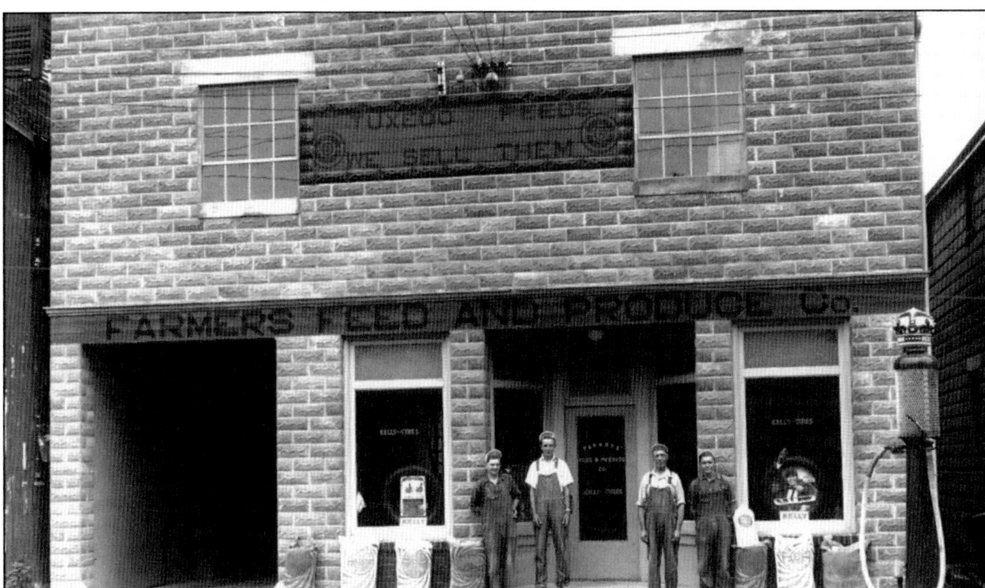

The Farmer's Feed and Produce Company built a new concrete store on East George Street opposite the Batesville Lumber Company in 1929. The building was two stories measuring 35 by 78 feet. In March 1937, the Farmer's Feed and Produce Company reported that eggs crashed to the floor. Reports from the seismological observatory at Xavier University verified the suspicion of an earthquake. (Paul Wycoff.)

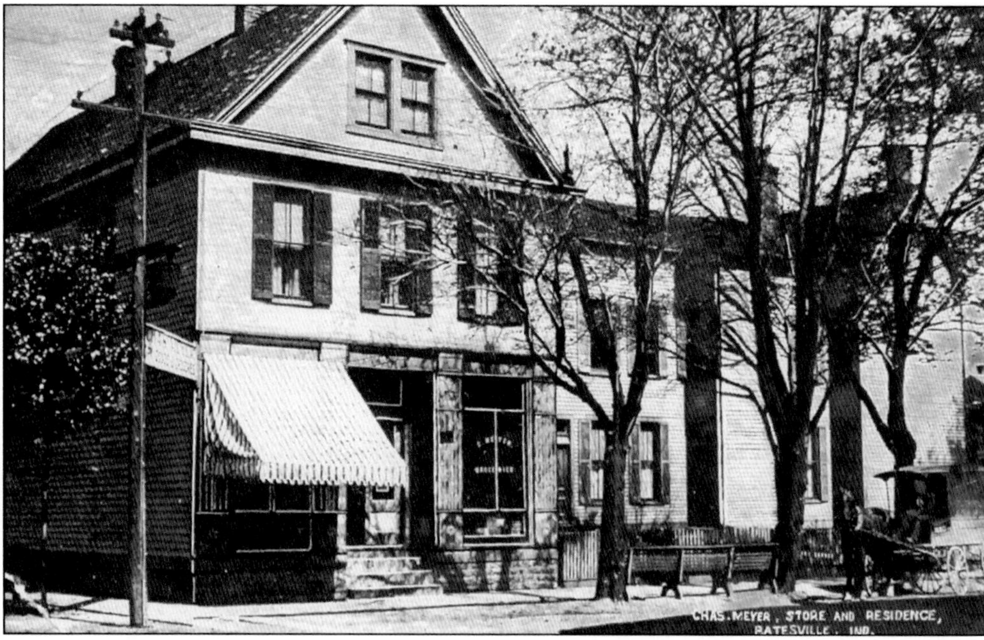

Charles Meyer operated a grocery store for many years at the northwest corner of George and Walnut Streets in Batesville. After selling the grocery store, which was kitty-cornered from the Baas Drug Store, Meyer was associated with his son, Chester Meyer, as express agents and managers of the Meyer Garage on West George Street. (Jean Struewing.)

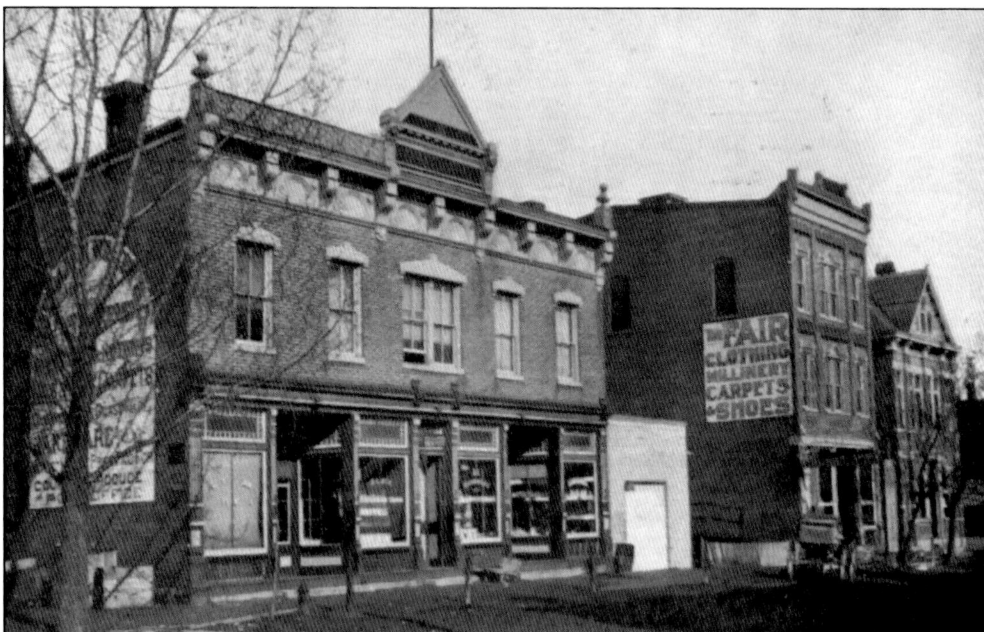

Greeman, Wilker and Company occupied their new brick store on Main Street in December 1910. The old frame building, not visible at the rear, was moved back from the street to accommodate the new brick addition and was used as a warehouse room. Owners of stock in this company were John H. Wilker, Michael Heinlein, Mrs. W. T. Greeman, and William Giesin. (Pat Hare.)

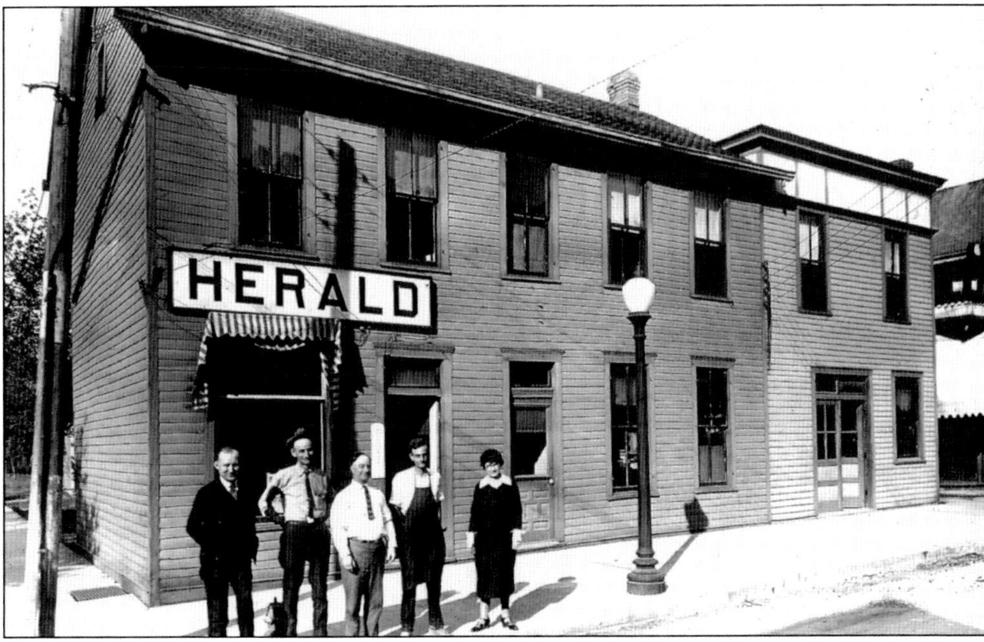

The *Herald* was a democratic paper located at the northeast corner of Main and Boehringer Streets, where Fran Telles now has his barbershop. The *Tribune* at that time was a republican paper. Boerstler's Jewelry Store occupied the store to the right of the Herald. People in the photograph were employees of the Herald. They are, from left to right, Clarence Andres, Harry Peetz, John Wintz, Leo Peetz, and Irene Goldsmith. (Women's Study Club.)

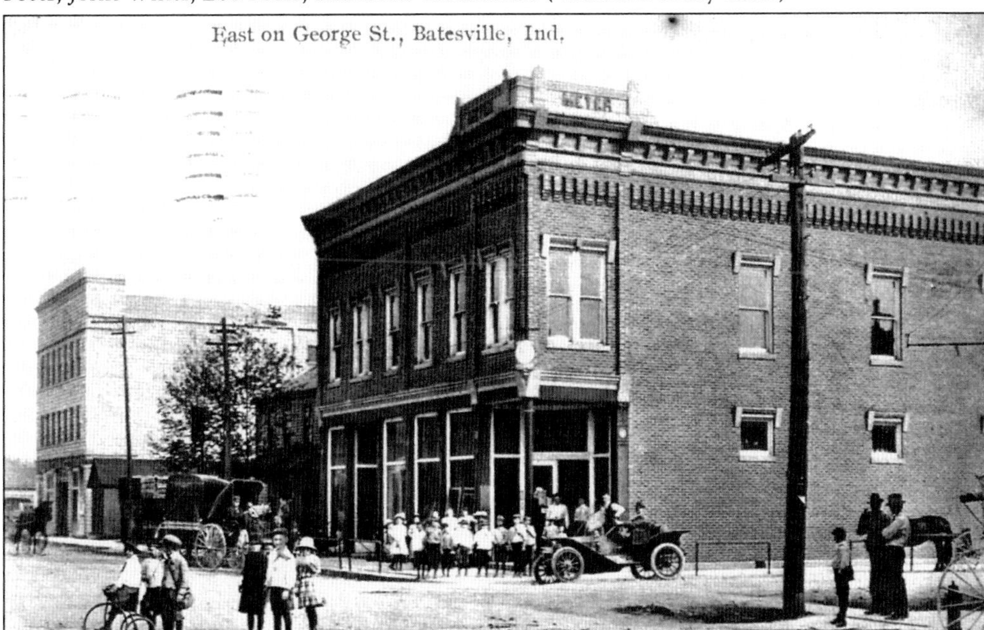

John Meyer built the large brick store at the corner of George and Main Streets and moved his hardware business into the new building. Later he enlarged the building to accommodate a line of furniture, developing the firm of Meyer and Company, Hardware and Furniture. His son Roman Meyer and son-in-law Quirin Walsman were also members of the firm. (Pat Hare.)

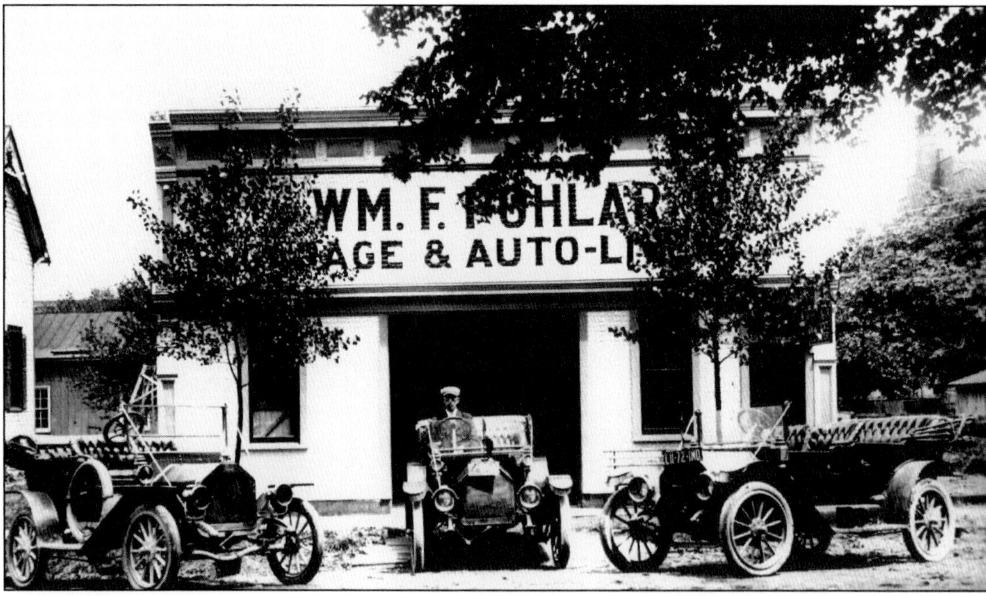

The Pohlar Garage, when first built, was one story high and measured 70 by 100 feet. It was built of brick with cement floors throughout. Monday night was drill night for the Liberty Guards, whose meetings convened at the Pohlar Garage during the year 1918. (Clinton Nolte.)

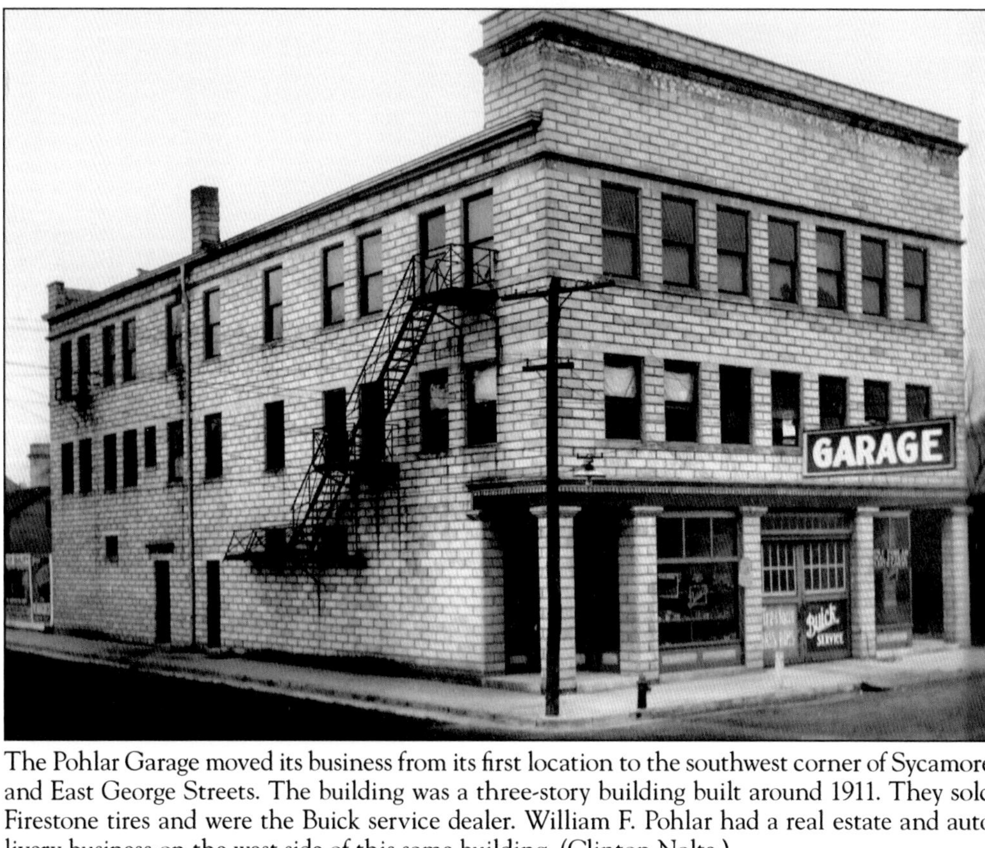

The Pohlar Garage moved its business from its first location to the southwest corner of Sycamore and East George Streets. The building was a three-story building built around 1911. They sold Firestone tires and were the Buick service dealer. William F. Pohlar had a real estate and auto livery business on the west side of this same building. (Clinton Nolte.)

Eight

HOMES

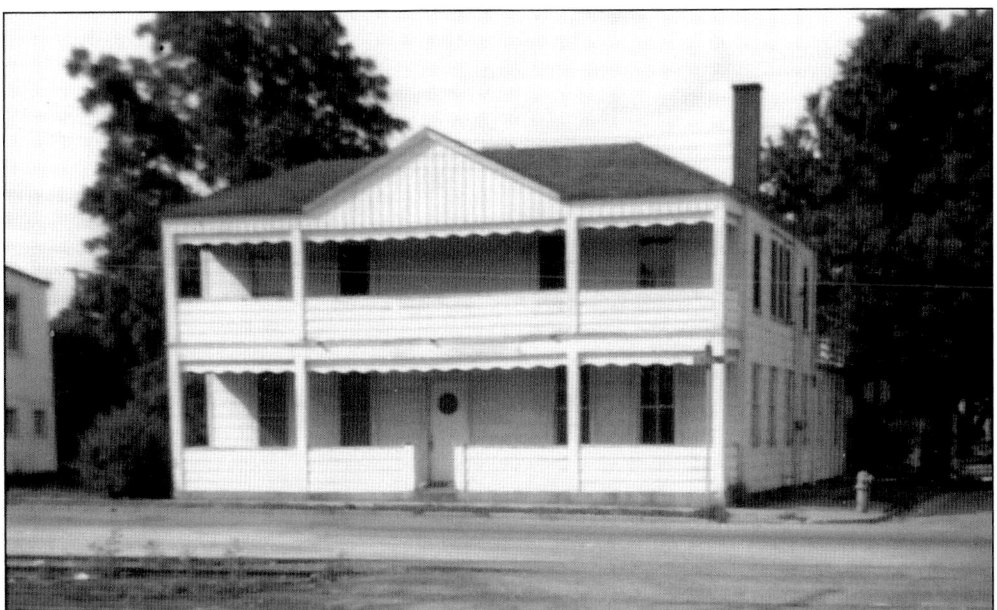

On January 3, 1877, John Hillenbrand Sr. purchased lots five and six on Broadway (now East Pearl Street) and Park Avenues, where he built this home. This house was the Hillenbrand family home during all the active years of Hillenbrand's life. Hillenbrand was born in Adams Township, Ripley County, on February 18, 1843. He died at Batesville on May 27, 1910. (Gary Moenter.)

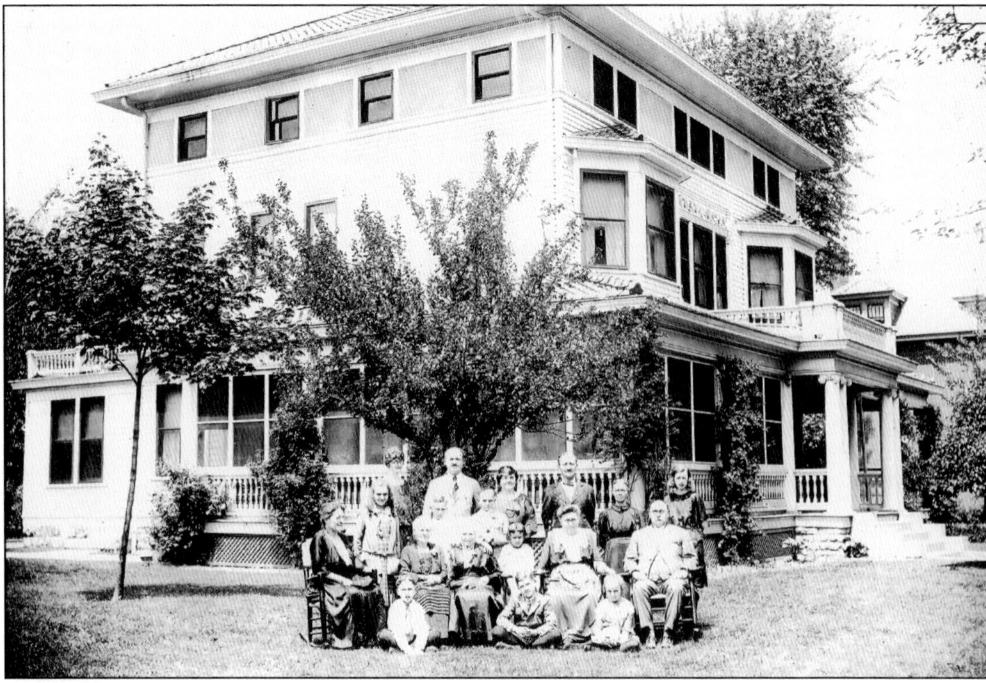

The photograph above is a side view of John A. Hillenbrand's home on North Walnut Street. Along with his family are Sophie and George M. Hillenbrand. The photograph below is a front view of the John A. Hillenbrand home, taken many years later. John A. married Clara Enneking on February 11, 1903. The couple lived on Main Street until 1908 when they moved to this house on Walnut Street, where they raised their family. Wide inviting steps lead visitors to the tall glass doors behind which broad halls open up the center of the house. Family life matured in the big house. After the deaths of Clara and John A., the house was given to the City of Batesville. The new public library was later built on that location. (Above, Paul Wycoff; below, BAHS.)

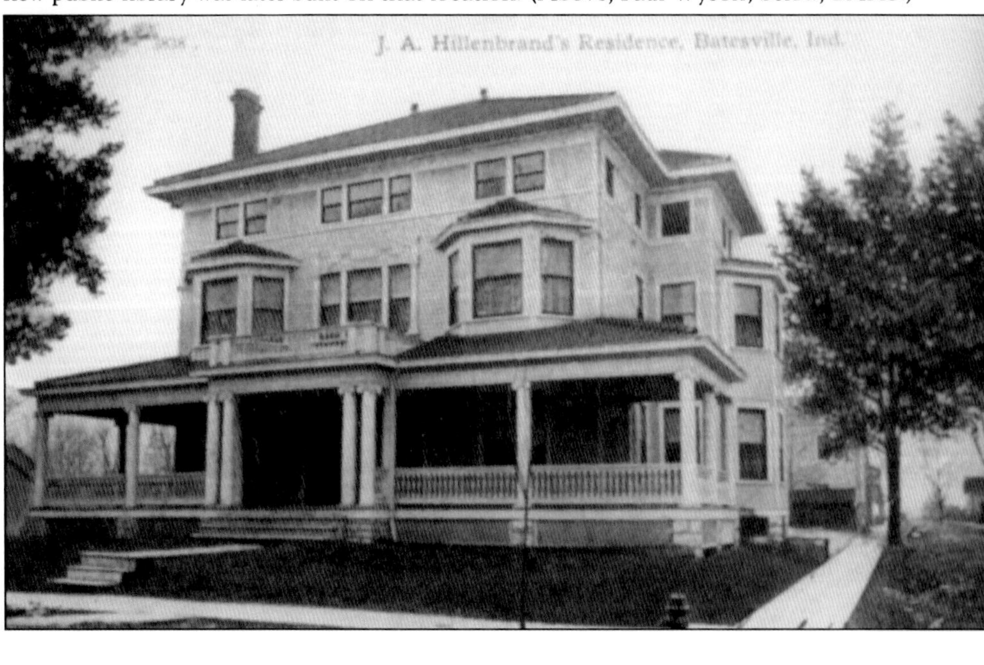

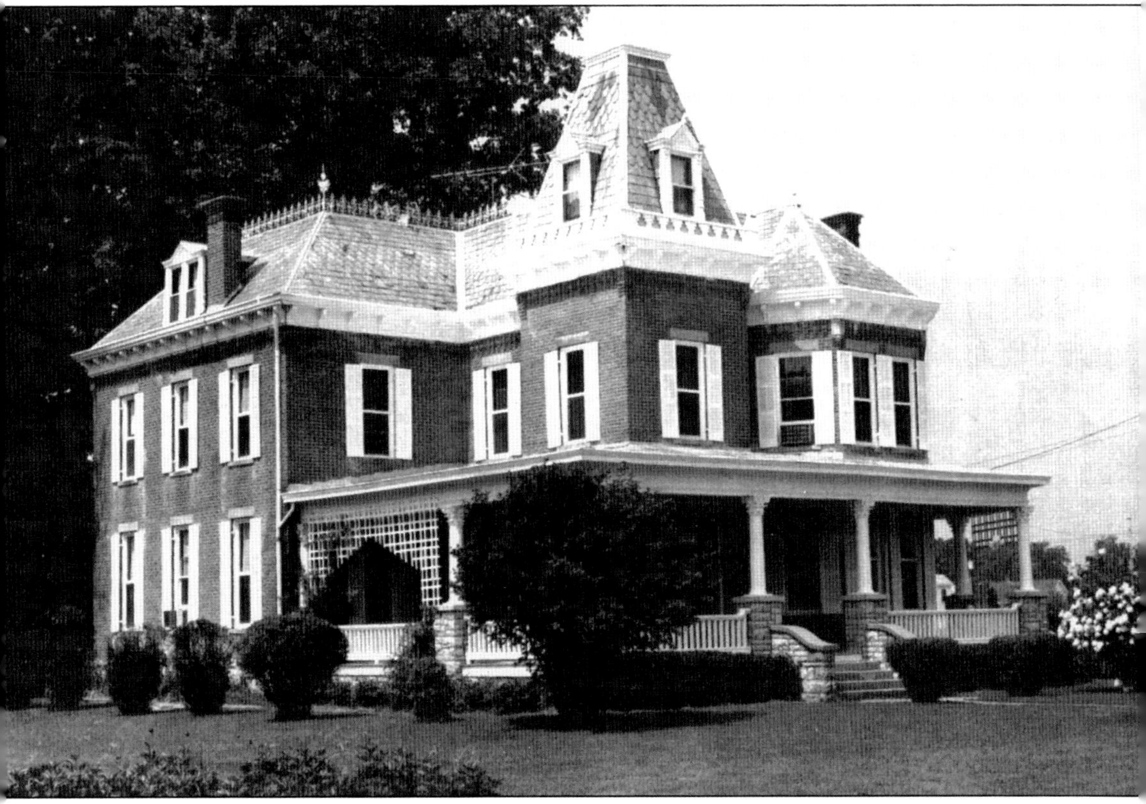

The Canfield house, showcasing the elegance of the early 1900s, is one of the older showplaces in Batesville. It was formerly the home of the late U.S. congressman Harry C. Canfield. Located on South Mulberry Street, the home was owned by Fred Kops, father of Washington, D.C., attorney Andrew Kops. The location was once known as Middletown. Fred's sister Anna Morgan built the house in 1896. The Canfields purchased the house in 1913 from Anna. This stately house has 11 rooms, 2 baths, and 3 halls. Upon entering the house, visitors encounter a beautiful hardwood floor featuring, in its center, a star made of different colored woods. One of the most unique rooms on the first floor is the dining room. Canfield had the famous cathedral painter Edward Peine of Oldenburg paint a continuous Dutch mural around the entire room near the ceiling. According to older residents of the community, there is a secret passage somewhere in the house. (BAHS.)

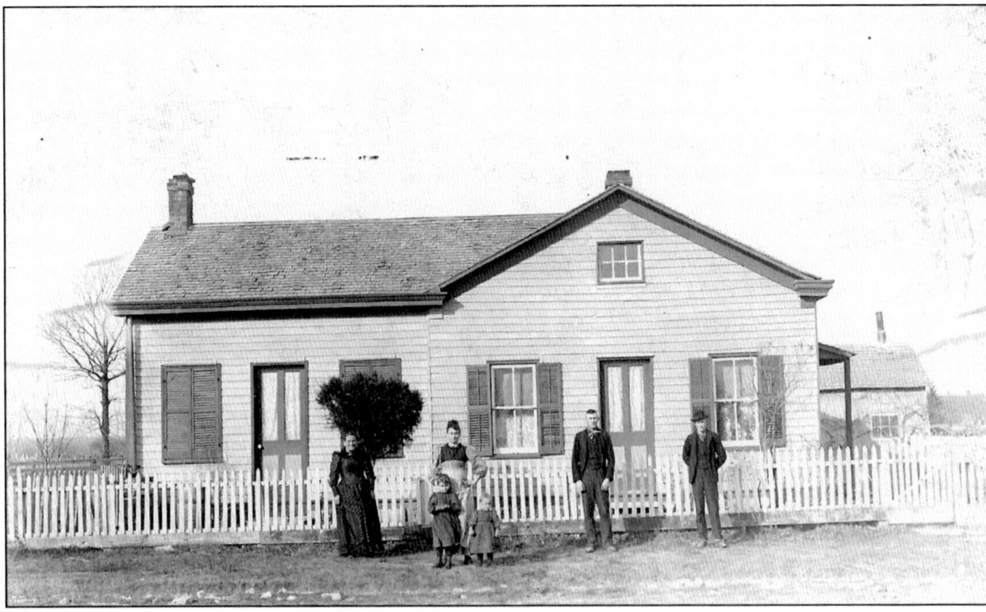

This was the home of Dr. Joseph X. Ziteke on South Walnut Street (the individuals in the photograph are unidentified). Ziteke was the leader in developing the sanitation of the new town of Batesville. He served as secretary of the board of health for many years. He died about 1916. (BAHS.)

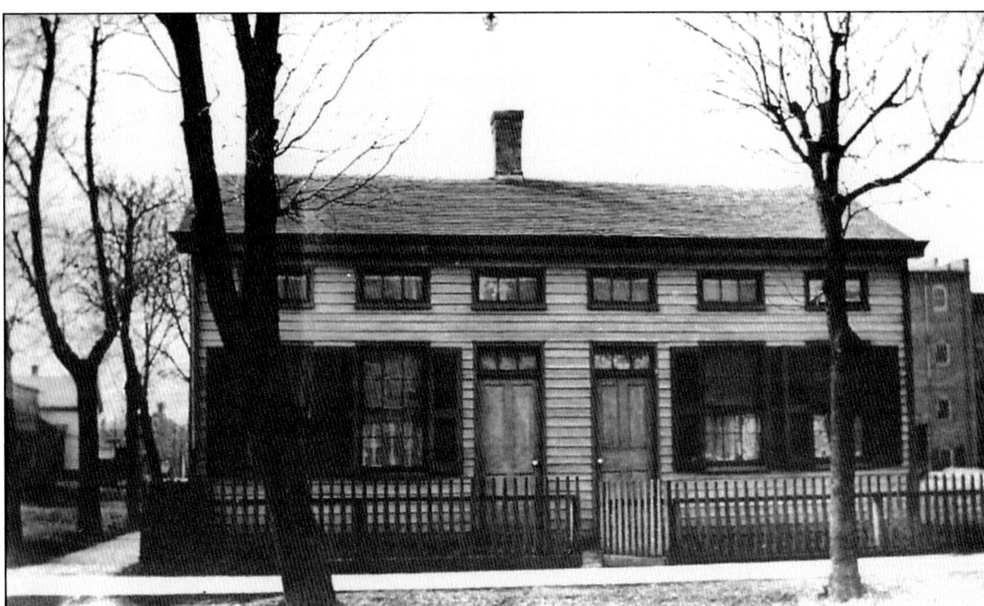

This is the home of John and Agnes Becher at the southwest corner of West Pearl and Elm Streets, across from the Eagles building. They were the parents of Emile Baas, who was the wife of George W. Baas, and Sophia Baas, who was the wife of Louis Baas. (Paul and Milt Baas.)

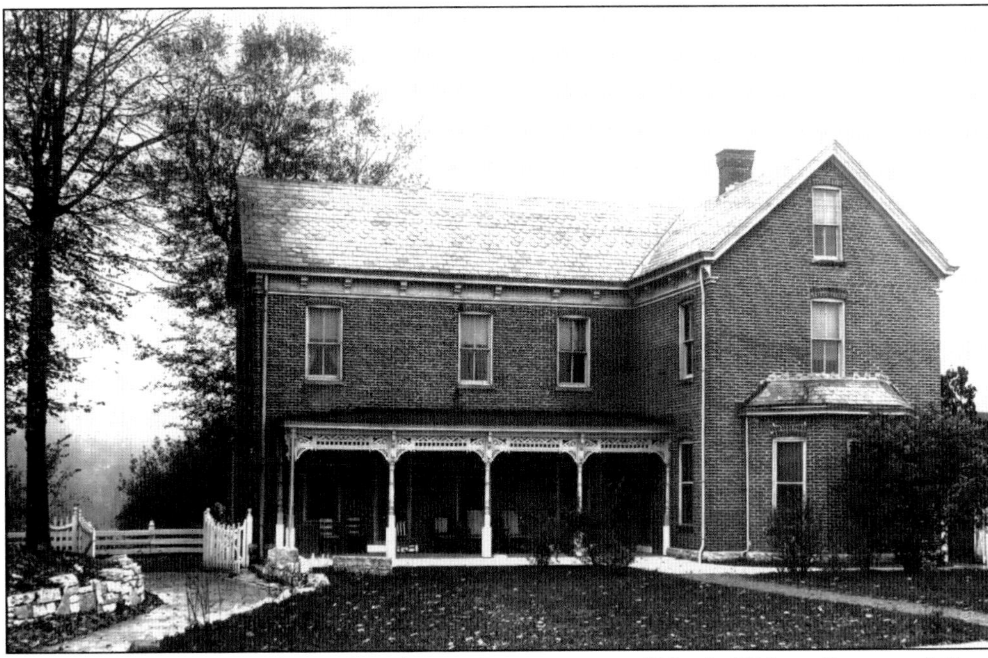

The Schrader home was located at the southwest corner of North Walnut Street and State Highway 46, where the Hillcrest Country Club now has a parking lot. The country club used this home as their clubhouse for many years until the new clubhouse was built across the street on the southeast corner in 1990. This home was built by Herman Schrader, who died in 1882. (Paul Wycoff.)

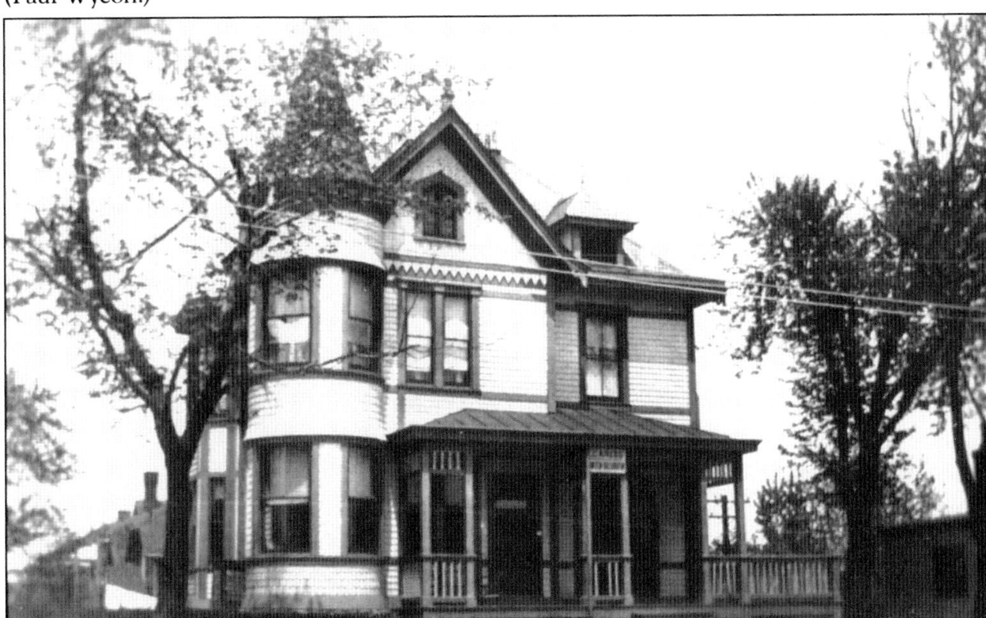

This photograph shows the Kaiser home that was built on the southwest corner of George and Walnut Streets, where the post office now stands. The Kaisers had a livery barn behind this house on Walnut Street. The round tower was removed when it was relocated one lot west facing George Street. It was later converted into Dr. Ali Daftary's medical office. (Jewelnita Luhring)

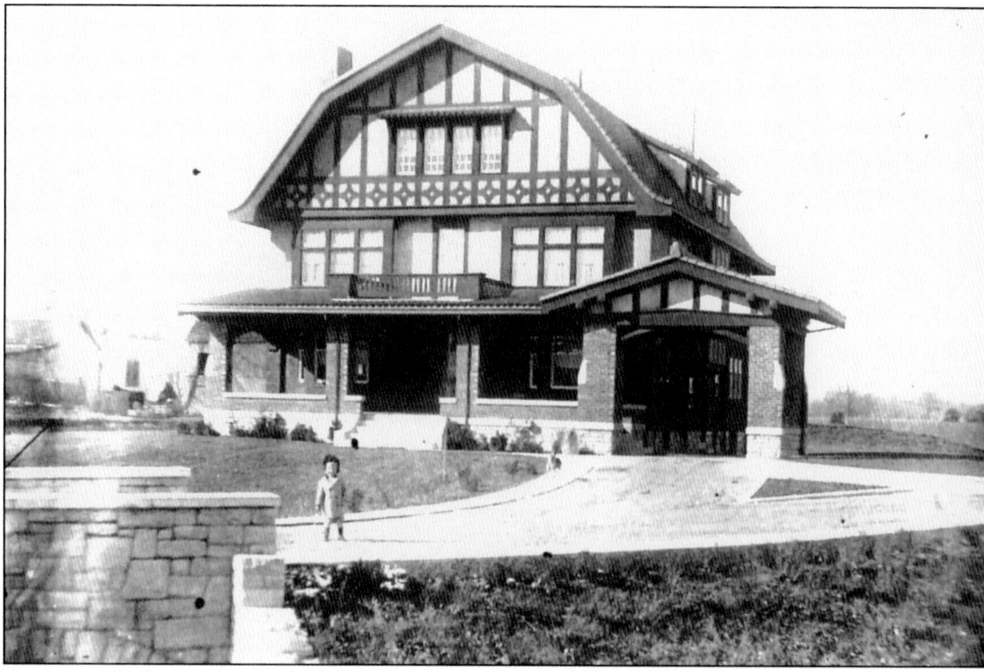

Anthony W. Romweber built this beautiful home in 1911 in what was called the Hillencrest of Batesville, adjacent to Rosemont and the golf course on North Walnut Street. This home and the home of George M. Hillenbrand formed the residential showcase of Batesville, featuring flowers, shrubbery, and landscape gardening on an elaborate scale. The home is now the John Schuerman Law Office. (Flora Stein Estate.)

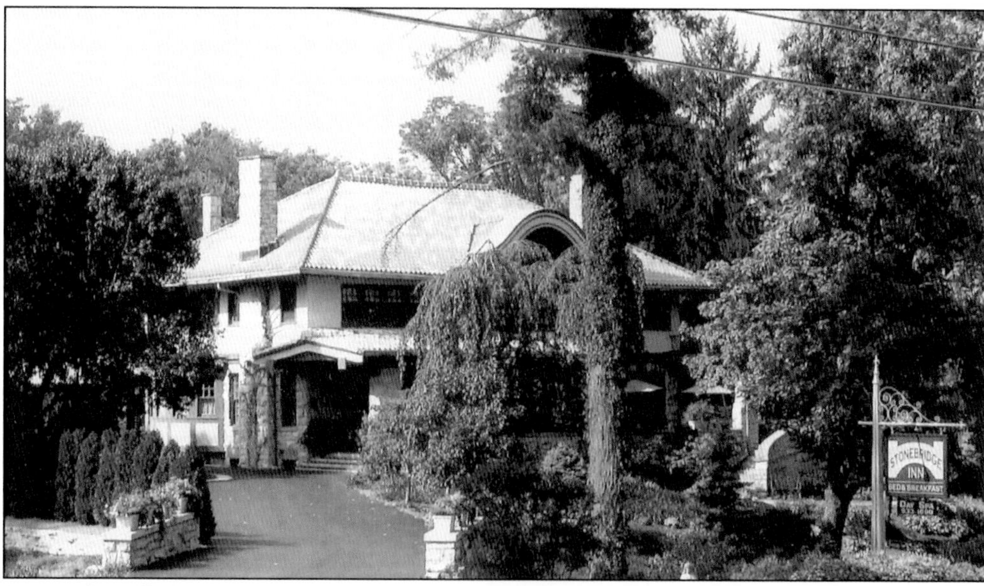

Originally called Hillencrest, and now home of the Stonebridge Inn, this beautiful estate home was built in 1910 for George M. and Sophia Hillenbrand. Its walls have heard the laughter and tears of almost one hundred years of family life. George M. was the first mayor of Batesville in 1882 when the town first formed its government. Sophia was an artistic and creative person who enjoyed her work decorating this home and running a hat-making shop. (Jean Struewing.)

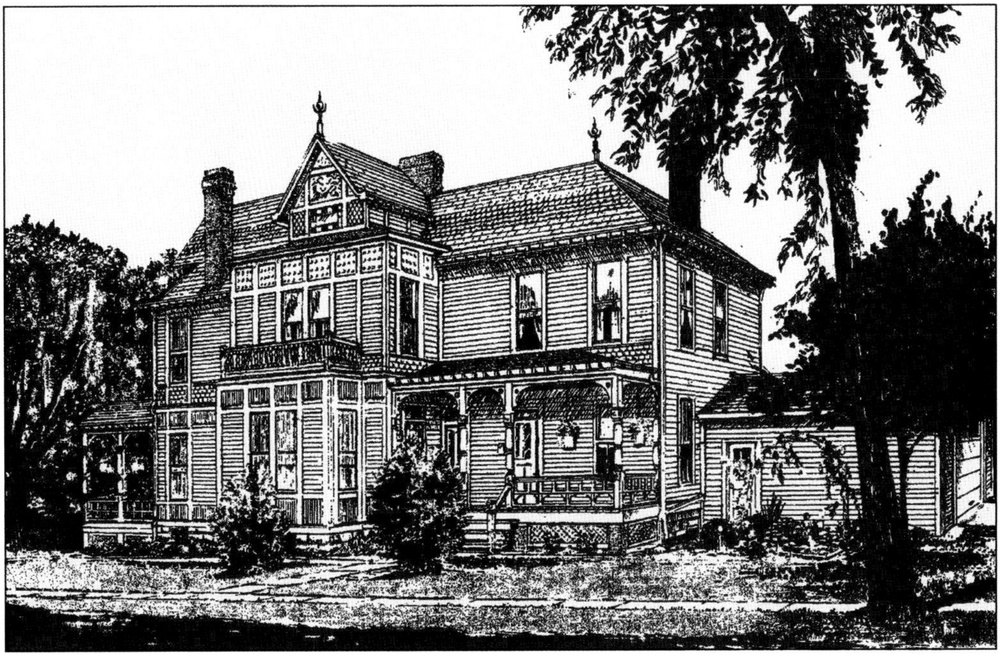

Dr. O. A. Bigham moved to Batesville in July 1921, succeeding the late Dr. Joseph X. Ziteke in the office on Walnut Street. This is an artist's sketch of Dr. Bigham's home on the southwest corner of South and Depot Streets. (BAHS.)

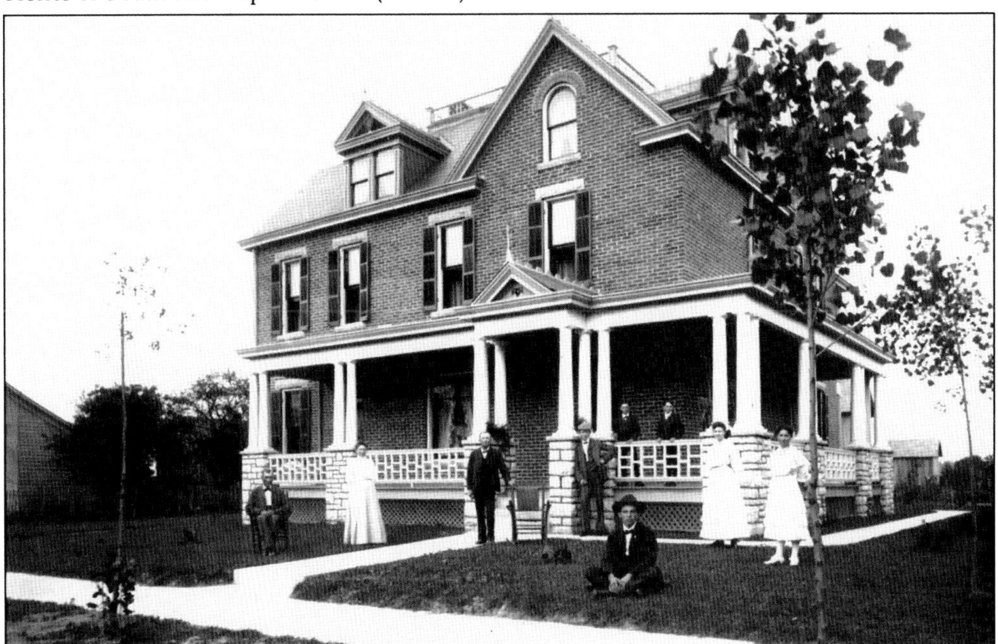

This photograph shows the Benz homestead on the east side of North Park Avenue. Sitting on grass is Michael Benz Jr. Sitting in the chair is Joseph Wilhelm. Standing in the yard are, from left to right, Mary (Wilhelm) Benz, Michael Benz Sr., Joseph Benz, Tillie (Benz) Wintz, and Martha (Benz) Hunteman. Standing on the porch are, from left to right, Hugo Benz and Leo Benz. The house is now a rental property owned by Doug Obermeyer. (Martha Hunteman.)

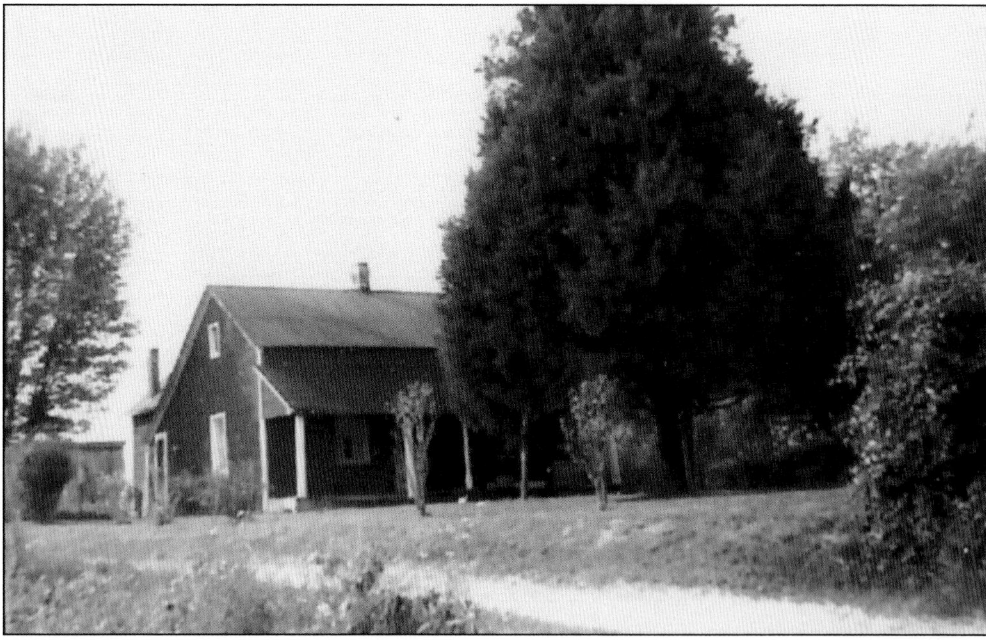

This is a photograph of the Adam Hoyer home at Steamboat Landing on the Walnut Fork of Laughery Creek. Adam was the grandfather of Howard Hoyer. Steamboat Landing was named because of a nearby store with a picture of a steamboat painted on the side. The area was known for the basket makers that practiced their trade there. (Ruth Hoyer.)

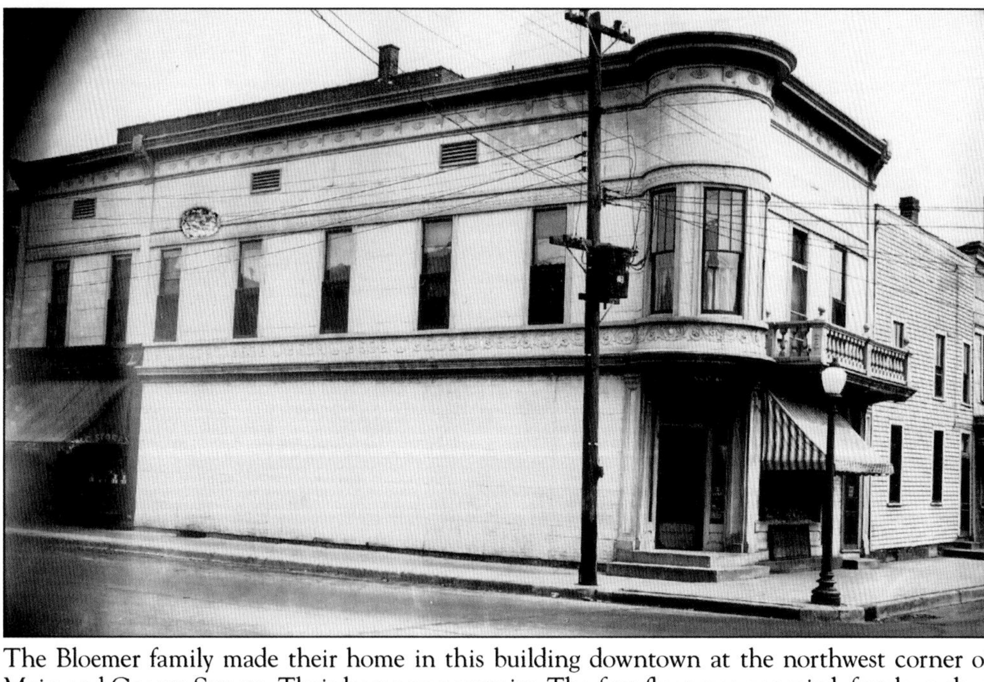

The Bloemer family made their home in this building downtown at the northwest corner of Main and George Streets. Their home was upstairs. The first floor was occupied, first by a shoe store and later by a dress shop. This picture was taken in the 1930s. Later, when the Hillenbrands owned the Sherman House, this building was added to the Sherman House property. (Alma Miller and Georgann Flory.)

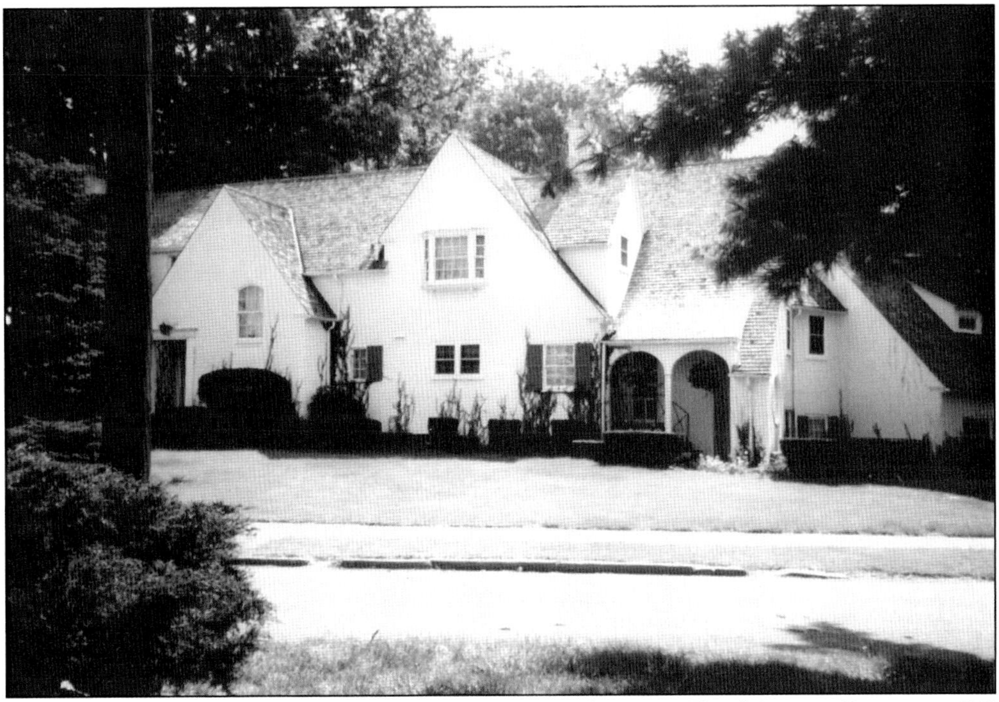

The address of this lovely home built by Anthony Romweber is 610 Floral Court in Rosemont. Bill and Denise Hillenbrand bought the house recently and have made some major improvements. The house again hears the patter of little feet as Bill and Denise have four children. (Jean Struewing.)

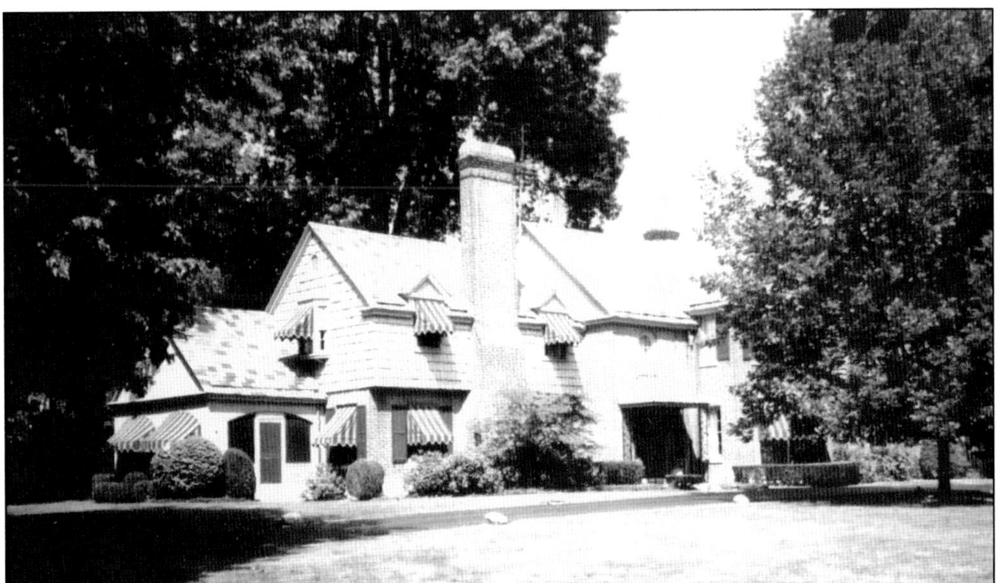

Paul C. Romweber built this home at 511 Floral Court in Rosemont. Paul C. was a part of the management of the Romweber Industries, makers of fine furniture including the Viking Oak series. The home is now owned by Jake and Nancy Flannery. (Jean Struewing.)

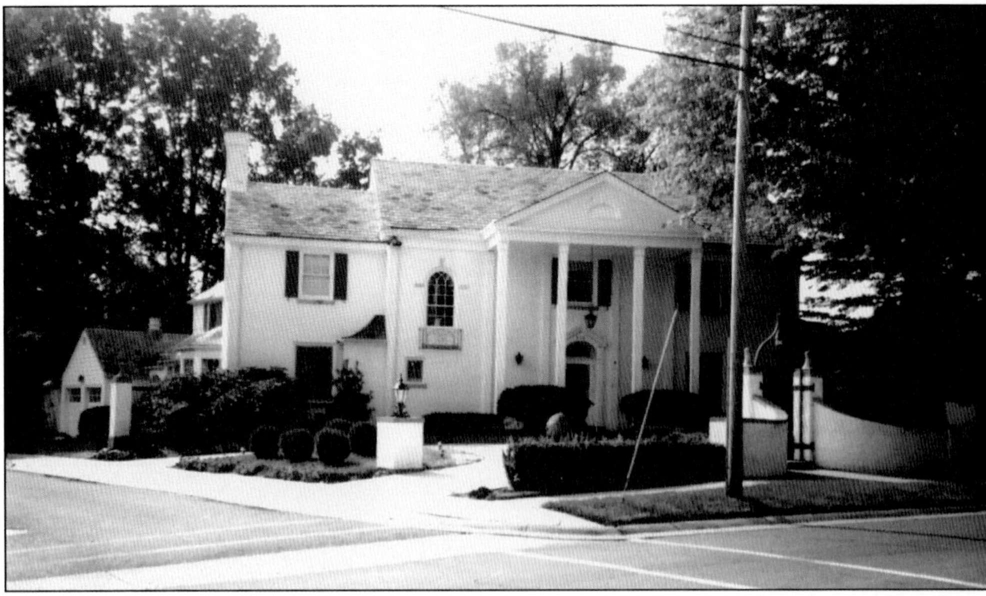

This beautiful home at 410 North Walnut Street was originally built by John W. Hillenbrand in 1936. The house is a classic example of antebellum style architecture. The house consists of 9,000 square feet of space including the basement. The floors are laid with solid oak slats in varying shapes and patterns. The James A. Fritsch family took ownership in 1992. (Jean Struewing.)

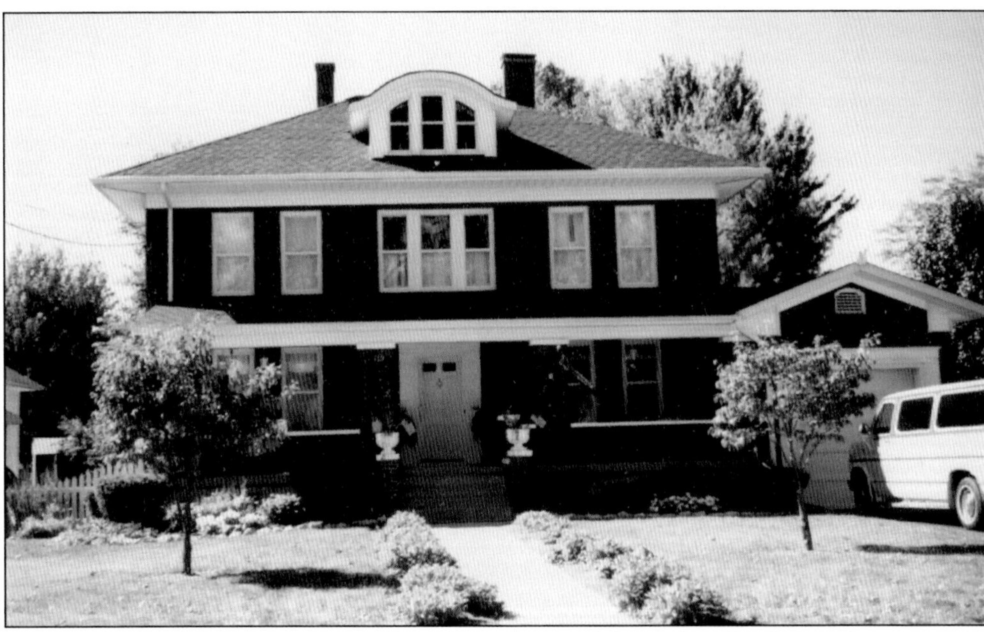

This American foursquare, two-story house has a low-pitch hipped roof with attic dormers, and a porch that spans the width of the front facade. The home was built by John Benham and served as his residence while he was a member of the U.S. Congress from 1918 to 1922. Current owners, Teri and Rick Fledderman, have made every effort to maintain the home's charm and character. (Jean Struewing.)

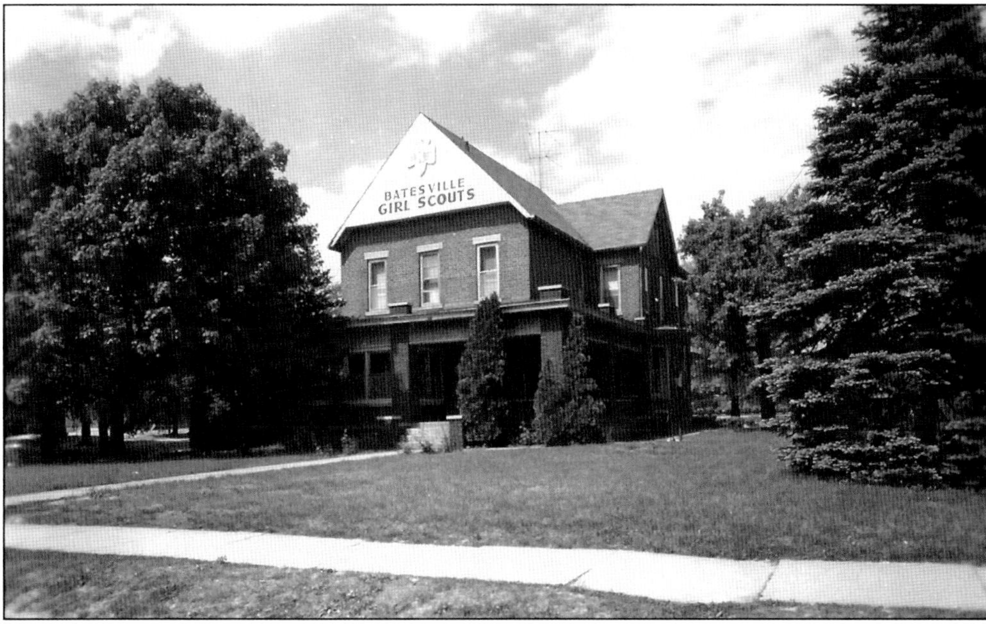

The John H. Wonning family once owned this house on West Pearl Street. The Wonning dairy farm was operated from this same property. After the dairy business was moved to the outskirts of town, Richard Flodder tells the story that in the field behind this house is where the circus performed when it came to town. In later years, this house was given to the Girl Scouts to use as their meeting place. (BAHS.)

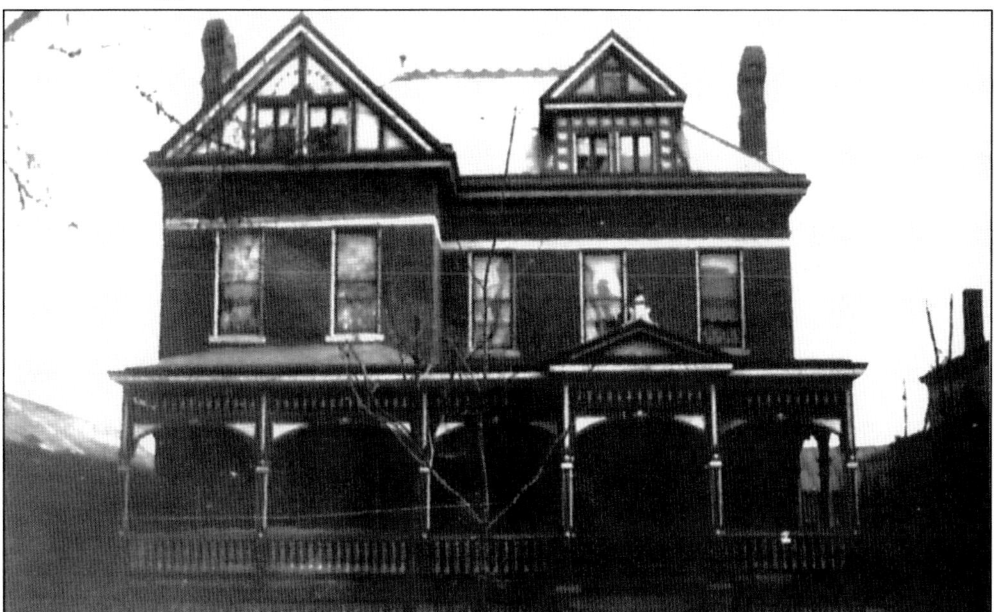
This home on West Pearl Street was once owned by Charles Green. It stood just west of the Lehmkuehler building, which was later the Herald Tribune office, and now Kevin Krekeler owns the building. After the Green family sold the house to the American Legion for their clubroom, the basement was remodeled to make a reception or party room. They named the party room the Fox Hole. (Rick Green.)

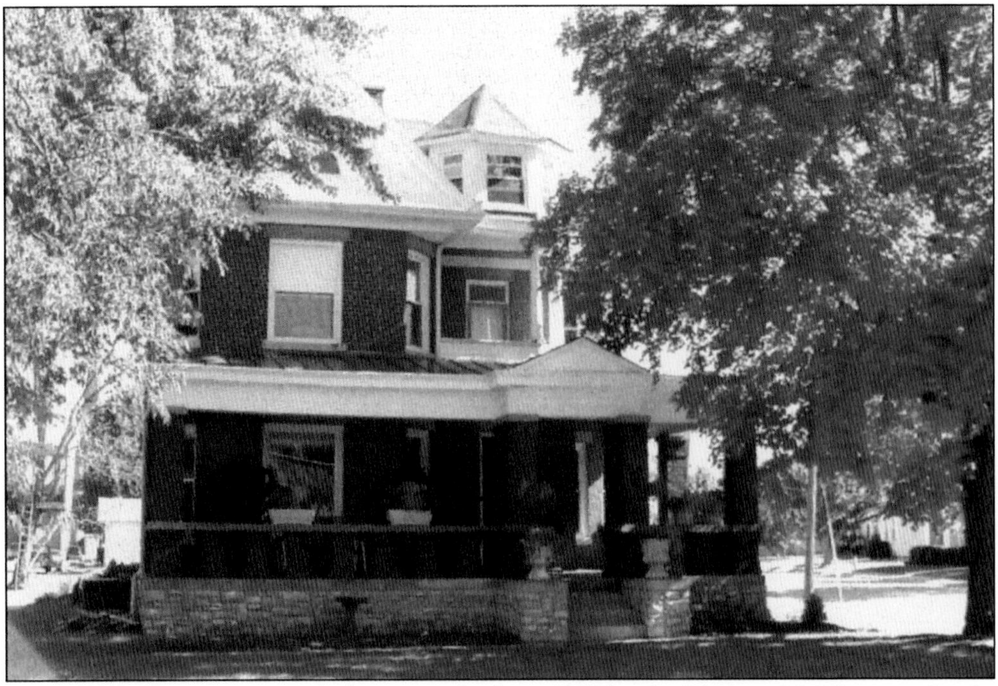

This stately Queen Anne–style home was built in 1907 by the Herman H. Wonning family. Harvey Wonning and his sister Nora Wonning lived in the home until their deaths. The home is shaded by the big maple trees and the four persimmon trees on the west side of the home. Laura and Chris Ault purchased the home in 1999 and added a few of their own touches. (Jean Struewing.)

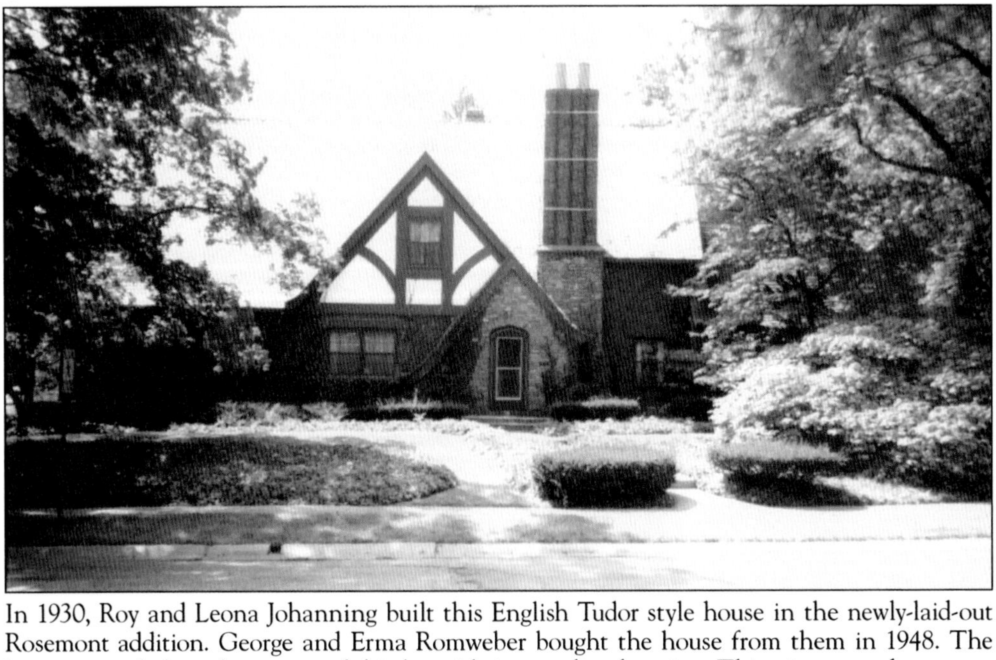

In 1930, Roy and Leona Johanning built this English Tudor style house in the newly-laid-out Rosemont addition. George and Erma Romweber bought the house from them in 1948. The house is nestled on the corner of this lot with its tree lined setting. This nine-room home was the home of Erma Romweber until her death on November 22, 2005. (Jean Struewing.)

Nine

People

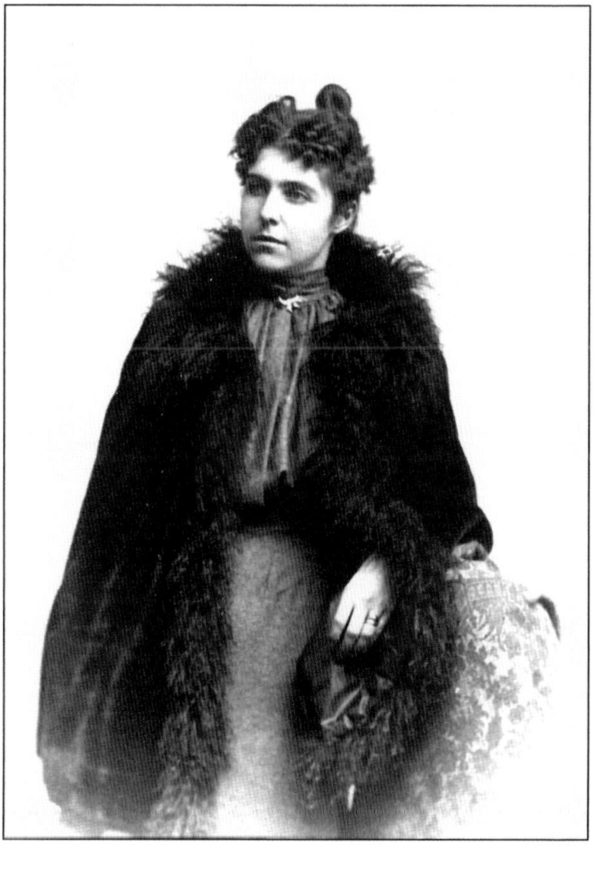

Minnie E. Wycoff was born near Cross Plains on August 11, 1874. She attended Moores Hill College and became a teacher. She married Albert B. Wycoff, and they had one son, Paul. In 1908, they moved to Batesville where she became very involved in civic life. She organized the American Legion Auxiliary and the Ripley County Historical Society and served as president of the Ripley County Tuberculosis Association and as supervisor of Red Cross activities. (Pat Hare.)

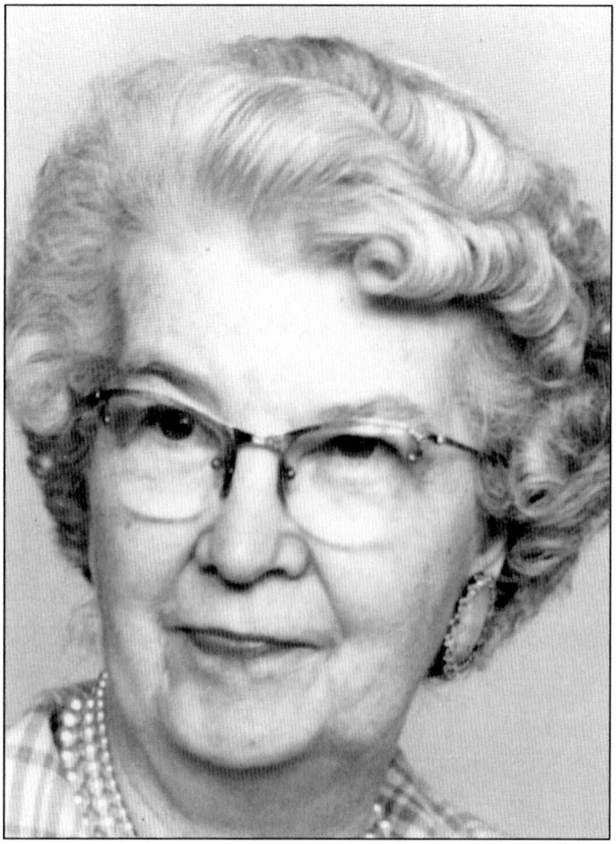

Miriam Mason Swain began her life in Goshen in 1900. She moved to Batesville during the late 1940s. The three important things in her life were church, culture, and reading. She decided to become a writer and began writing children's books. Her first published book was *Little Story House*, which appeared in 1935. During her career, she wrote over 50 books for young people. During her later years, she also served as a consultant for primers produced for elementary school students. Included in her works were books about her grandson Andy Beck and her daughter Kathleen (Kitsi) Beck. The book about Andy was entitled *A Small Farm for Andy* and appeared in 1958 when Andy was seven years old. The book about Kathleen was entitled *Katie Kittenheart* and was published in 1957. Swain remained a Batesville resident until her death in 1971. (Carol Roberts and Marge Reverman.)

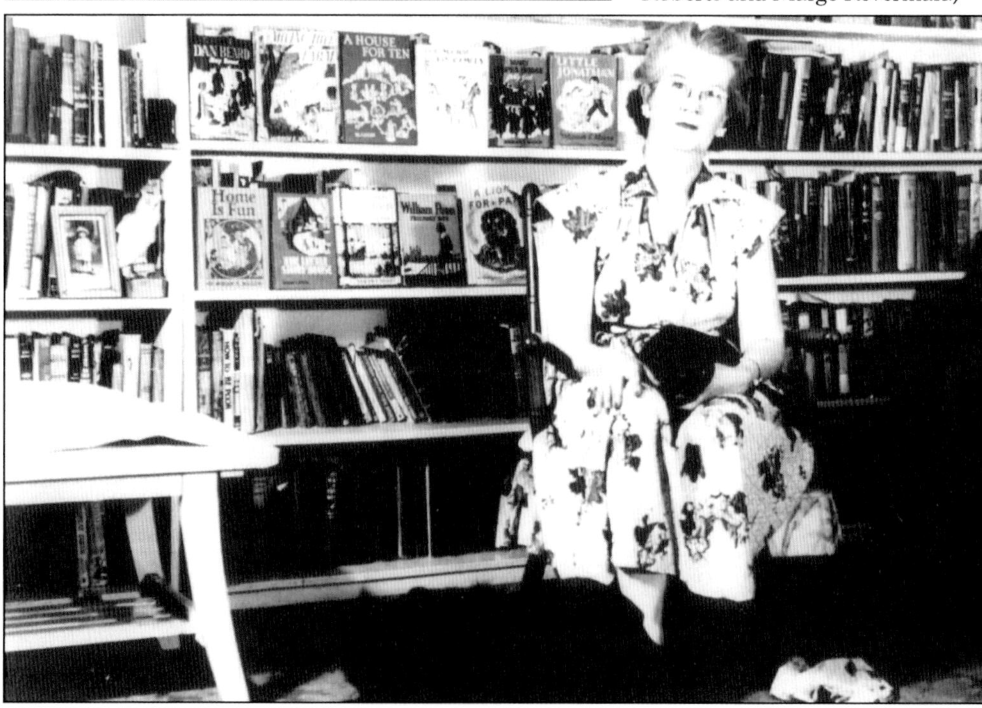

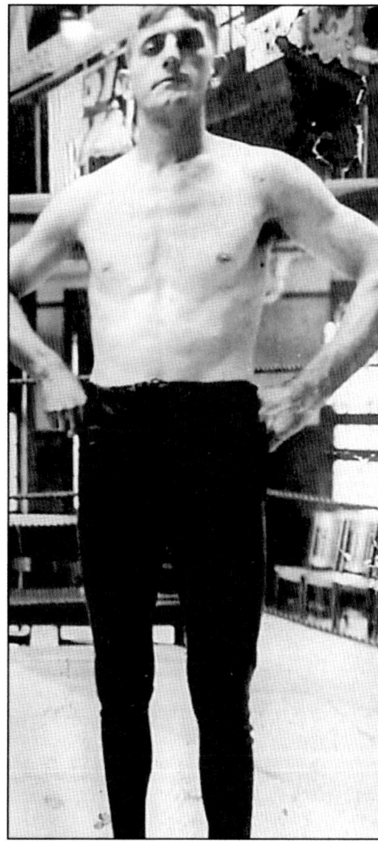

This man is Peter Karbowski, whose skill as a wrestler won him the Olympic Gold Medal in Stockholm in 1912. He was awarded his medal in Chicago in 1913. He was in the welterweight class, meaning he could not weigh over 145 pounds. He was then a young man of 25 and had gained his training in Chicago where he resided at that time. He had previously won a gold medal at the Hawthorne Men's Club on April 26, 1912, in the middleweight division. Karbowski was famous for some of his wrestling "holds" and relied on them to overcome his opponents. When he was a young man, he visited an aunt who lived in Batesville. He grew to like the city so much; he decided to move to Batesville in 1915. (Don Karbowski.)

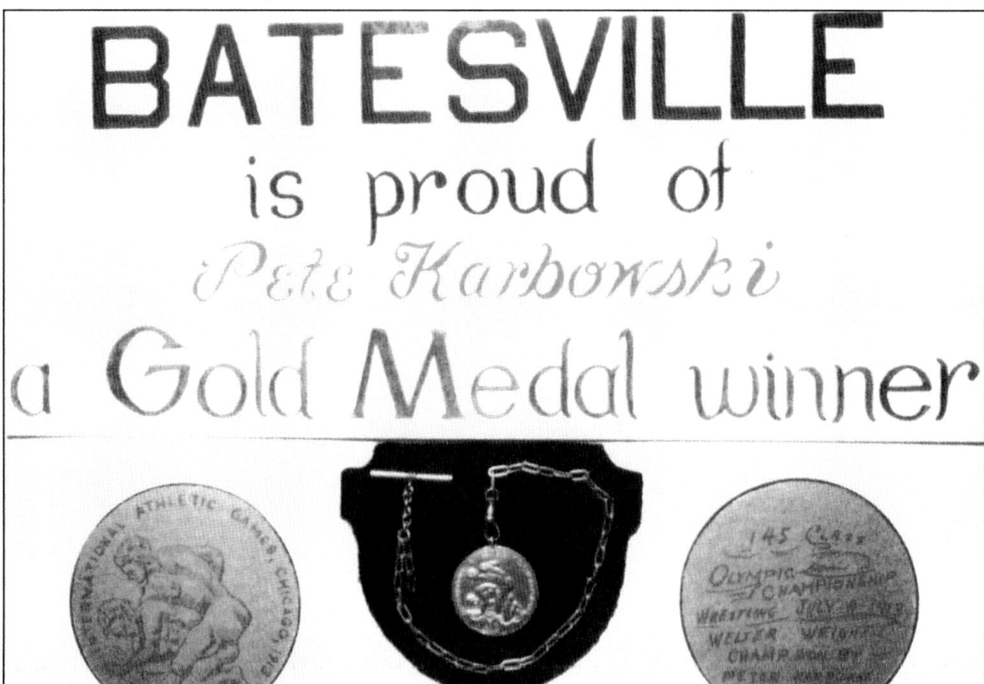

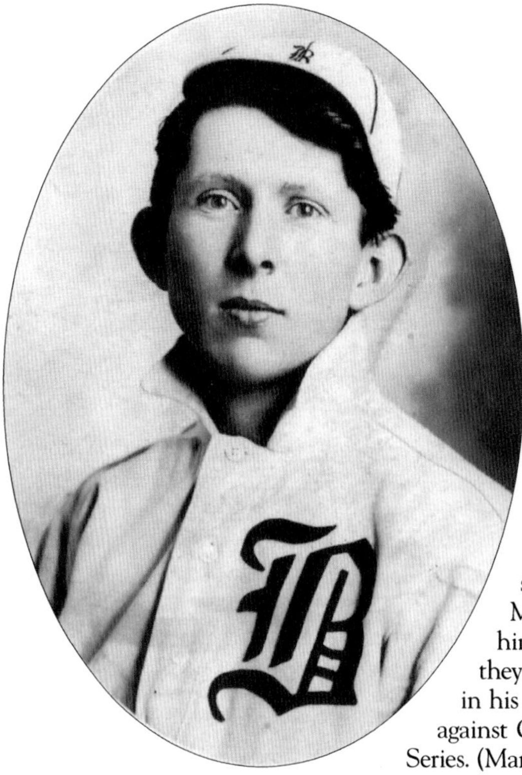

Joe Benz's story begins in New Alsace, the place of his birth. When he was 17 and a senior in high school, his father, an avid White Sox fan, decided it was up to him to help his son determine his career. He took Joe to Chicago to the White Sox owner, Louis Comiskey. "Mr. Comiskey," he said "Benz is my name. My son Joe here believes that he is a baseball player, what's your opinion?" He signed his contract with the White Sox team in March 1910. The media in Chicago had tagged him with the nickname "Butcher Boy Benz" when they learned that his family owned a slaughterhouse in his home town. Joe pitched one no-hitter in 1914 against Cleveland and also pitched in the 1917 World Series. (Martha Hunteman.)

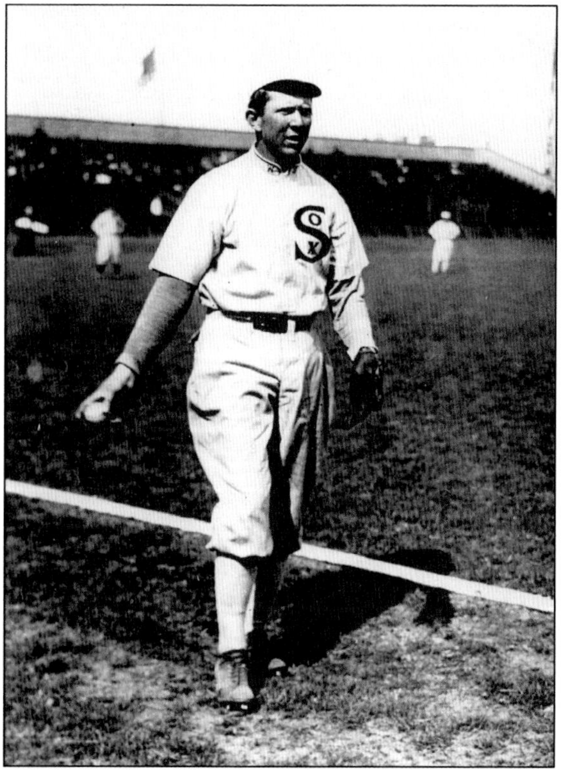

John Hillenbrand Sr., as he came to be called, was born in Adams Township, Spades, on February 18, 1843. He is one of the outstanding men of his time in Batesville industrial and political life. Hillenbrand transferred most of his industrial and business holdings to his sons and sons-in-law as they developed business ability. Hillenbrand married Margaret Herr in 1862. (BAHS.)

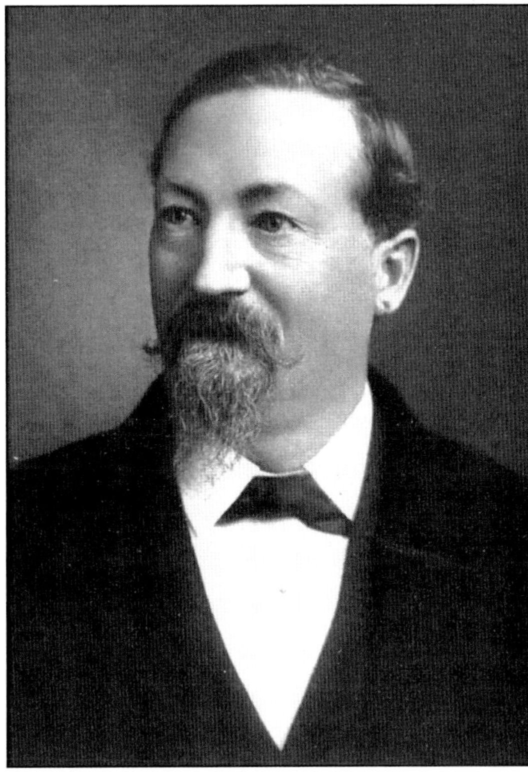

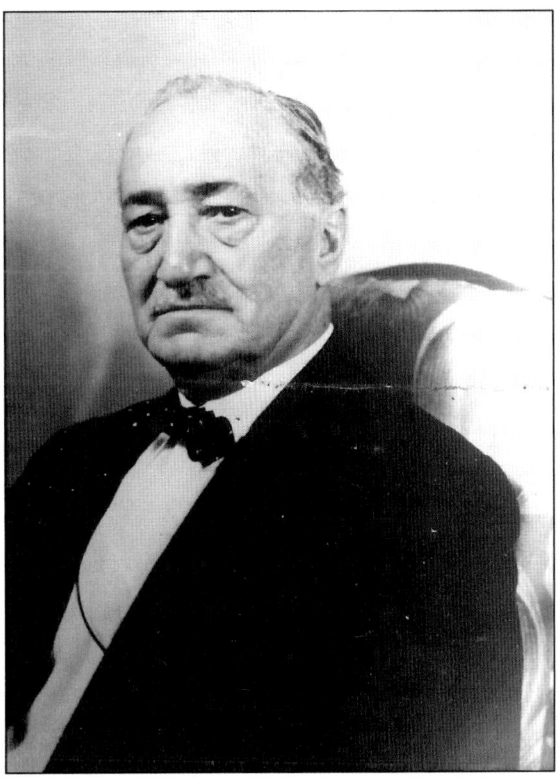

It has been more than 100 years since John A. Hillenbrand founded Batesville Casket Company, but the advice he received from his father is just as meaningful today as it was then. Like his father, John A. combined hard work and ingenuity to create several Hillenbrand family enterprises. In 1906, John A. seized an opportunity to rescue the Batesville Coffin Company from bankruptcy and make it into a successful company. (Women's Study Club.)

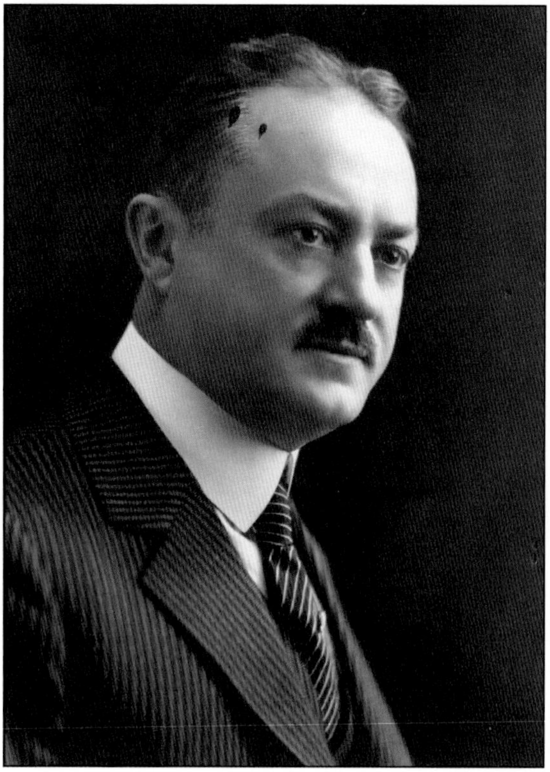

George M. Hillenbrand was a charming man and a born salesman. He was one of the owners of the American Furniture Company, which was founded in 1881. Hillenbrand was the first mayor of Batesville in 1882 when the town first formed its government. Hillenbrand and his wife, Sophia, were gracious and generous. In 1920, they donated the land that the community now enjoys as Liberty Park, as one of their many acts of generosity. (BAHS.)

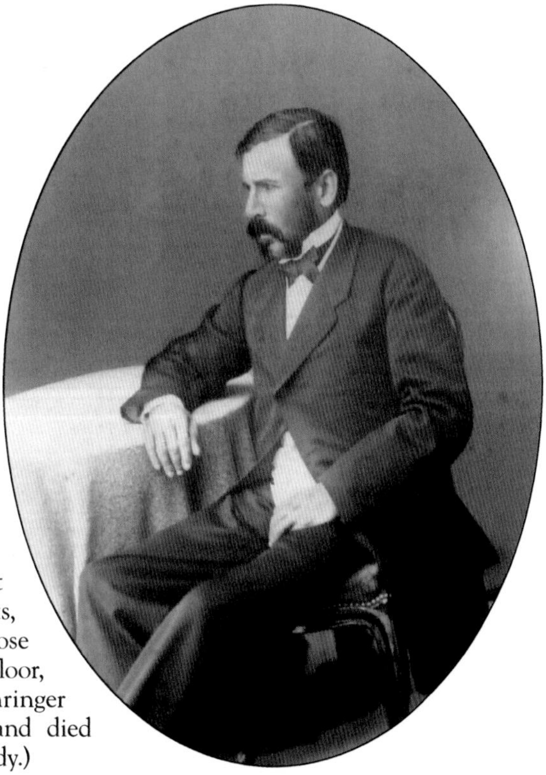

In the 1860s, Henry Boehringer was buying land and developing property in Batesville. He built homes along Boehringer Street, which was named in his honor. He built Boehringer Hall at the corner of East Pearl and Depot Streets, now the Big Four. It was a multi-purpose building including his home, a dance floor, a boardinghouse, and office space. Boehringer was born June 19, 1824, in Germany and died October 24, 1871, in Batesville. (John Moody.)

Fredrick W. Greeman was born in 1824 in Hanover, Germany, and came to Indiana by way of Cincinnati in 1863. Three years later, he established the Batesville Carving Company, the first real furniture factory foundation company. Over a period of years, it developed into the Greeman Brothers Manufacturing Company. His oldest son, William F. Greeman, succeeded him as active head of the carving company. Fredrick died in 1910. (Pat Hare.)

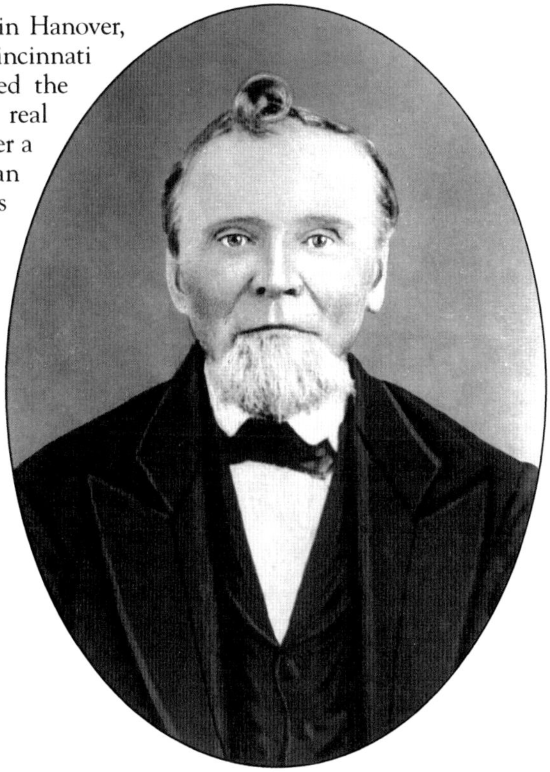

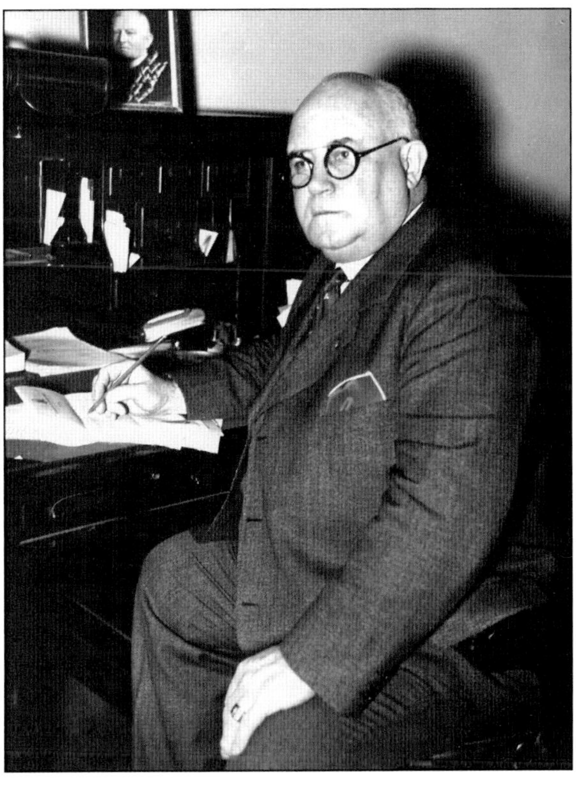

Harry C. Canfield came to Batesville in the late 1890s as an employee of the Western Furniture Company. When William H. Schwier retired, Canfield took over the entire stock and reorganized the company. Canfield lived on Eastern Avenue until 1913 when he bought the Fred Morgan residence on South Mulberry Street. Canfield was elected to Congress in 1922 and re-elected for four succeeding terms. (Susie Canfield.)

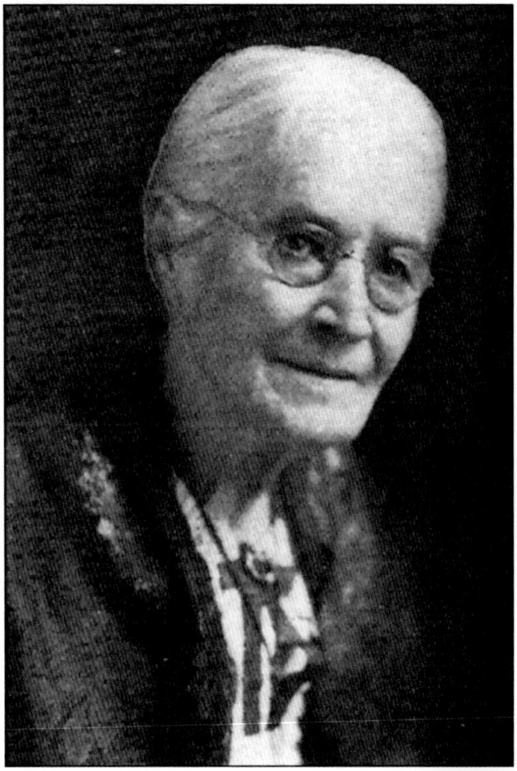

Margaret Hillenbrand, originally Margaret Herr, was born at Dahn, Germany, on June 14, 1842, and died at Batesville on February 1, 1929. She married John Hillenbrand of Spades in 1862. Margaret donated money in her will to build Margaret Mary Hospital. Her dream was realized by the added gift of money by her daughter Mary Mitchell and her son George M. Hillenbrand's gift of the land for the hospital. (BAHS.)

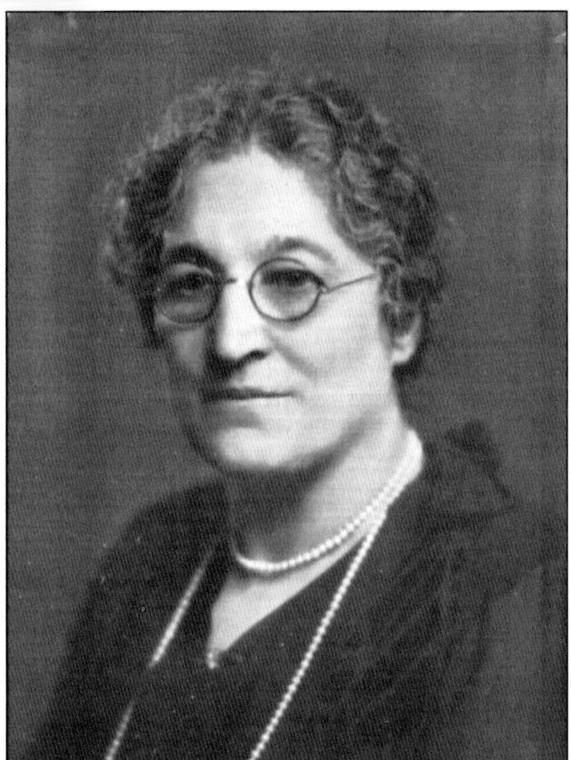

Mary A. (Hillenbrand) Mitchell was born on February 23, 1867, and came to Batesville with her parents in 1876. She graduated from Immaculate Conception Academy, Oldenburg, and married Joseph Fragge Jr. in 1886. After her husband's death in 1888, she married George Mitchell. They built their home, a two-storied frame dwelling, on the northeast corner of Main Street and Hillenbrand Avenue, now owned by Doug Obermeyer. (MMCH.)

Michael Benz II was a butcher who came to Batesville in 1891. His business, the Benz Brothers Meat Market was in the John Pfalsgraf building on Main Street. The business developed into one of the most efficient and largest meat markets in southeastern Indiana. He died on February 6, 1941. He was the grandfather of Martha Hunteman. (Martha Hunteman.)

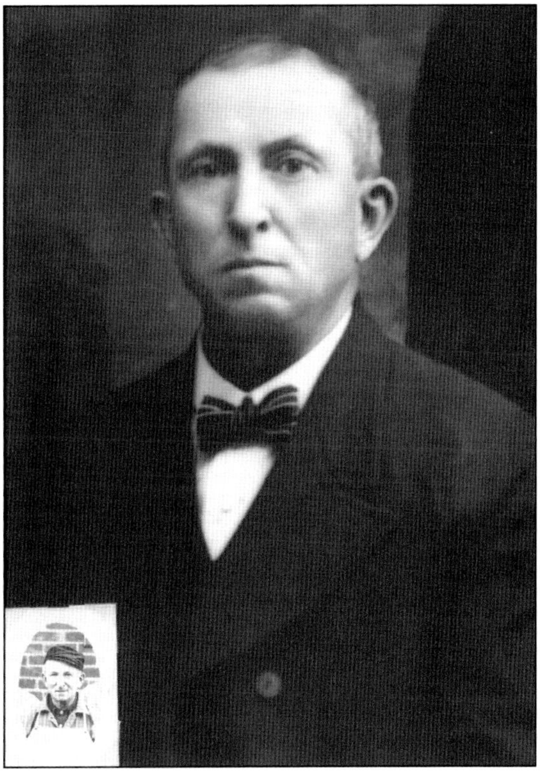

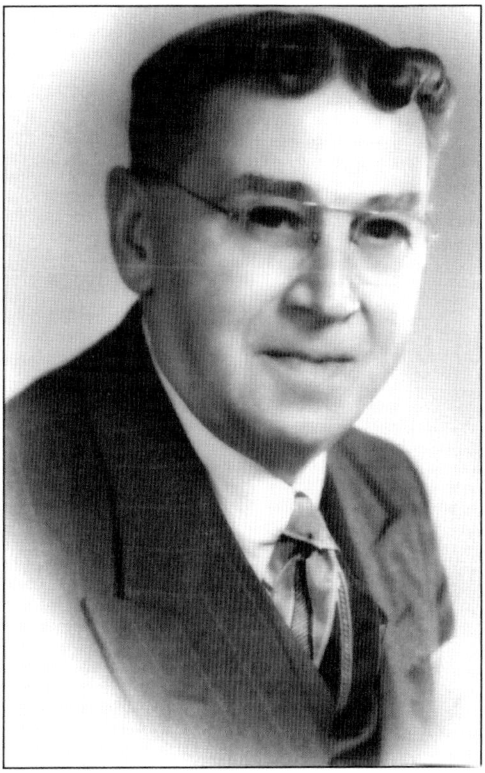

Frank E. Kellerman was mayor of Batesville from 1948 until his untimely death, while still in office, on February 19, 1951. He defeated Andy Benz by 127 votes in the election held on Tuesday, November 4, 1947, for the office of city mayor. (Mary Ann Meyer.)

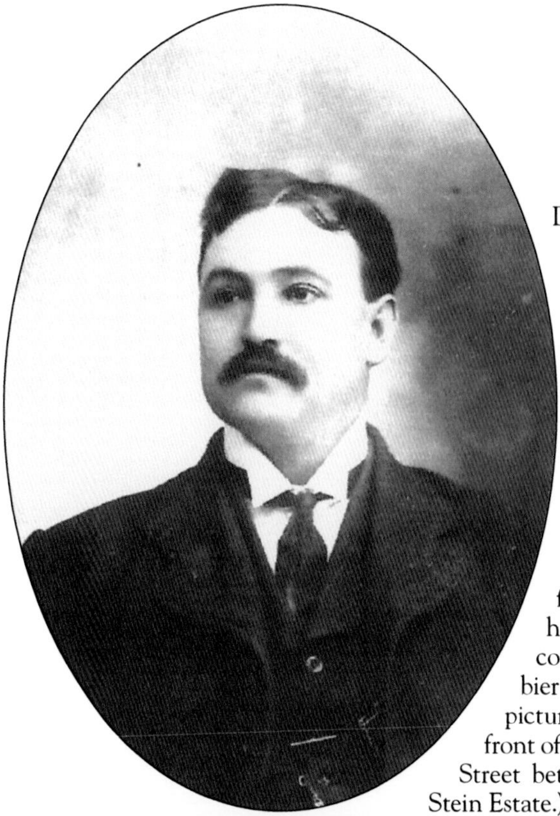

Dr. Charles W. Gibson was born at Gardersville, Kentucky, on November 13, 1870. Dr. Gibson began his practice of medicine at Goforth, Kentucky. He later moved to Morris and in 1909 moved to Batesville and bought the property of Dr. Frederick Schlosser at the corner of Walnut and Boehringer Streets. He lived in this house until his death on May 14, 1924. He built the Gibson Theatre and the Gibson Garage; both were ambitious undertakings. He was twice elected mayor of Batesville. His funeral was held in the theater that carried his name. The whole city and surrounding community passed in long lines before the bier of their beloved physician and friend. The picture below shows him in his automobile in front of his office on the north side of Boehringer Street between Walnut and Main Streets. (Flora Stein Estate.)

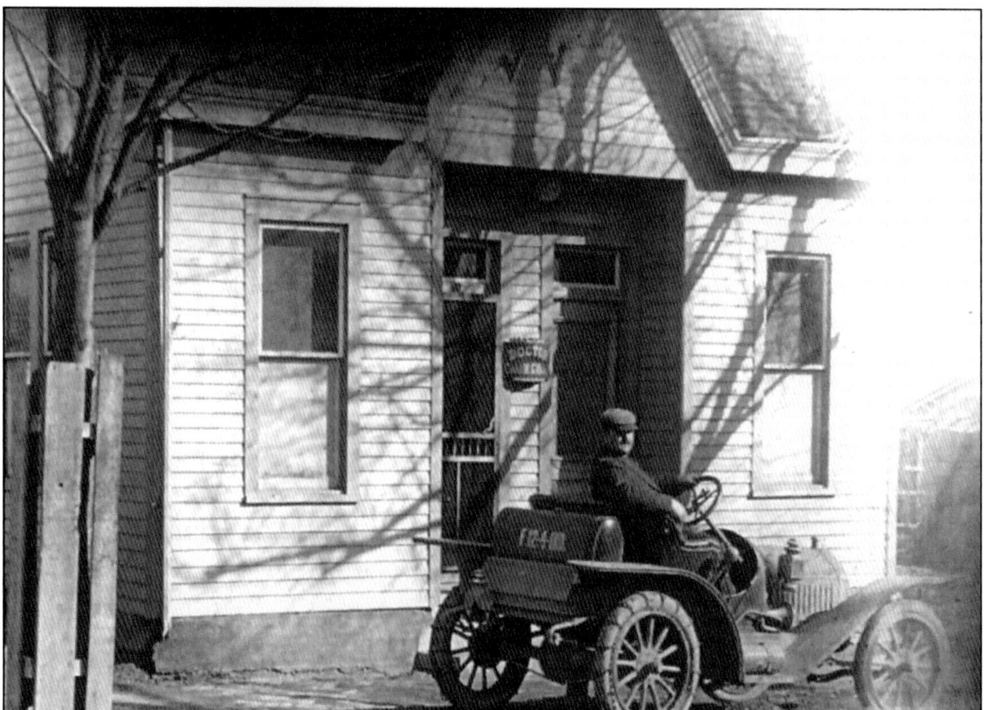

A new doctor moved to Batesville in July 1921, Dr. Orville A. Bigham of St. Anthony, Dubois County. He occupied the former office of Dr. Joseph X. Ziteke on South Walnut Street. Bigham's home was on South Street across from the Depot Street City Park. (BAHS.)

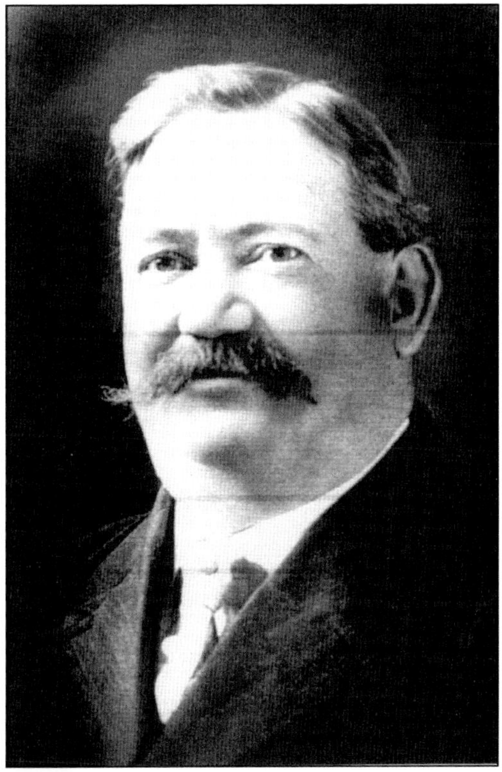

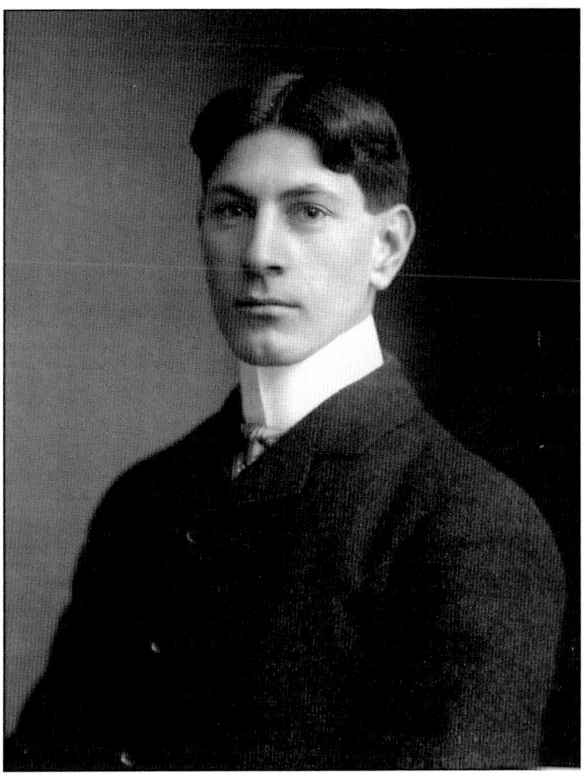

Edwin B. Schultz entered the employment of the Baas Drug Store as an apprentice and clerk. He eventually succeeded George A. Baas as the "leading druggist of Batesville," as their slogan stated. Schultz bought out the store's entire stock in 1909. He was a permanent member of the Batesville male quartet. The Schultz brothers, Wesley, Edwin, Theodore, and Arthur, had a male quartet of their own. (Clinton Nolte.)

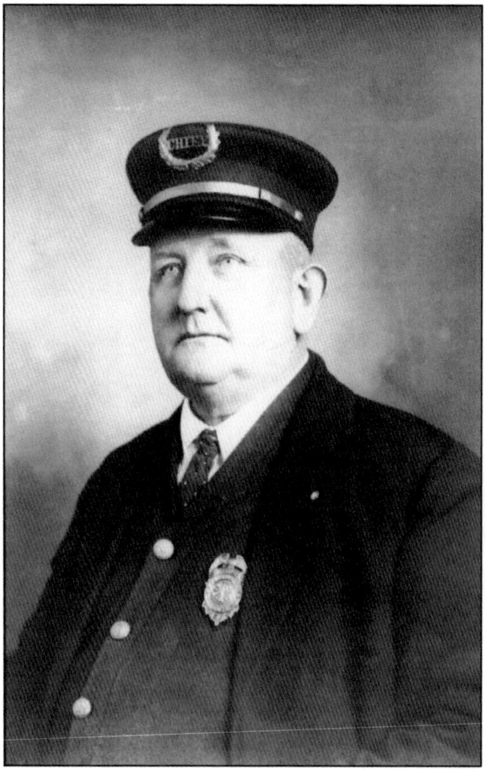

Fred "Fritz" Brummer was appointed fire chief on January 1, 1922, by Mayor Quirin Vonderheide. His record with the fire department dated from 1892. He was made assistant chief in June 1905 and served in that position until he was appointed chief. He had not missed a fire drill from 1892 until November 1907, and only two in his 30 years of service. (Betty Macke.)

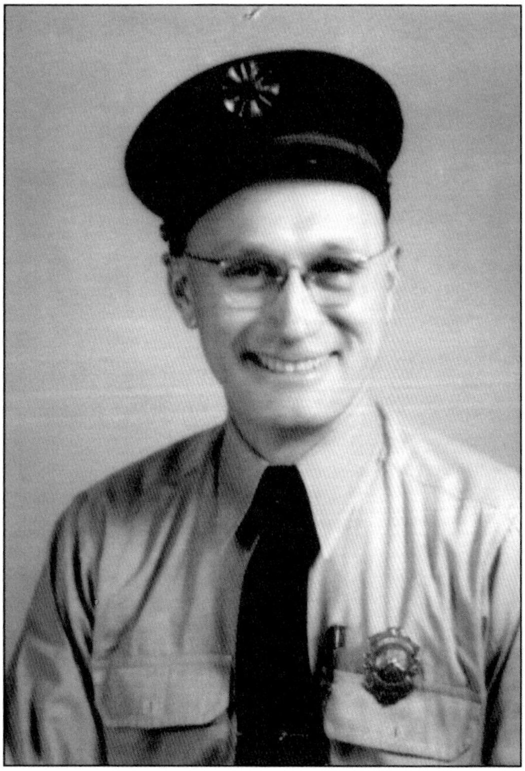

Clarence "Pop" Roell was born at Oldenburg on February 17, 1904. He was the son of Adam and Susan Roell. In 1945, he was appointed fire chief, a position he held for 15 years. In 1957, he was given the Good Government Award by the local Jaycees for meritorious service to the city as fire chief. He died in November 1960. (Betty Macke.)

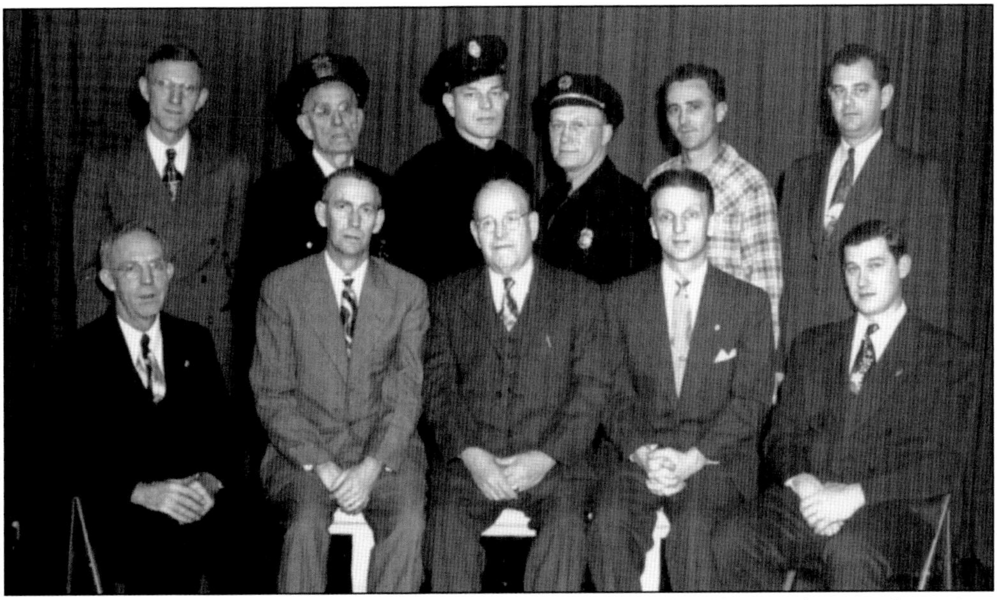

City council members from 1948 to 1951 are, from left to right, (first row) councilman Leo Walke, councilman Robert Stewart, Mayor George Schumacher (replaced Frank Kellerman), councilman Paul Lindenmeyer, and councilman Harold Narwold; (second row) clerk-treasurer Harry Johnson, police chief Richard Lightner, police chief Orvall Armbrecht, Fire Chief Clarence "Pop" Roell, street commissioner Charles Hirt, and attorney Bill Greeman. Not pictured is Mayor Frank Kellerman, who died in office February 19, 1951. (BAHS.)

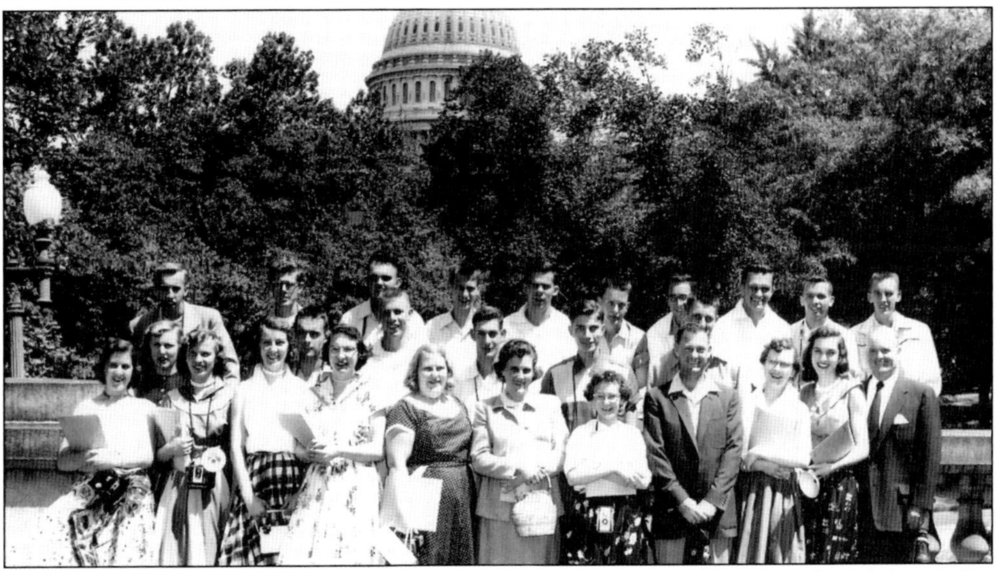

Member of the class of 1955 senior trip to Washington, D.C., seen here are, from left to right, (first row) Janet Winland, Marlene Federle, Jean Flodder, Genarose Hunefeld, Margie Pursley, JoAnn Gardner, Gala Gardner, Roy Gardner, Maxine Shook, Kathleen Uhlmansiek, and Earl Wilson; (second row) Janice Huneke, Alton Gibson, Clifford Schrader, Raphael Grossman, John Cook, and Floyd Werner; (third row) Bob Dillhoff, Dick Becker, Ken Weber, Bob Schutte, Kenny Emsweller, Ralph Kuntz, Jim Doll, Virgil Obermeyer, Bob Erne, and Lloyd Klusman. (Jean Struewing.)

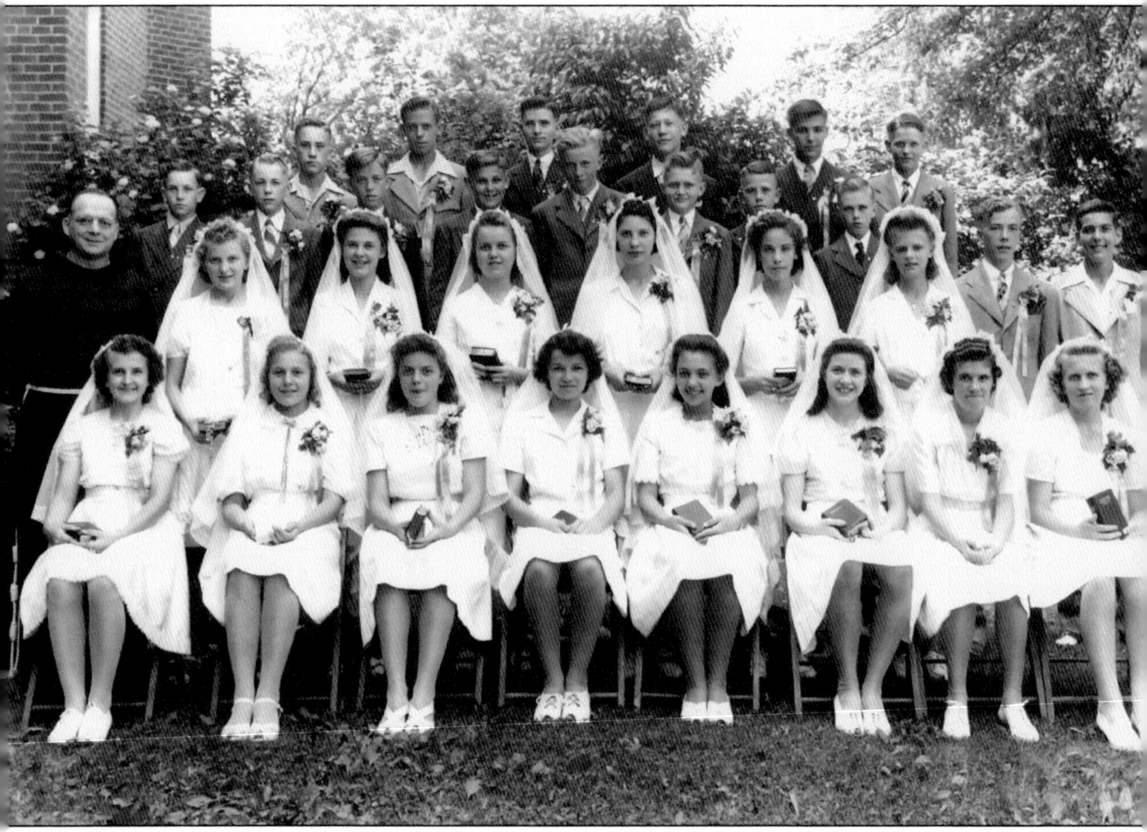

This photograph shows the St. Louis School eighth grade graduation, class of 1943. Eighth grade graduation was called solemn communion. Seen here are, from left to right, (first row) Gertrude (Langferman) Krieger, Irene Hoff (became a nun), Gretchen (Romweber) Lammers, Virginia (Laudick) Meyerose, Mitzi (Hillenbrand) Lally, Rita (Smith) Schneider, Ruthie Hermesch, and Arvilla "Tuttie" (Siefert) Prickel; (second row) Fr. Matthias Heile, Mary Jane (Laudick) Prickel, Roberta (Blandford) Pioli, Zeta Mae (Bierbusse) ?, Helen Rose Muckerheide, Alyce Jean (Dietz) Baker, Mary (Mollaun) Weigel, Virgil "Pete" Flodder, and Tom Hellmich; (third row) Paul "Mousie" Kruseman, Dick Hertel, John Bohl, Leroy Freeland, Alvin Starke, Eugene "Gene" Becker, Adrian Schene, and Eugene "Moon" Wenning; (fourth row) James Fischer (killed in service), John Pohlman, Leroy Grossman, Jack Thrine, Walter Freeland, and Ed Forthofer. (Leroy Grossman.)

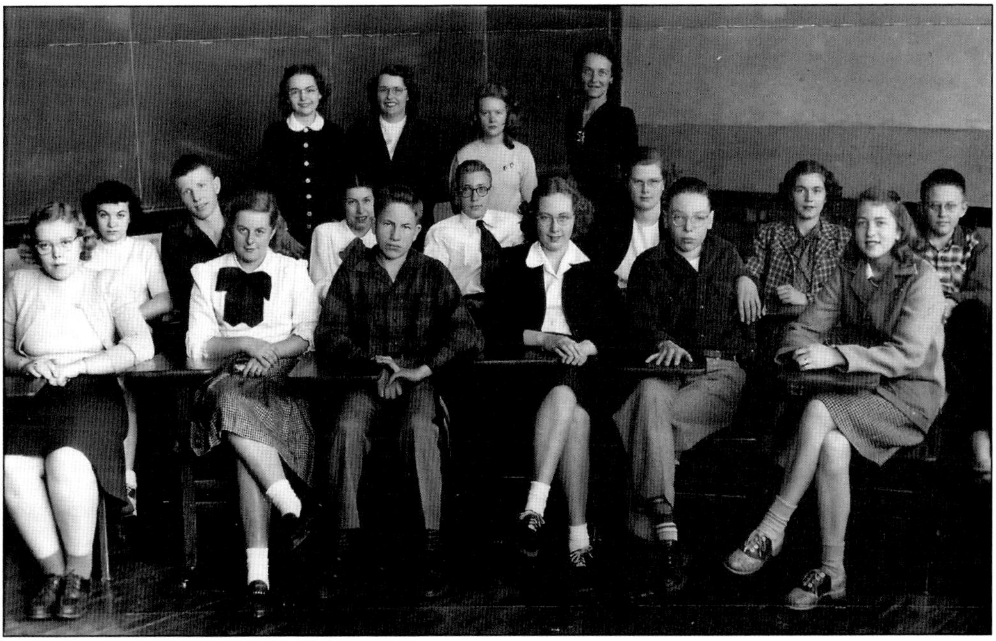

The Latin Club of Batesville High School was organized in September 1948 by Thelma Feeler and was open to all Latin students. The club members are, from left to right, (first row) Mary Dwenger, Margie Grieshop, Dan Ferkinhoff, JoAnn Glusenkamp, Bruce Beihl, and Helenrose Hammerle; (second row) Doris Bentfield, Jim Prentice, Dorothy Loew, John Huneke, Mary Lou Thielking, Elaine Thie, and Donald Steinkamp; (third row) two unidentified, Betty Jo Gutzwiller, and Thelma Feeler. (Women's Study Club.)

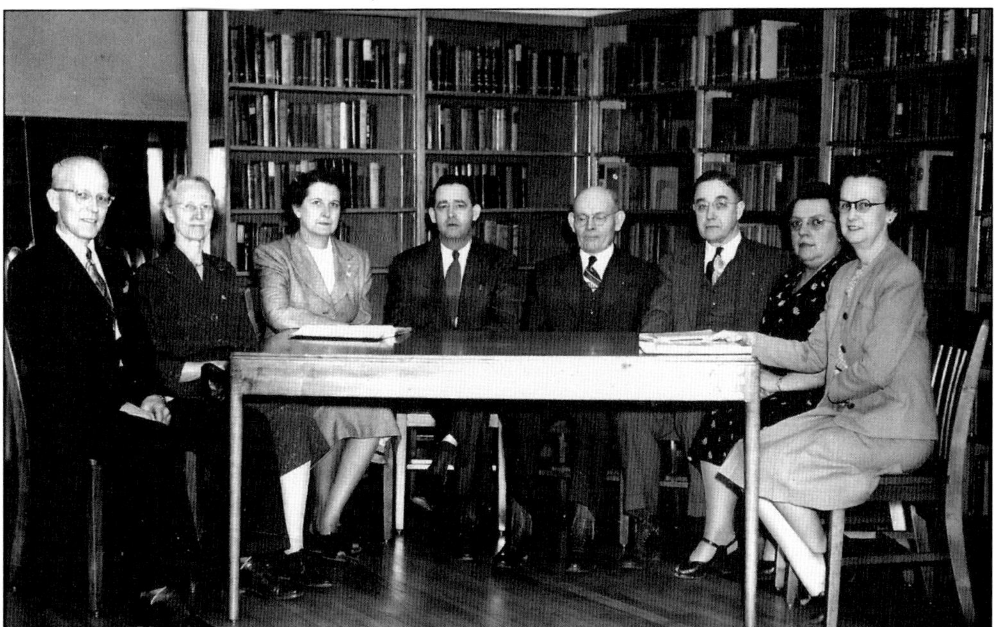

The Batesville Community School Board of 1952 met monthly in the library. Board members are, from left to right, Dick Laudick, Elma Gelvin, Nora Wonning, John Frushour, Walter Westerman, Elmer Gesell, Estella Kaiser, and Hazel Andres. (Women's Study Club.)

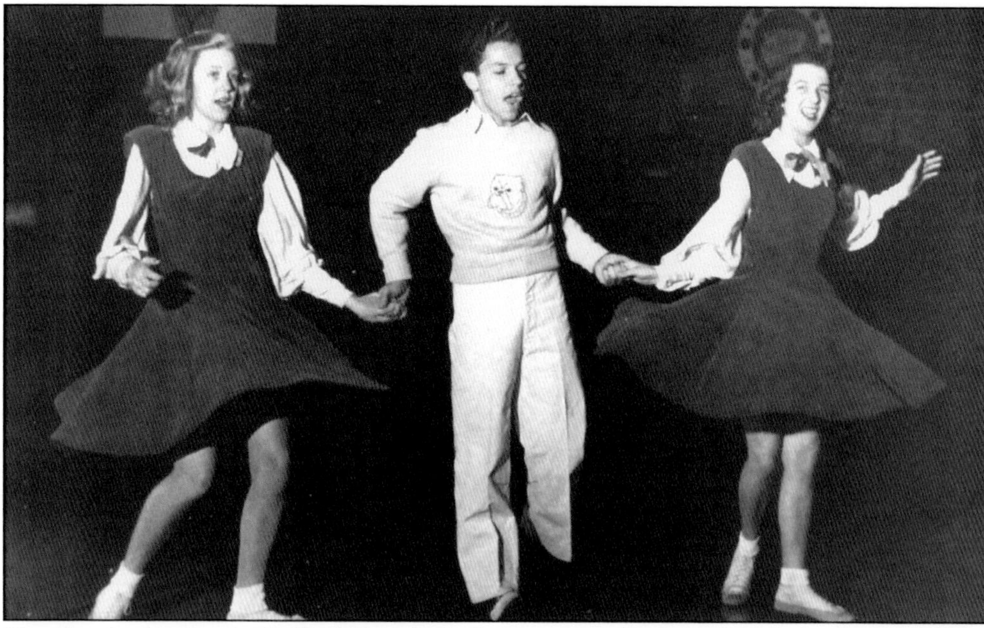

The cheerleaders for the 1947–1948 basketball season seen here are, from left to right, Marilyn Pohlman, Johnny Simmermeyer, and Marian Craig. The team they cheered for (not pictured) consisted of Jim Hortemiller, Tom Wiegel, Tom Lampert, Dick Meyer, Don Kellerman, Larry Brockman, Pete Schorr, Bob Raver, Norman Haverkos, Herb Oesterling, Eddie Thielking, and Calvin Doyle. Student managers were Lloyd Weber and Ralph Wenning. The team was coached by Red Anderson. (Women's Study Club.)

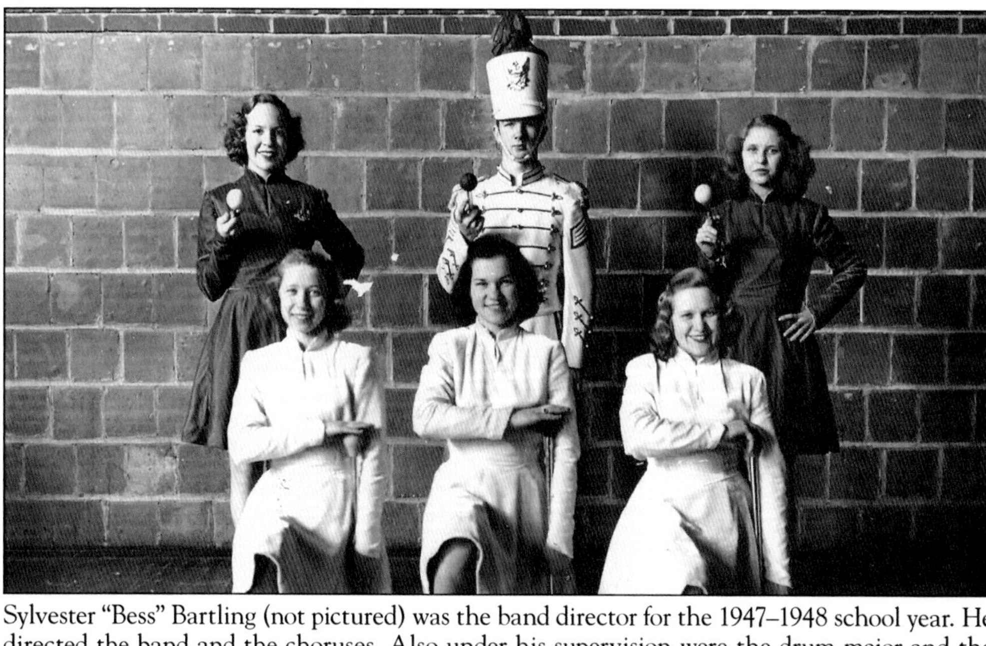

Sylvester "Bess" Bartling (not pictured) was the band director for the 1947–1948 school year. He directed the band and the choruses. Also under his supervision were the drum major and the majorettes who are shown here. They are, from left to right, (first row) Doris Laudick, Bonnie Fritsch, and Virginia Becker; (second row) Mary Carolyn Wintz, Joe Decker, and Marian Uphaus. (Women's Study Club.)

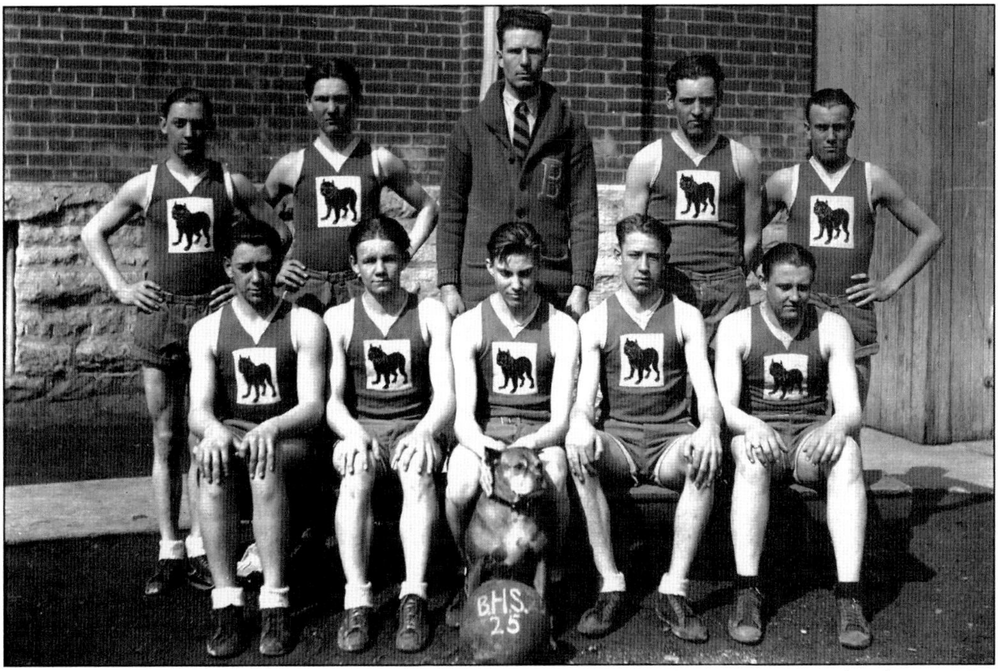

Batesville High School's first basketball team was organized in the 1920–1921 school year. The team played their first games in an unheated barn at Liberty Park. By the time this picture was taken in 1925, the team was better organized. They even had a live bulldog for their mascot. Their coach was Richard "Doc" Prentice (second row, center), and the player on the far right in the first row is Nelson Steinkamp; others are unidentified. (Clinton Nolte.)

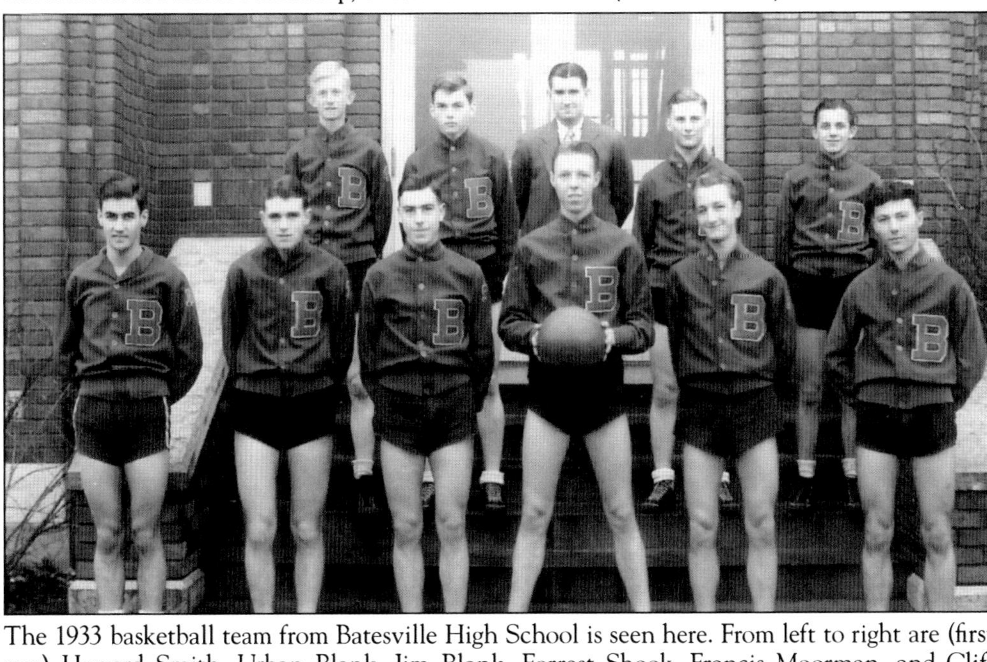

The 1933 basketball team from Batesville High School is seen here. From left to right are (first row) Howard Smith, Urban Blank, Jim Blank, Forrest Shook, Francis Moorman, and Cliff Fritsch; (second row) Richard Flodder, Russell Green, coach Jim Hickey, Clarence Huber, and Carl Fritsch. (Richard Flodder.)

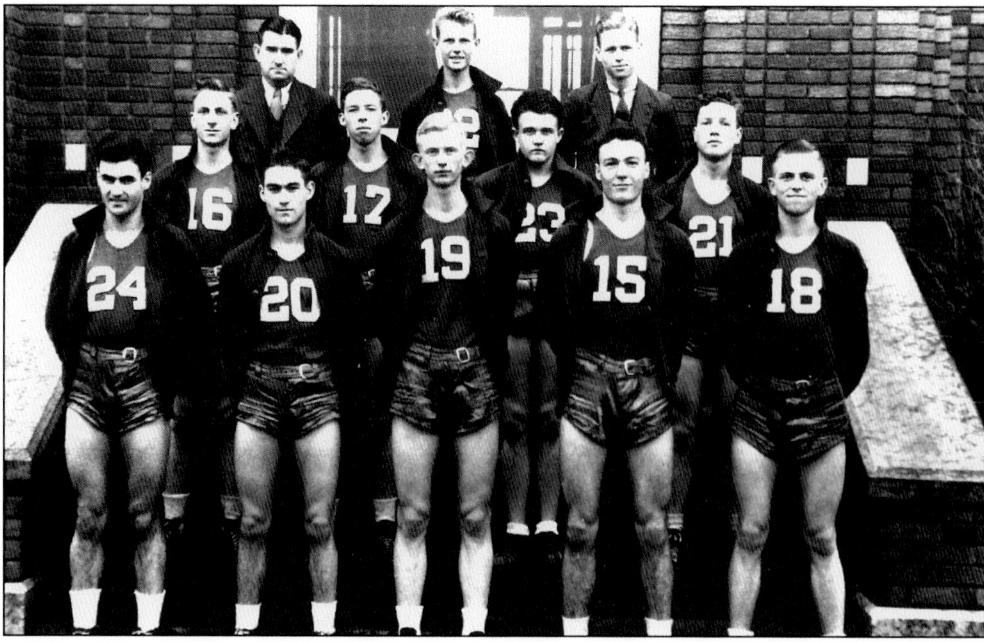

The players and staff of the 1935 Batesville High School basketball team are, from left to right, (first row) Howard Smith, Richard "Duck" Schroeder, Richard Flodder, Herb Fichtner, and John Fritsch; (second row) Frank Tekulve, George Shook, Harold Steinkamp, and Mac Lightner; (third row) coach Jim Hickey, Julius "Dude" Mollaun, and student manager Paul Timmerman. (Richard Flodder.)

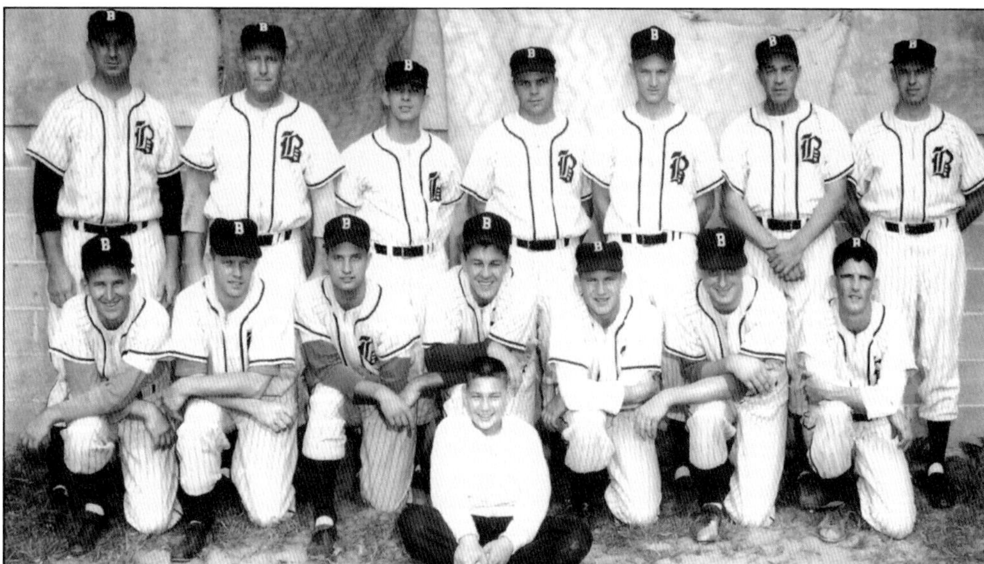

This photograph of the Batesville City League baseball team was taken sometime in the 1950s. Sitting in front is batboy Ronnie Barrett. From left to right are (first row) Louie Ensinger, Ralph Wenning, Thomas "Ace" Moorman, Paul "Ham" Wernke, Ernie Schutte, Dick Erhardt, and Clete Walsman; (second row) Dick Struewing, Raymond "Boz" Bloemer, Bob Christopher, Ben Federle, Herman "Ham" Struewing, coach Urb Huser, and Larry Miller. (Herman "Ham" Struewing.)

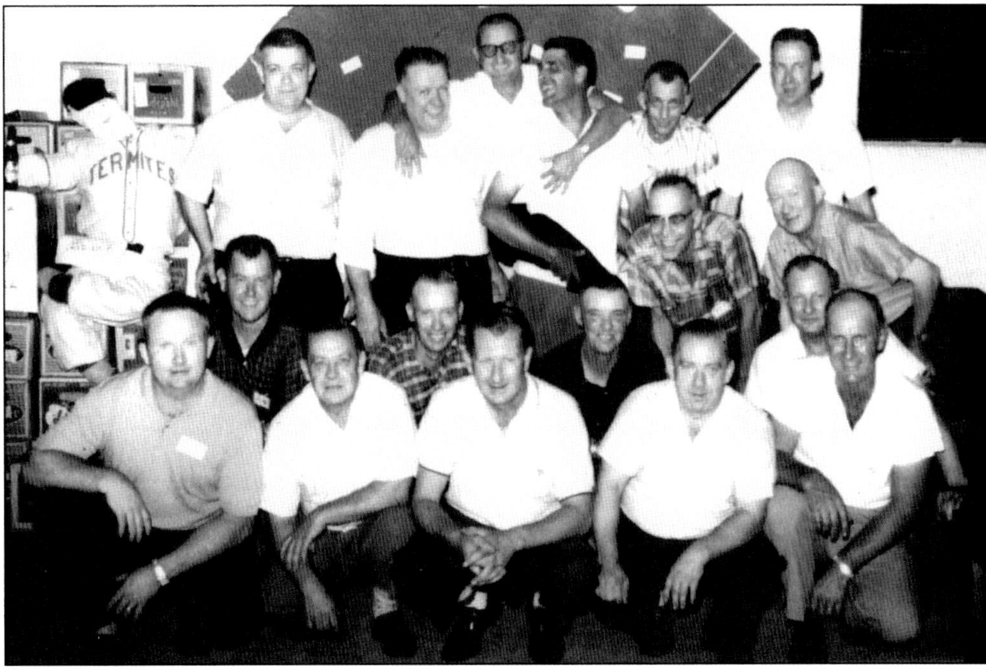

The 1930 Termites baseball team consisted of the following, from left to right, (first row) Eugene "Red" Maple, Carl Roth, Bob Decker, Norbert "Pro" Roth, and Paul Hortemiller; (second row) Ferdinand "Ferg" Abplanalp, Bob Huneke, Floyd Harlemart, Nick Osier, Art Bergman, and Gus Moorman; (third row) Leonard "Lum" Wernke, Charles "Chuck" Prickel, Horace "Hap" Rodgers, Ray Wallpe, Merle Johnson, and Ray Moorman. (Nick and Anna Mae Osier.)

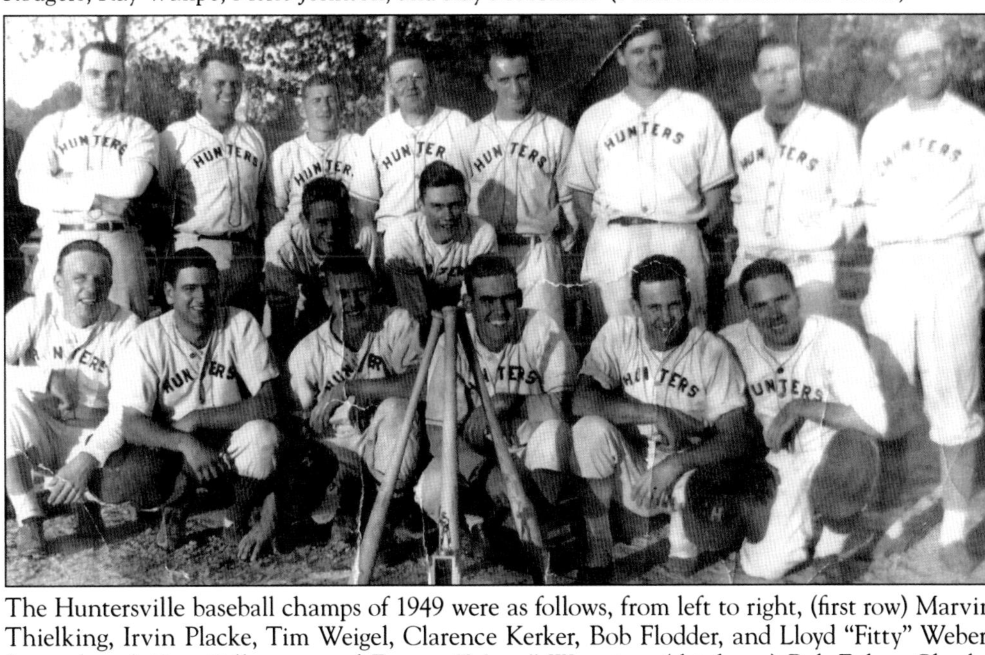

The Huntersville baseball champs of 1949 were as follows, from left to right, (first row) Marvin Thielking, Irvin Placke, Tim Weigel, Clarence Kerker, Bob Flodder, and Lloyd "Fitty" Weber; (second row) Don Kellerman and Eugene "Moon" Wenning; (third row) Bob Fisher, Charles Koester, Joe Wissel, Clarence "Chick" Wessel, Herb Moody, Harold "Hintz" Narwold, Irvin Wessel, and Art Flodder. (Bob Flodder.)

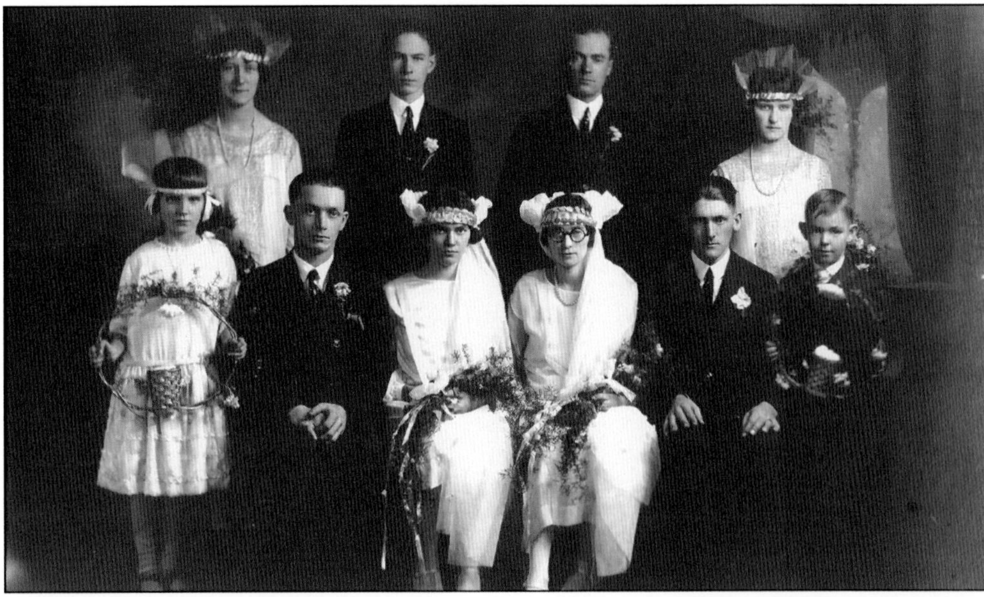

St. Mary's Church at Hamburg was the scene of a pretty double wedding ceremony on October 28, 1925, when Raymond Ford married Eleanor Thrine (the couple on the left), and her sister Clara Thrine became the bride of Raymond Grossman (the couple on the right). In the first row beside the bride and grooms are flower girl Agnes Kramer and ring bearer John Ford. In the second row, from left to right, are Leonarda Artmire, Herman Artmire, Frank Thrine, and Antoinette Grossman. (Rosalie Geis.)

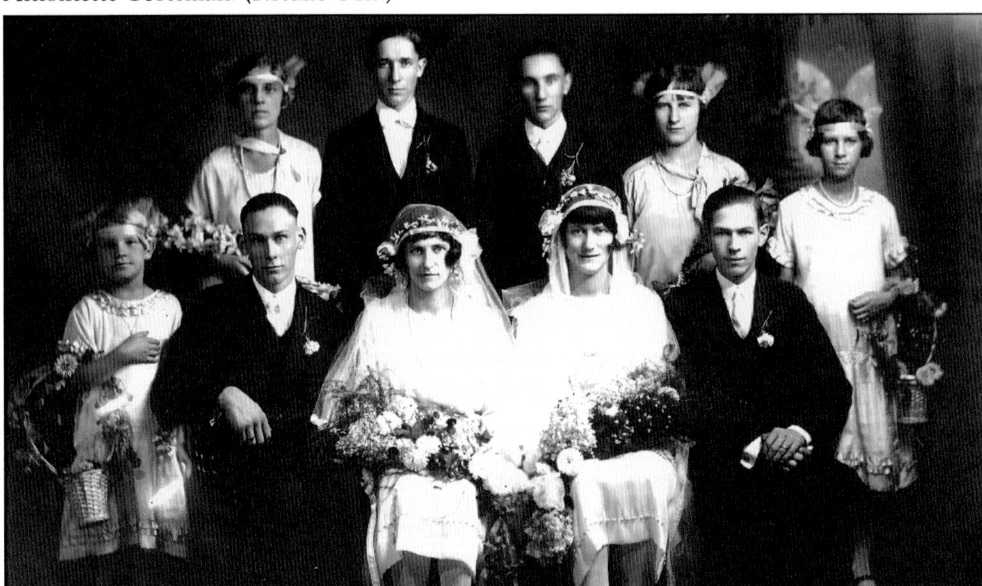

The St. Anthony's Catholic Church at Morris was the scene of another double wedding ceremony on September 1, 1926, when John R. Wessler was married to Antoinette Grossman (the couple on the left), and her sister Leonarda Grossman was married to Herman Artmire (the couple on the right). In the first row beside the bride and grooms is the flower girl Mildred Wessler. In the second row, from left to right, are Florence Wessler, Lloyd Bryne, Roy Wilhelm, Rosie Artmire, and Bertha Bosse. (Rosalie Geis.)

The Hillenbrand men take a break from the duties of industry. Pictured are, from left to right, John A. Hillenbrand II, Daniel Hillenbrand, Ray Hillenbrand, and August Hillenbrand, standing. (Tim Dietz.)

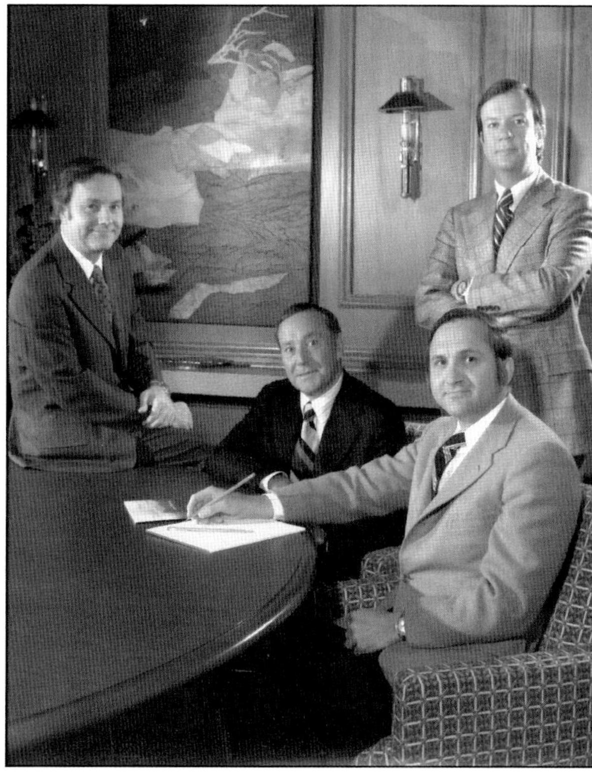

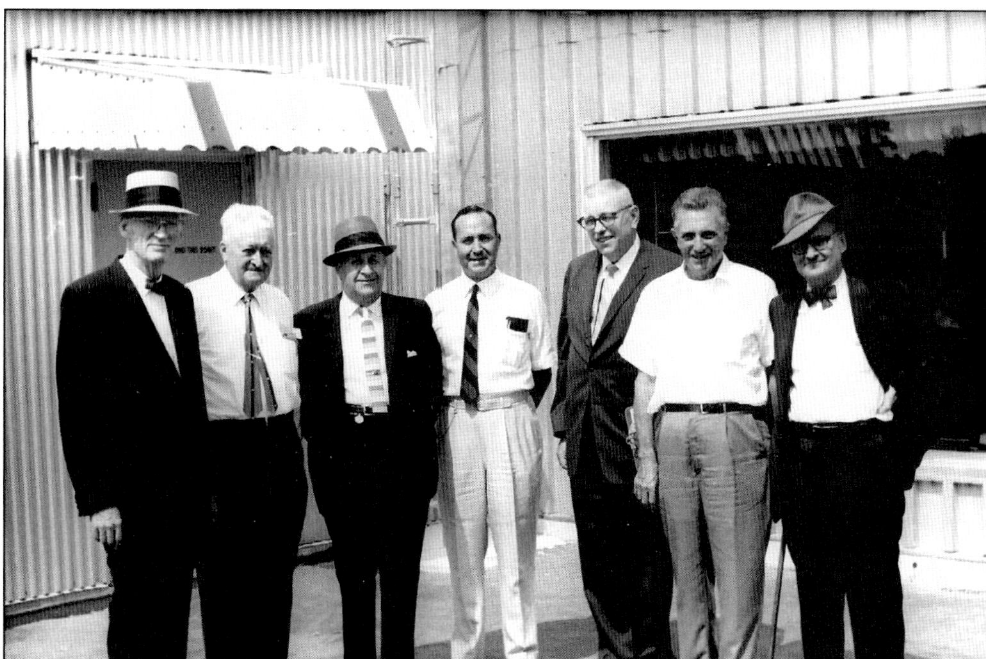

Executives of the Hillenbrand Company gather outside one of their factories. Pictured are, from left to right, Will Gelvin, Fred Heitzman, Sim Ward, Daniel Hillenbrand, Bob Bere, Ed Reverman, and George Carl Hillenbrand. (Women's Study Club.)

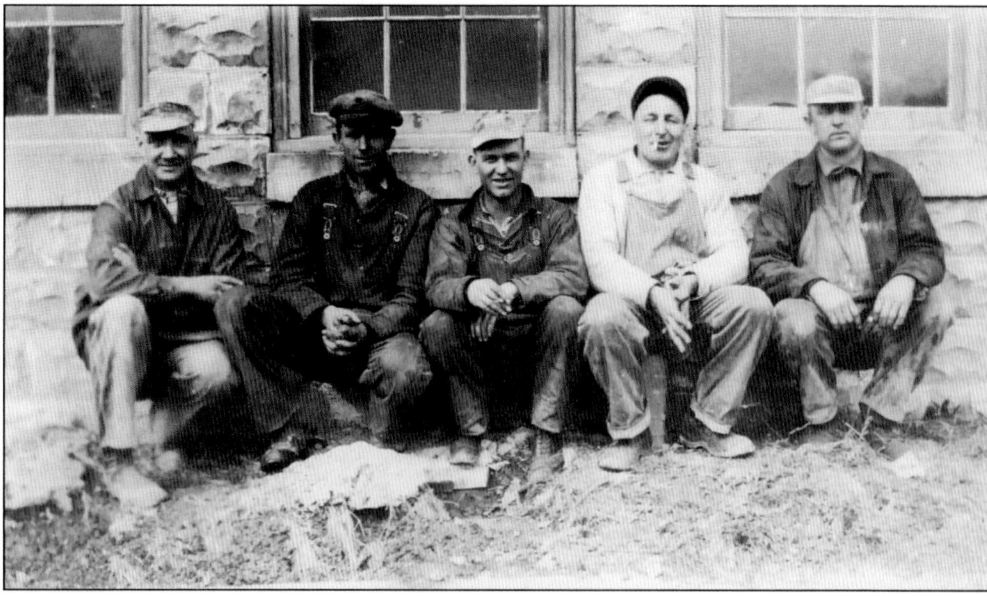

This photograph, taken in February 1924, is of a group of Steinkamp and Company workers taking a break. They are, from left to right, Fred Baas, Walter Borchelt, Irvin Brunner, Clarence "Cap" Heidt, and Robert "Bob" Hoyer. (Betty Koester.)

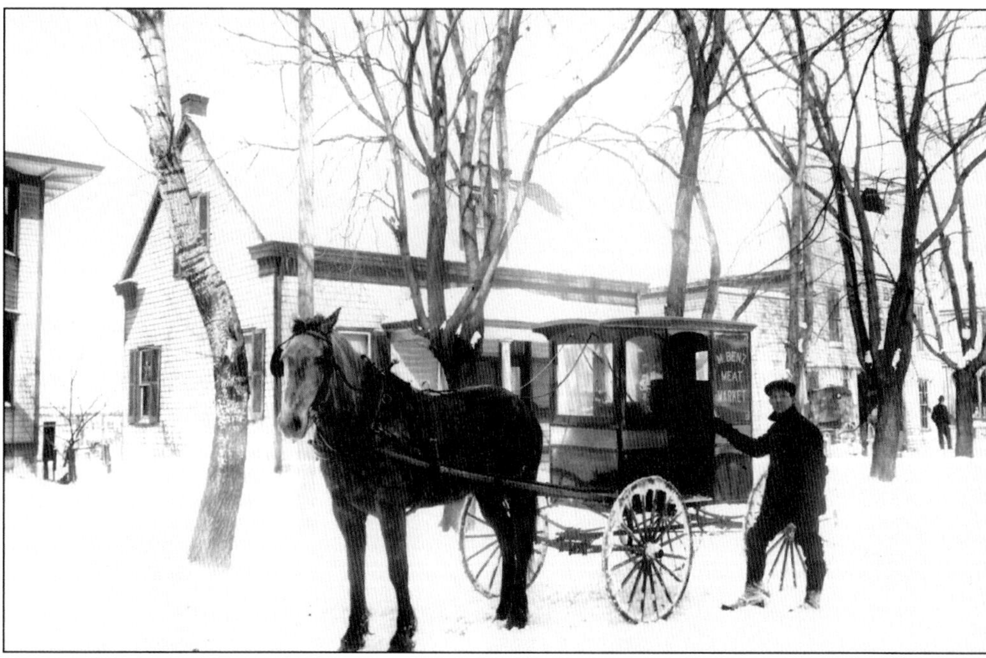

Michael Benz Jr. drove his meat wagon around town, ringing the bell to draw housewives' attention. His daily routine included getting up at 1:30 a.m. to cut the meat and load his wagon, then going home for a big breakfast and finally making the rounds to service his customers. Out poured the ladies to peek under the mosquito net to make their selections of meat. Those were great memories. (Martha Hunteman.)

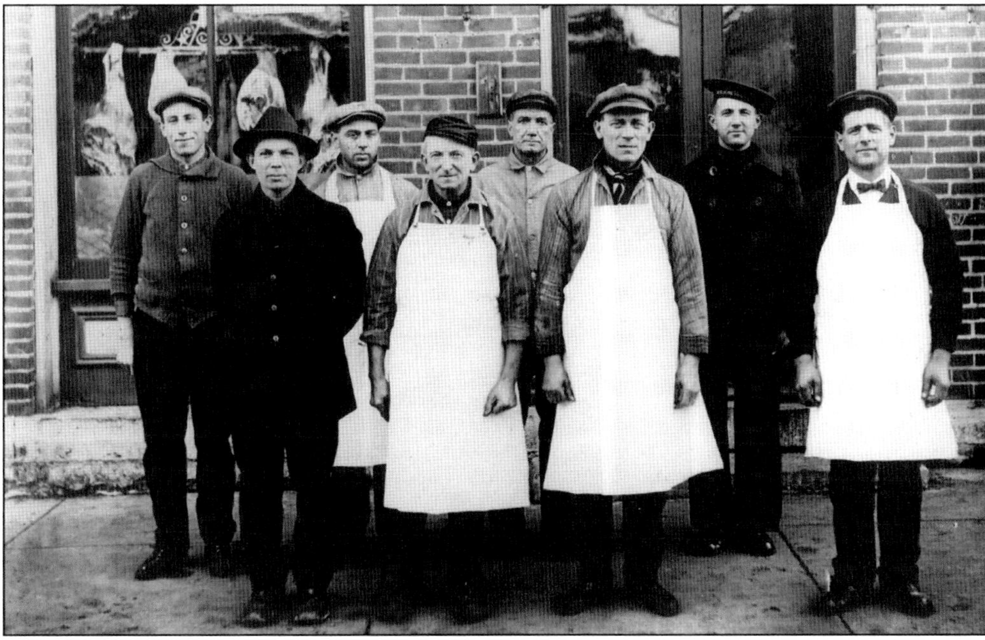

Michael Benz Jr. came to Batesville in 1891 as a butcher, locating his business in the John Pfalsgraf building on North Main Street. The business firm was known as the Benz Brothers. The men pictured are, from left to right, (first row) Michael Benz Jr., Michael Benz Sr., unidentified, and Joe Boehmer; (second row) Tony Stein, Frank Kellerman, Charles Brum, and Hugo Benz. (Martha Hunteman.)

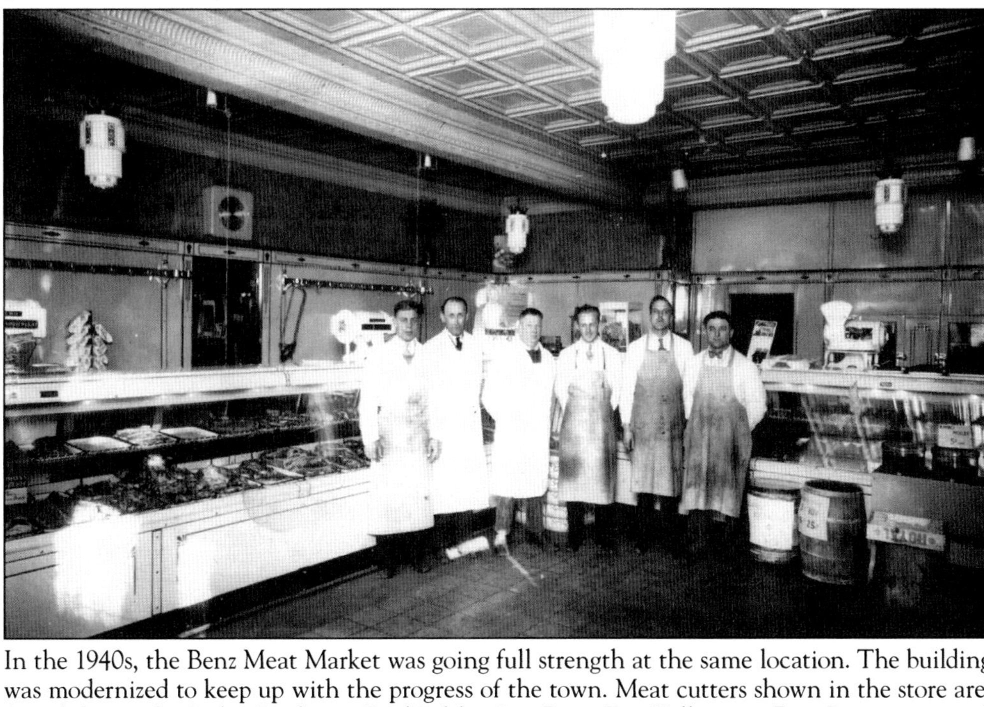

In the 1940s, the Benz Meat Market was going full strength at the same location. The building was modernized to keep up with the progress of the town. Meat cutters shown in the store are, from left to right, Jackie Boehmer, Fred Pohlar, Leo Benz, Des Kellerman, Ray Crusemeyer, and Jake Cook. (Esther Crusemeyer.)

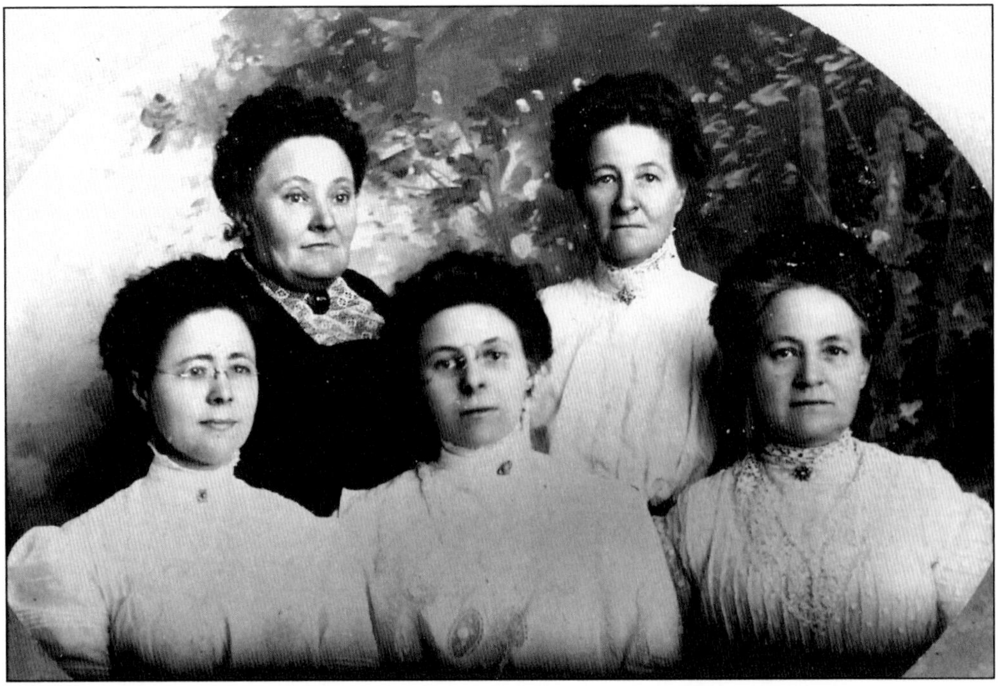

This is a picture of the Severinghaus sisters, daughters of John Henry "Squire" Severinghaus. Pictured in this photograph are, from left to right, (first row) Nora Wortman, Elma Wohld, and Emily Beck; (second row) Lizzie Schepper Fink and Claire Fichtner. (Pat Hare.)

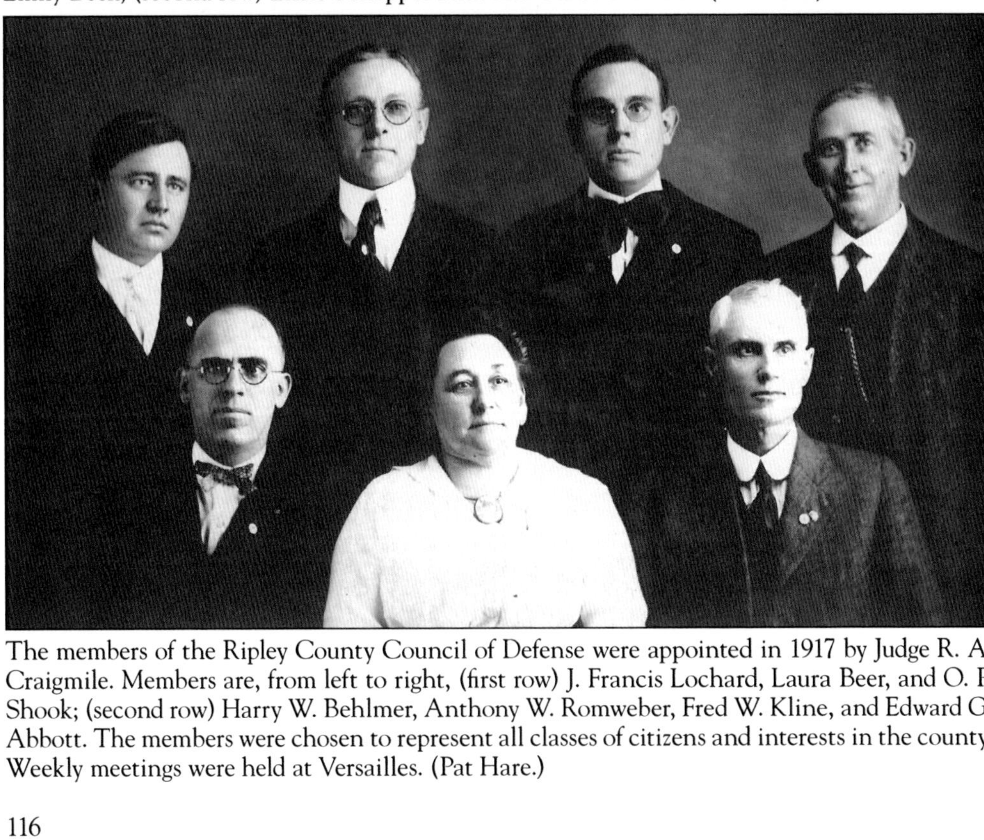

The members of the Ripley County Council of Defense were appointed in 1917 by Judge R. A. Craigmile. Members are, from left to right, (first row) J. Francis Lochard, Laura Beer, and O. P. Shook; (second row) Harry W. Behlmer, Anthony W. Romweber, Fred W. Kline, and Edward G. Abbott. The members were chosen to represent all classes of citizens and interests in the county. Weekly meetings were held at Versailles. (Pat Hare.)

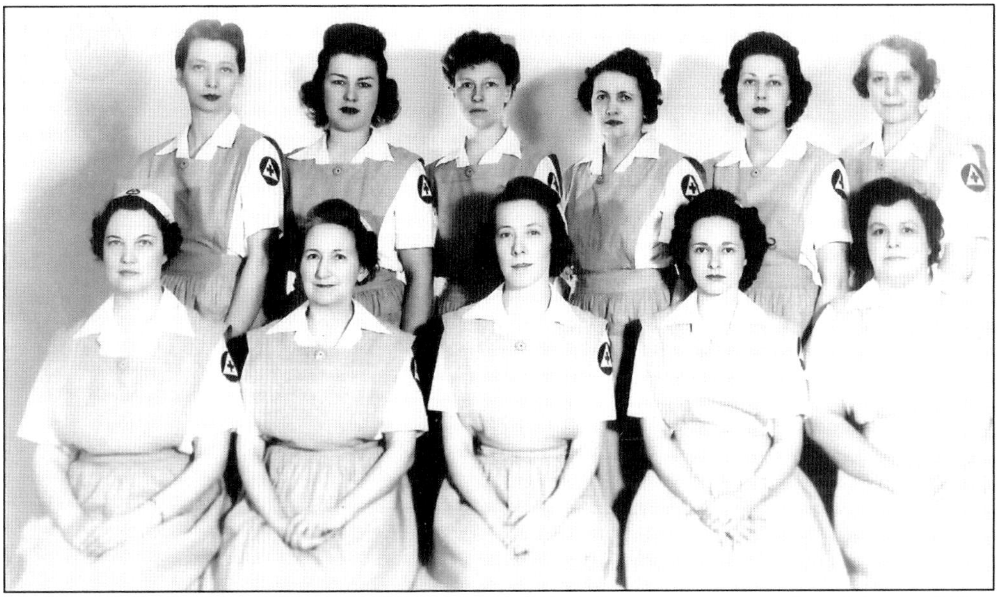

The first Ripley County Chapter of the American Red Cross was organized on Memorial Day 1917. This is a later chapter of the Red Cross. From left to right are (first row) Sylvia Wonning, Mary Schroeder, Irma Romweber, Jean Burst, and Flora Fritsch; (second row) Lucille "Ludy" Broerman, Juanita "Neetz" Wonning, Hilda Currin, Estella Gauck, Mary Helen Pictor, and Sophia Bohland. (Nancy Raver.)

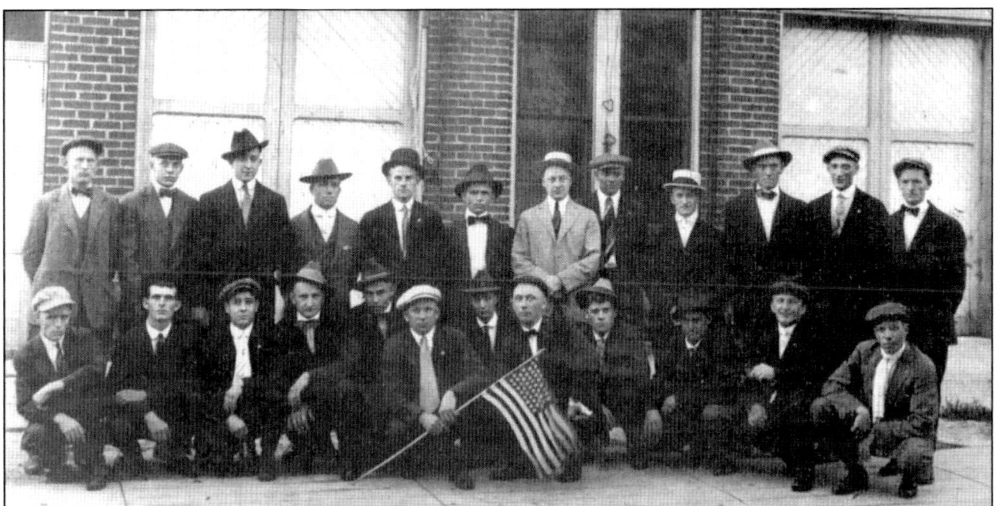

In this photograph are the men of this vicinity who were the first to be called for duty in World War I. The picture was taken at Batesville City Hall Sunday, on or about September 13, 1917. From left to right are (first row) Leo Benz (holding the flag) and Arthur Schein; (second row) Charles Green, John L. Bland, Louis Boehmer, William L. Brummer, Frank Burst, Lester Breckensiek, William Crowell, Albert Drescher, George Engel, and William Nordmeyer; (third row) Frank Metz, Roy Johanning, Alvin Kramer, Quirin Walsman, Anthony Kurtz, Walter Maple, Frank Gauck, Clinton Meister, Arthur Schene, Louis Walterman, William Wernke, and Matt Weigel. (BAHS.)

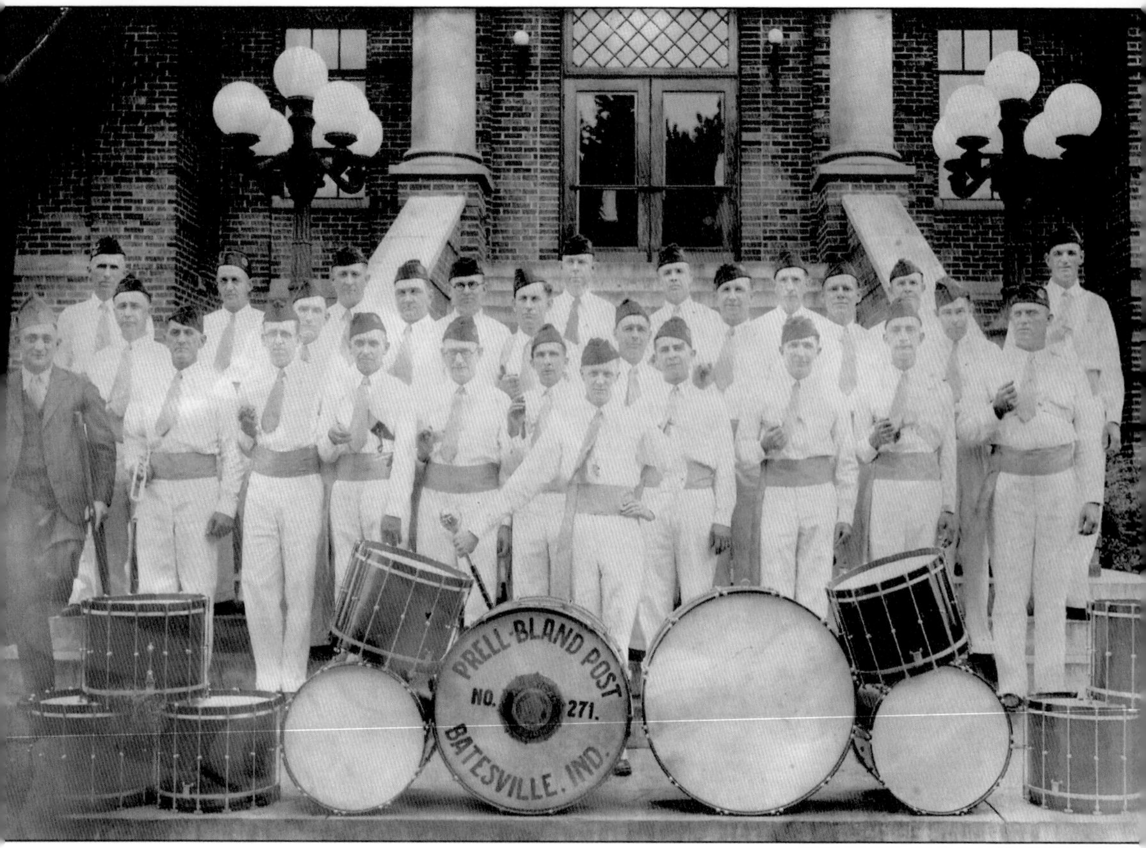

Members of the Prell-Bland Post of the American Legion are C. Theobold, C. Kretzmeyer, E. Gesell, P. Karbowski, C. Miller, E. Kleiner, C. Bosse, possibly C. Lambert, Ed Wisman, F. Baas, W. Hoff, W. Burst, A. Irrgang, D. Foley, P. Wycoff, E. Boese, L. Boehmer, W. Dietz, G. Goyert, C. Lampert, R. Benz, M. J. Baas, W. Bloemer, R. Firsich, H. Goyert, F. Burst, E. Huneke, and B. Winsor. (Pat Hare.)

When the Civil War broke out in 1861, John Schultz Jr., pictured here in his Civil War uniform, was anxious to enlist. His parents, having but one child, did not want him to do so, especially as he was still under 18 years of age. He finally ran away and enlisted without their consent and was assigned to the 53rd Ohio Infantry. He was discharged in 1865. (June Moenter.)

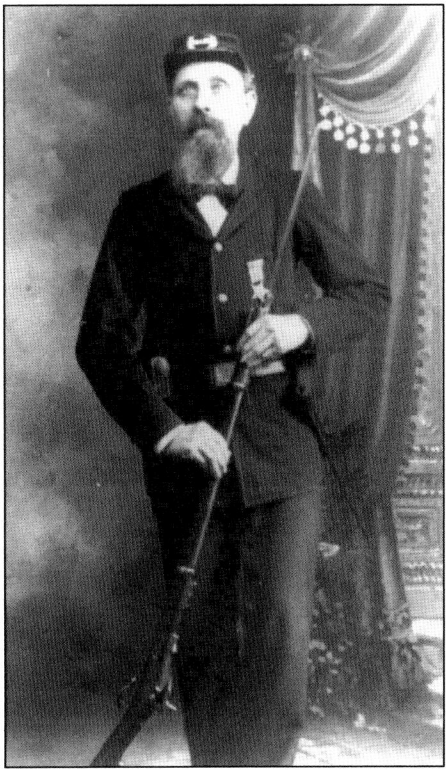

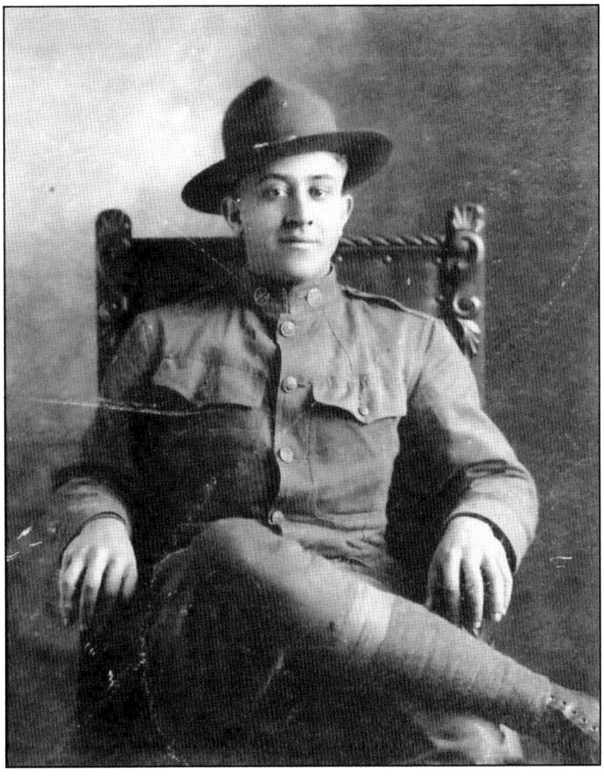

Alvin Henry Cramer trained at Camp Taylor and Camp Grant from September 20, 1917, to March 4, 1918. He was sent overseas to Genecourt, France, from March 14, 1918, to June 14, 1919. He returned to the United States on June 25, 1919, and discharged at Camp Sherman on July 3, 1919. He is the father of Dolores Amberger. (Dolores Amberger.)

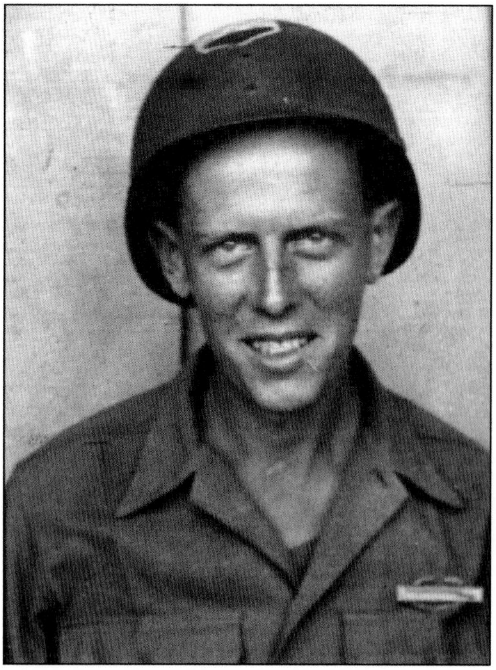

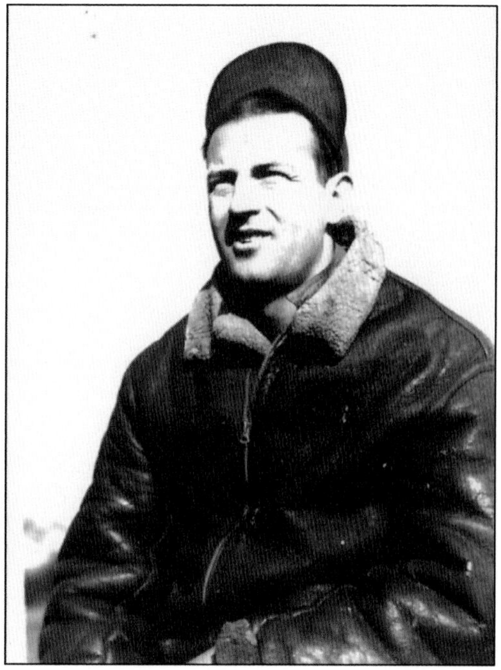

These were two Batesville men who fought in World War II. On the left is Sgt. Albert H. Mollaun, who served with the 393rd infantry in Germany. He was awarded the Purple Heart for wounds received in action against the enemy. On the right is Sgt. Albert F. Giesting who was awarded the Bronze Star Medal and selected as outstanding crew chief in the Thunderbolt Fighter Group. (Women's Study Club.)

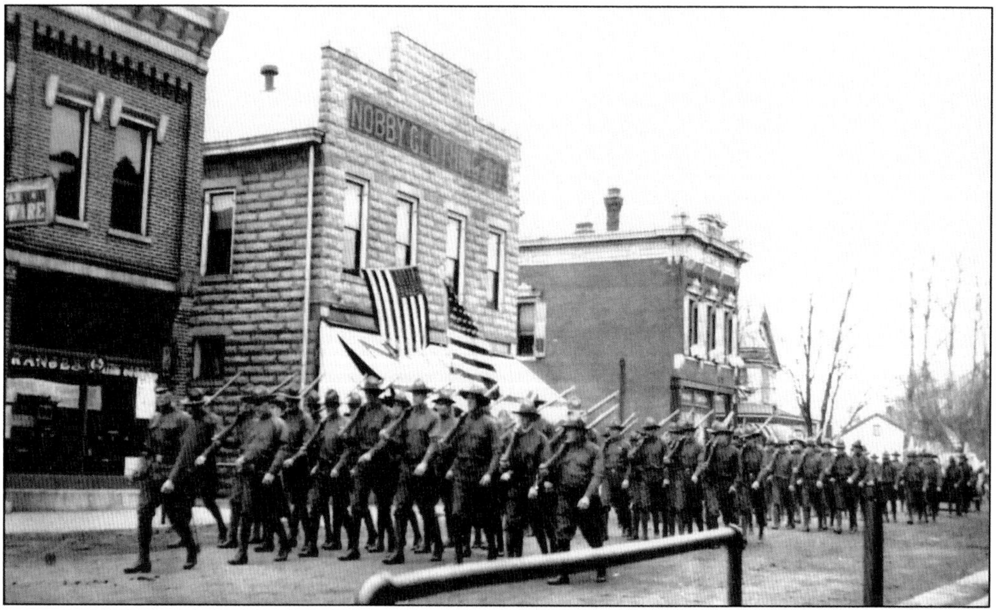

On January 4, 1918, 65 men were sworn in as Liberty Guards. Monday night of each week was set for drill night with meetings to convene at the Pohlar Garage on George and Sycamore Streets. From there, the guards marched to the Fair Grounds Hall for drill maneuvers. The marching was part of their drill practice. (Women's Study Club.)

Ten

Centennial Celebrations

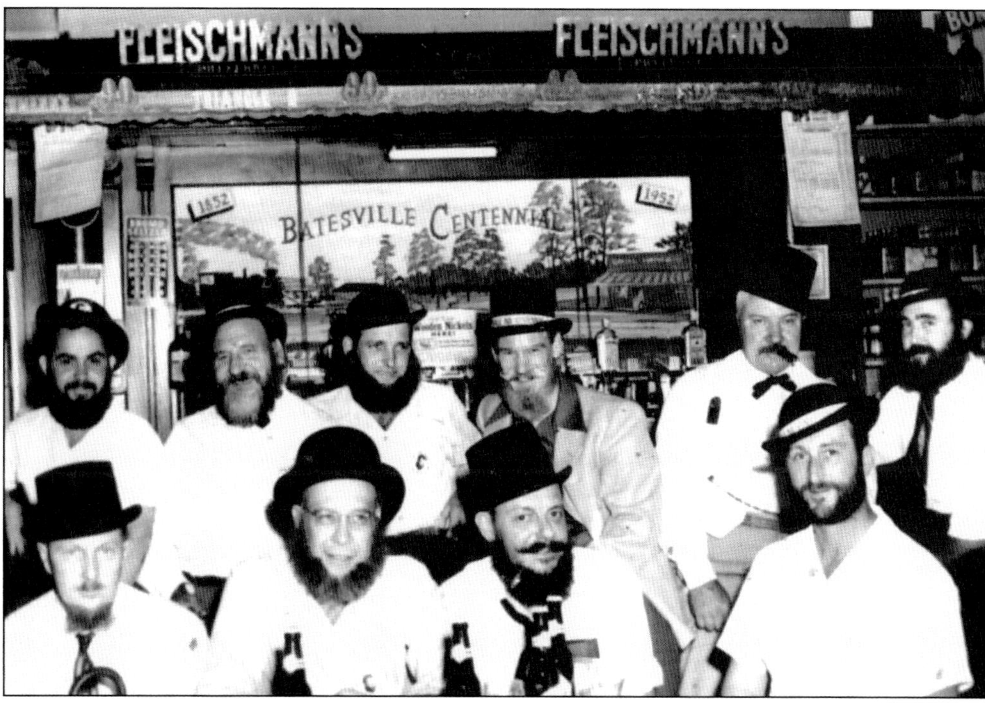

Participants in the "Brothers of the Brush" beard contest in the 1952 Batesville centennial celebration included, from left to right, (first row) Art Bergman, Nick Osier, Ed Burkhardt, and Florentine Decker; (second row) Edgar Kramer, Lester Moody, Melvin Brinkman, Jim Obermeyer, Ray Smith, and Joe Suttmiller. In this picture, they were socializing at the Triangle B bar and restaurant at the corner of Walnut and Pearl Streets. (Women's Study Club.)

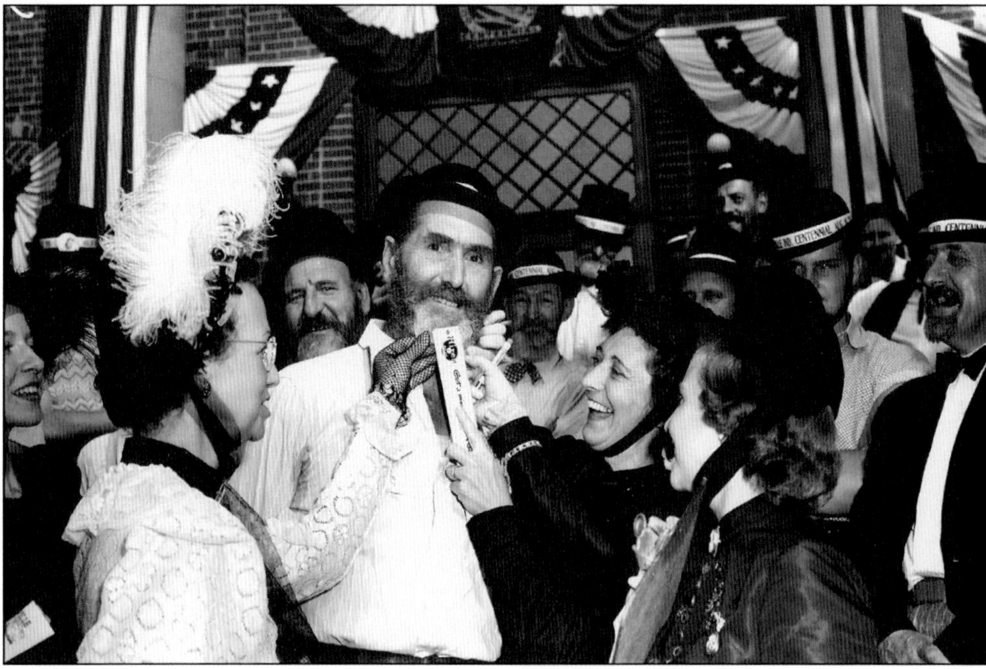

One of the categories to be judged for the "Brothers of the Brush" beard contest was the longest beard. Here, from left to right, Hazel Andres, Freda "Fritzie" Kellerman, and Ella Hisrich are measuring the length of this unidentified man's beard. This makes one wonder if he was the winner of the prize. (Mary Ann Meyer.)

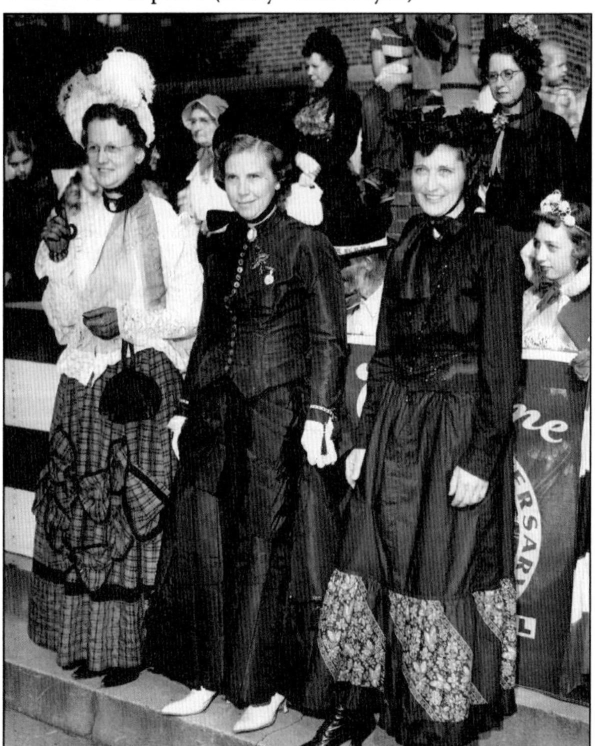

These ladies were the winners of the "Period Dress" contest at the 1952 Batesville centennial. From left to right are (first row) Hazel Andres, who won third place; Ella Hisrich, who won second place; and Freda "Fritzie" Kellerman, who won first place as the most authentic costumes. Behind them, from left to right, one can see Esther Hahn (in the bonnet), Drew Flodder, Irene Gannon, and "Centennial Queen" Nancy (Raver) Broerman. (Mary Ann Meyer.)

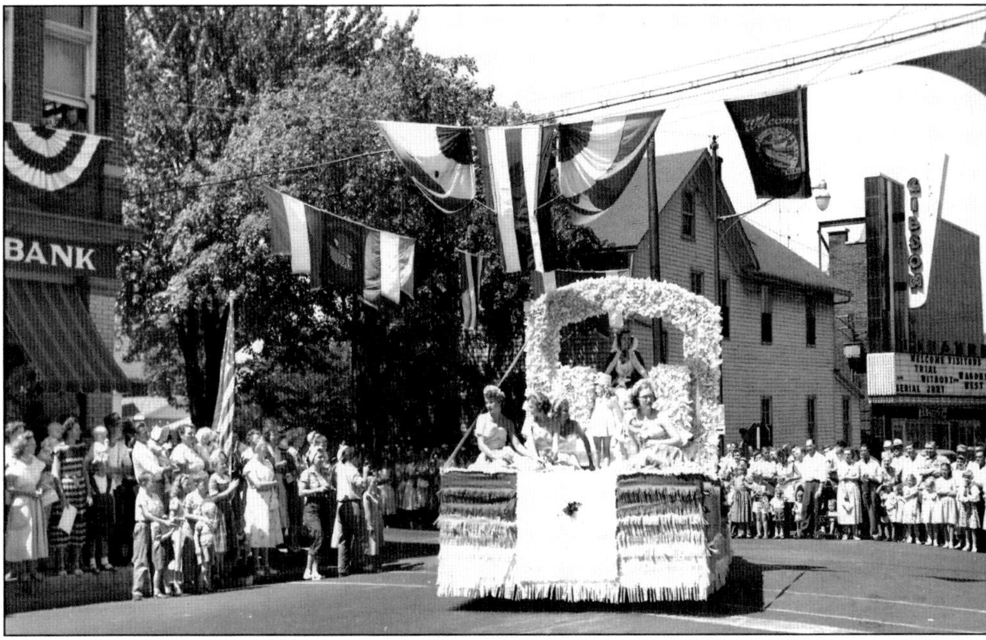

This photograph features the Centennial Queen Nancy Broerman (under the arch) and her court, including little Miss Centennial. The float has just turned the corner from Boehringer Street to Main Street. The Gibson Theatre can be seen in the background. (Women's Study Club.)

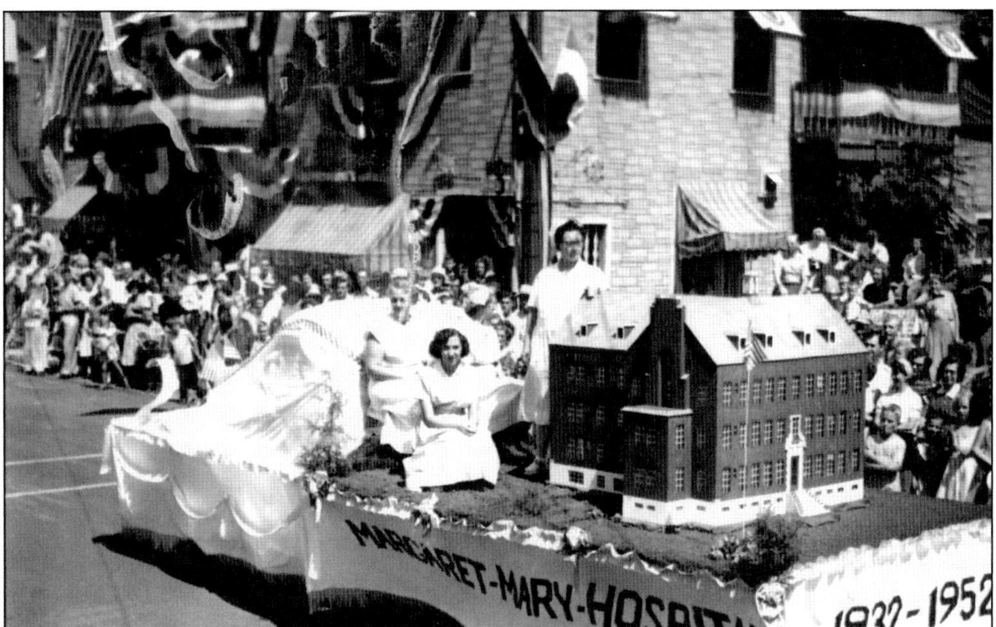

There were many really beautiful floats in the 1952 centennial parade. This is the Margaret Mary Hospital float. The photograph was taken on Main Street in front of Burkhart's Grill, which was the teenage hangout in the 1950s. (BAHS.)

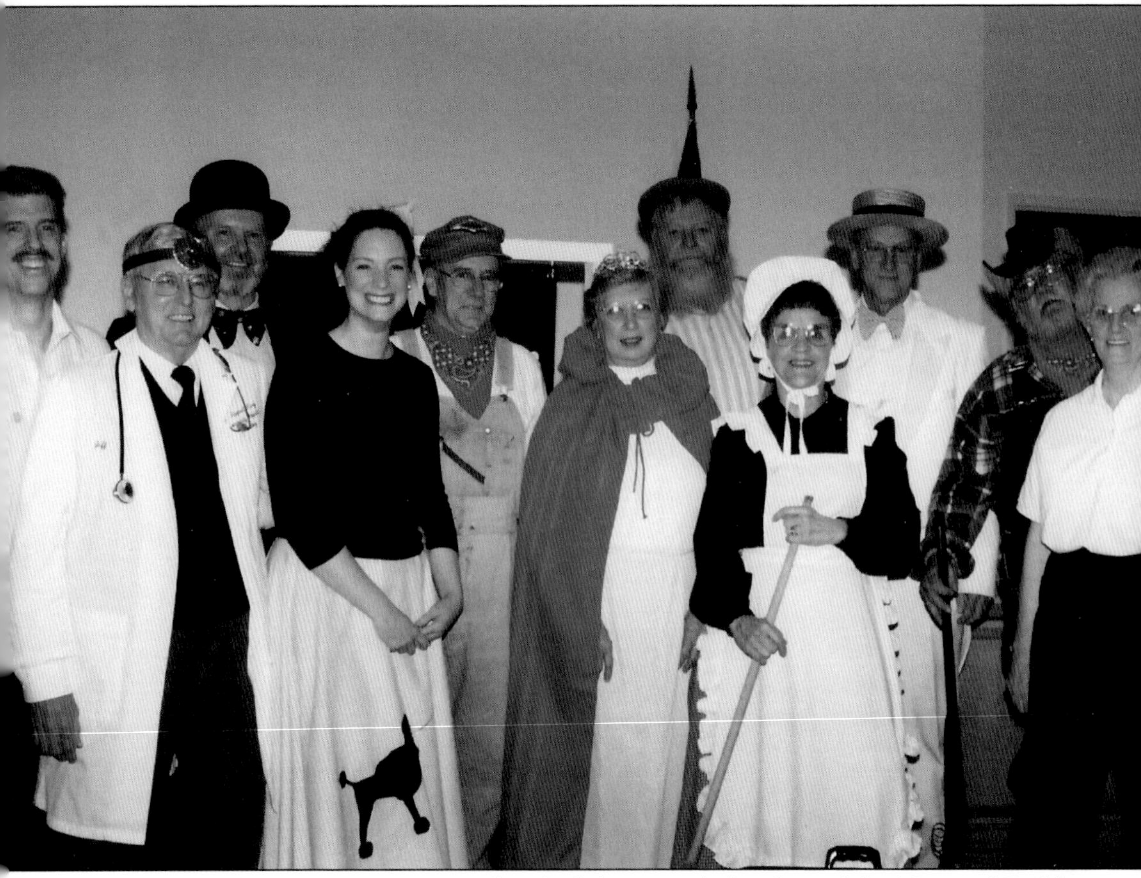

On January 3, 2002, a capacity crowd packed the council chambers of the Memorial Building to attend the opening ceremonies of Batesville's sesquicentennial. A short history of Batesville's first 150 years was performed by the following people, who are, from left to right, Chris Ault as the 1950s jitterbug dancer, Don Karbowski as Dr. Charles Gibson, Leonard Nobbe as Mr. John Hillenbrand, Laura Ault as Chris's 1950s jitterbug dance partner, Joe Greiwe as George H. Dunn, Nancy Raver as the queen of the 100-year celebration, Bill Schrader as Joshua Bates (whom the town was named after), Lou Voegele as Nancy Amack, Ham Struewing as John Callahan, Joe Little as Teunis Amack, and Jean Struewing as the emcee. (BAHS.)

John A. Hillenbrand II served as the emcee for the 150-year celebration. Instead of referring to the celebration as the sesquicentennial celebration, the phrase "Century and a Half" was used as the slogan during the festivities. Many activities were planned during the whole year of 2002, but the climax was the week of August 4–10, 2002. (BAHS.)

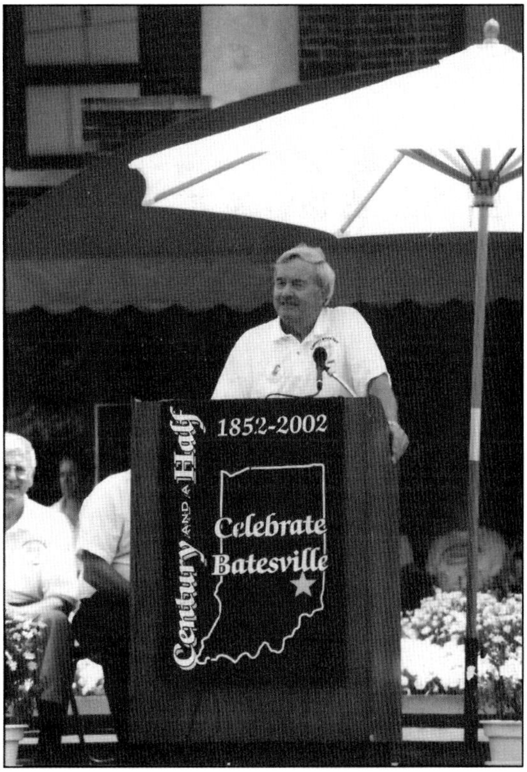

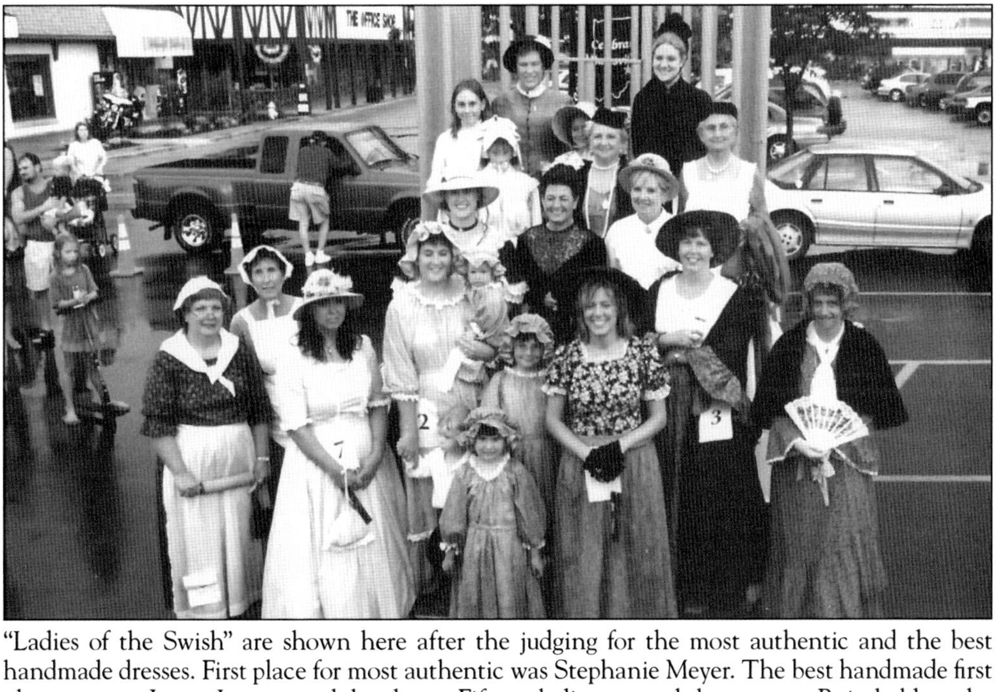

"Ladies of the Swish" are shown here after the judging for the most authentic and the best handmade dresses. First place for most authentic was Stephanie Meyer. The best handmade first place went to Janna Irrgang and daughters. Fifteen ladies entered the contest. Rain held up the judging for a while, but it cleared up and the festivities continued. The contest was held in the village green on Main Street. (BAHS.)

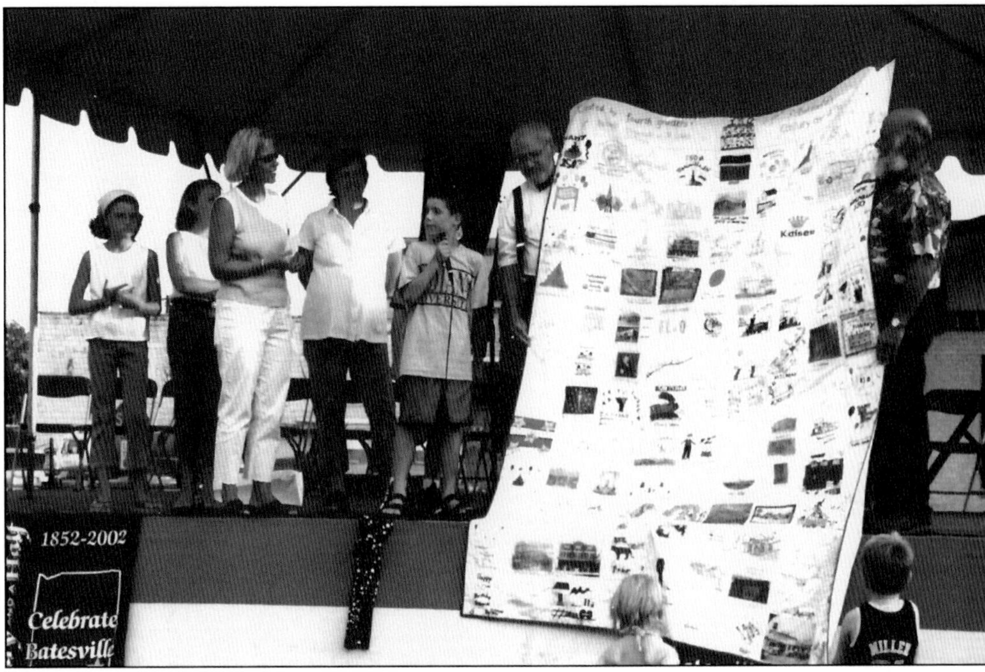

The school children also got into the spirit of the "Century and a Half" celebration by making a quilt with pictures of the different landmarks and symbols of Batesville's first 150 years. Their teachers and members of the historical society helped educate the children about the interesting events and happenings of the past. Teacher Amy Weigel took a lead in this endeavor. (BAHS.)

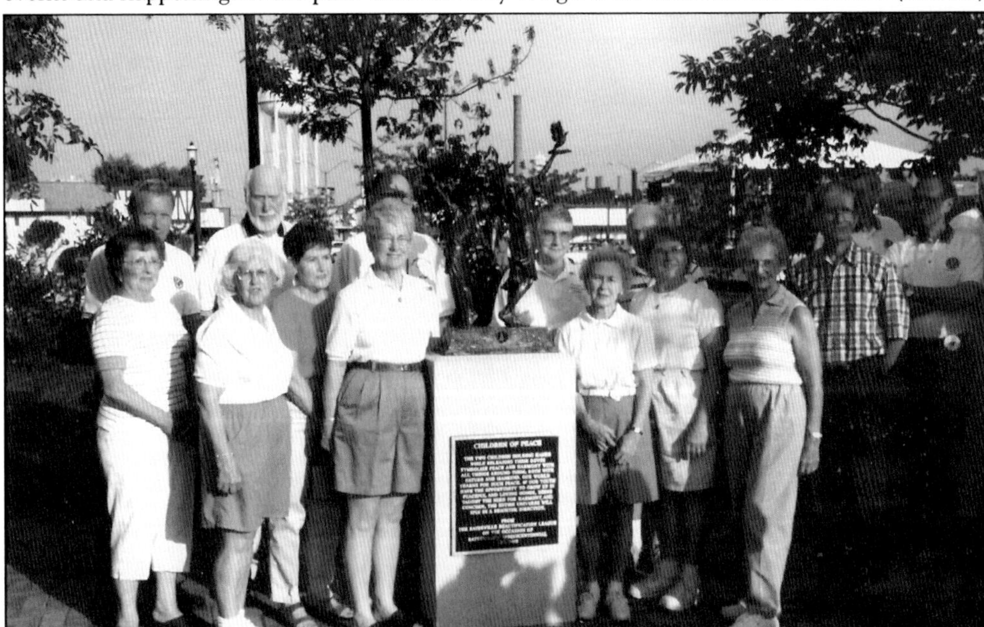

The Beautification League erected an impressive bronze statue titled *Children of Peace* in the village green. The Kiwanis Club arranged for a time capsule to be enclosed in the base of the statue. They plan to open the capsule at the bicentennial ceremonies in 50 years. The ceremonies took place the week of August 4–10, 2002. (BAHS.)

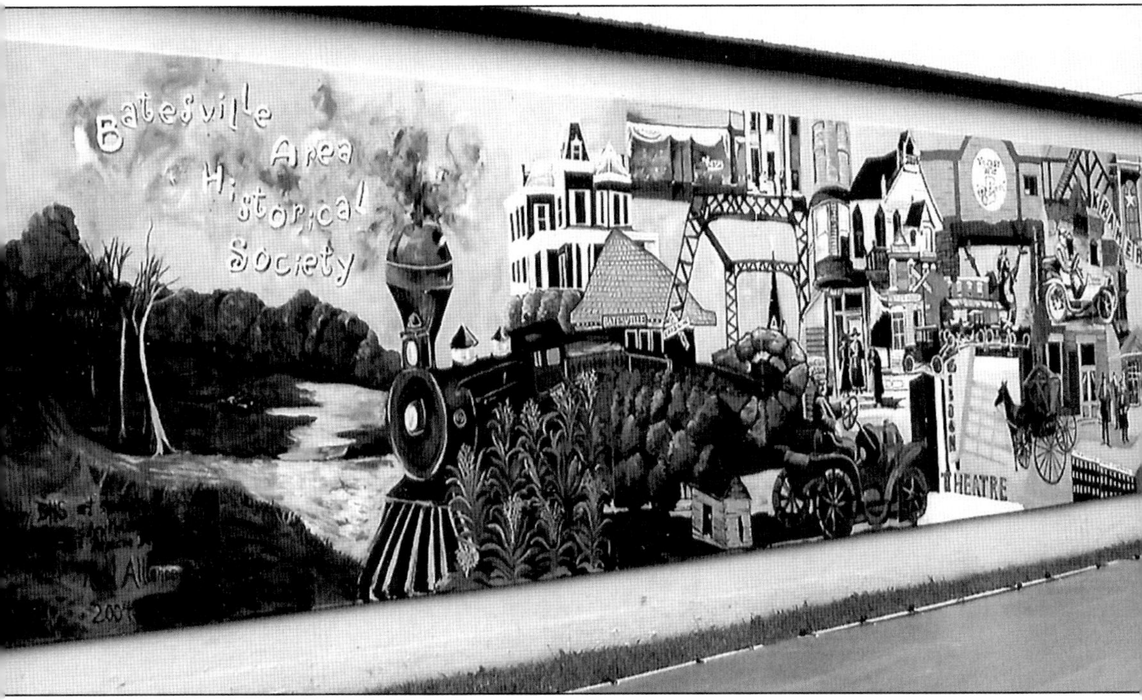

The Batesville Area Historical Society (BAHS) had this mural painted on the side of the building, located at 10 West Boehringer Street, which was used as the society's museum from October 2003 until July 2007, when the library asked the BAHS to vacate because they were in need of the extra space for their use. The senior art classes at Batesville High School, the Rural Alliance for the Arts, and the BAHS worked together to achieve this striking mural. The BAHS would like to thank everyone who purchases this book. Every effort has been made to present the correct facts, dates, and names on each caption. (Nick Stewart.)

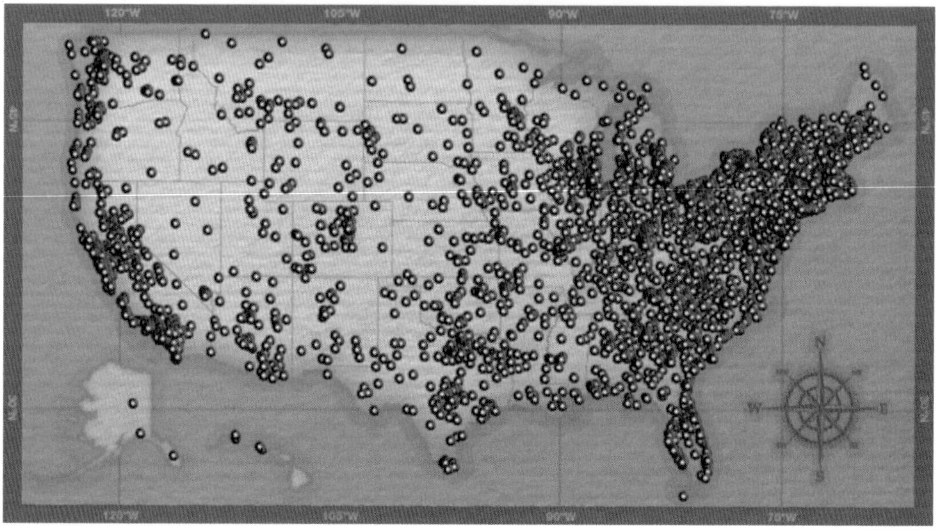